Praise for *Does Scripture Speak for Itself?*

From common sense realism in the nineteenth century to the Museum of the Bible, American Protestants, and white evangelicals in particular, have approached the Bible with a kind of willful naïveté, confident that they understand its meaning. In their "close reading" of the Museum of the Bible, Jill Hicks-Keeton and Cavan Concannon demonstrate that any approach to the Bible is complicated by allegiances, prejudices, economics, privilege, and cultural location. This is a very worthy and thought-provoking book.

– Randall Balmer, Dartmouth College

Does Scripture Speak for Itself? uses one book and one museum to unpack with incisive reflection the manifold ways that white evangelicalism has leveraged a particular rendering of biblical Christianity for political gain. Combining business history with exegesis, cultural analysis with media studies, ethnography with sharp scrutiny of power, Jill Hicks-Keeton and Cavan Concannon's outstanding book is a must-read for anyone trying to grasp the institutional juggernaut that is the modern religious right.

– Darren Dochuk, University of Notre Dame, author of Anointed With Oil: How Christianity and Crude Made Modern America

This book shows how contemporary white Americans manufacture the Bible they need to achieve the political future they want. In this incisive work, two brilliant scholars offer a coruscating view of how scripture operates as an ideological weapon. Required reading for students of religion, race, and politics in the U.S.

– Kathryn Lofton, Yale University

A compelling read and fascinating tour. As our author-guides walk us through the exhibits and back rooms of the Museum of the Bible, we come to see it as a kind of bible-making machine, built to produce and promote a form of biblicism that in turn reproduces and further promotes white Christian privilege. Along the way, we gain a deeper and richer understanding of the rise of American evangelicalism and the religious right.

– Timothy Beal, Case Western Reserve University, author of When Time Is Short: Finding Our Way in the Anthropocene

This fascinating book represents the pivot in orientation toward critical transdisciplinarity among academic scholars of the Bible that I have long called for. I especially appreciate the authors' readings of "the Bible" and other cultural and political "scriptures," which will make readers aware of the complex inheritance of and participation – with unintentional or willful ignorance – in the construction and ongoing advancement of white supremacy. With its honest questioning, analysis, and close reading, the book models the possibility of a refocused and reoriented field.

– Vincent Wimbush, Institute for Signifying Scriptures

Hicks-Keeton and Concannon provide an incomparable tour of the Museum of the Bible, placing it within the broader context of white evangelicalism and illuminating the theological and ideological agendas animating its work. Engaging and incisive, this brilliant book is a must-read for anyone who wants to understand the battle for the Bible in the American public square.

– Mark Chancey, Southern Methodist University

A keen, insightful reading of the white evangelical Bible that the Museum of the Bible hallows, magnifies, and markets with such zeal in the nation's capital. A learned excursion through the museum's acutely politicized exhibitions that is a tour de force both for biblical studies and American religious history.

– Leigh Eric Schmidt, Washington University in St. Louis

Does Scripture Speak for Itself leaves no doubt that the Museum of the Bible speaks loudly for white evangelicals. Hicks-Keeton and Concannon offer an eye-opening tour of the worlds within and around this new institution, shining a critical light on the values that inform its exhibits and the funders that underwrite its mission. Anyone interested in the still-bustling intersection of Christianity and American public life will find this an absorbing read.

– Heath Carter, Princeton Theological Seminary

DOES SCRIPTURE SPEAK FOR ITSELF?

Is the Bible the unembellished Word of God or the product of human agency? There are different answers to this question. And they lie at the heart of this book's powerful exploration of the fraught ways in which money, race, and power shape the story of Christianity in American public life.

The authors' subject is the Museum of the Bible in Washington DC, arguably the latest example in a long line of white evangelical institutions aiming to amplify and promote a religious, political, and moral agenda of their own. In their careful and compelling investigation, Jill Hicks-Keeton and Cavan Concannon disclose the ways in which the museum's exhibits reinforce a particularized and partial interpretation of the Bible's meaning.

Bringing to light the museum's implicit messaging about scriptural provenance and audience, the authors reveal how the MOTB produces a version of the Bible that in essence authorizes a certain sort of white evangelical privilege, promotes a view of history aligned with that same evangelical aspiration, and above all protects a cohort of white evangelicals from critique. They show too how the museum collapses vital conceptual distinctions between its own conservative vision of the Bible and "The Bible" as a cultural icon. This revelatory volume above all confirms that scripture – for all the claims made for it that it speaks only divine truth – can in the end never be separated from human politics.

Jill Hicks-Keeton is Associate Professor of Religious Studies at the University of Oklahoma. She is the author of *Arguing with Aseneth: Gentile Access to Israel's Living God in Jewish Antiquity* (Oxford University Press, 2018), for which she was awarded the Manfred Lautenschlaeger Award for Theological Promise.

Cavan Concannon is Associate Professor of Religion at the University of Southern California. He is the author of *Profaning Paul* (University of Chicago Press, 2021), *Assembling Early Christianity: Trade Networks and the Letters of Dionysios of Corinth* (Cambridge University Press, 2017), and *"When You Were Gentiles": Specters of Ethnicity in Roman Corinth and Paul's Corinthian Correspondence* (Yale University Press, 2014).

Does Scripture Speak for Itself?

The Museum of the Bible and the Politics of Interpretation

Jill Hicks-Keeton

Cavan Concannon

CAMBRIDGE
UNIVERSITY PRESS

CAMBRIDGE
UNIVERSITY PRESS

University Printing House, Cambridge CB2 8BS, United Kingdom

One Liberty Plaza, 20th Floor, New York, NY 10006, USA

477 Williamstown Road, Port Melbourne, VIC 3207, Australia

314–321, 3rd Floor, Plot 3, Splendor Forum, Jasola District Centre,
New Delhi – 110025, India

103 Penang Road, #05–06/07, Visioncrest Commercial, Singapore 238467

Cambridge University Press is part of the University of Cambridge.

It furthers the University's mission by disseminating knowledge in the pursuit of
education, learning, and research at the highest international levels of excellence.

www.cambridge.org
Information on this title: www.cambridge.org/9781108493314
DOI: 10.1017/9781108681247

First published 2023

Printed in the United Kingdom by TJ Books Limited, Padstow Cornwall

A catalogue record for this publication is available from the British Library.

Library of Congress Cataloging-in-Publication Data
Names: Hicks-Keeton, Jill, 1983– author. | Concannon, Cavan W., 1979– author.
Title: Does scripture speak for itself? : the Museum of the Bible and the politics of
interpretation / Jill Hicks-Keeton, Cavan Concannon.
Description: Cambridge, United Kingdom ; New York, NY, USA : Cambridge
University Press, [2023] | Includes bibliographical references and index.
Identifiers: LCCN 2021045483 (print) | LCCN 2021045484 (ebook) | ISBN
9781108493314 (hardback) | ISBN 9781108681247 (ebook)
Subjects: LCSH: Bible – Evidences, authority, etc. | Bible – Criticism, interpretation,
etc. – United States. | Museum of the Bible. | Christianity – United States.
Classification: LCC BS480 .H44 2023 (print) | LCC BS480 (ebook) | DDC 220.1/3–dc23
LC record available at https://lccn.loc.gov/2021045483
LC ebook record available at https://lccn.loc.gov/2021045484

ISBN 978-1-108-49331-4 Hardback

Contents

Illustrations

Introduction

BIBLES ARE NO STRANGERS TO WASHINGTON DC'S National Mall. When the Smithsonian Institute's Museum of the American Indian opened in 2004, for example, one of the permanent exhibits included a wall of bibles. The installation showcased the complex history of Christian colonialism by starkly juxtaposing the bibles with guns and (broken) treaties. Visitors were invited to meditate on how biblical translations by ambitious missionaries – often well-meaning and inspirational – were accompanied by violence and deceit, even as the translated messages also became resources for Indigenous resistance to colonizers.[1] But none of the bibles on that wall would have included the apocalyptic pronouncement and warning from Jesus found only in a much older bible, Codex Washingtonianus, held across the Mall at the Smithsonian Institute's Freer Gallery of Art. "The measure of the years of Satan's authority has been filled up," Jesus says here, "But other dreadful things are coming."[2] Codex Washingtonianus is part of a collection some biblical scholars have dubbed an "American treasure trove," and this saying of Jesus is known as the "Freer Logion" because of its exclusive appearance in this manuscript. This bible is the most famous of those displayed in a special exhibit that opened at the Arther M. Sackler Gallery in 2006. Entitled "In the Beginning: Bibles before the Year 1000," the installation was created in partnership with the Bodleian Library in Oxford and included significant early Hebrew and Christian biblical texts.[3] The press release announcing the exhibit

1

extolled the particularity of each bible on display. "Each one has a tale to tell," it read, "and opens up a landscape populated with colorful human stories."[4]

Elsewhere on the Mall, the coverless, worn bible of nineteenth-century enslaved preacher and rebellion leader Nat Turner is on display at the National Museum of African American History and Culture (NMAAHC).[5] Its small size – only about four inches long by three and a half wide – marks a strong contrast to the cavernous underground exhibit hall in which it has found a home, within an impressive museum installation treating enslavement and freedom in Black history in the United States. Having lost its beginning and end, Turner's bible no longer stretches from Genesis to Revelation but instead opens with the fourth chapter of Leviticus. Legend has it that Turner was holding this bible when he was captured, and historical records tell us stories of how its contents fired the religious visions that animated his violent revolt against white slavers. In between its possession by Turner, who was valued as property at $375 and was hanged in 1831, and its present location on the National Mall, this bible was gifted by the Virginia courthouse responsible for Turner's execution to a white family whose ancestors had died in the revolt.[6] The bible's travels raise stark moral questions that lay bare the persistent legacy of racism and white supremacy in American Christianity. Its context now in the NMAAHC underscores the necessity of tackling difficult issues of ownership – of bibles, of bodies – in our country's history and present, questions that come into view most clearly when we foreground dynamics of race and oppression, privilege and power.

Another bible featured on the National Mall invites us to reflect on the complex, and at times ambiguous, dynamics of scripture and society among our nation's founders. Thomas Jefferson's *The Life and Morals of Jesus of Nazareth*, popularly known as "The Jefferson Bible," is now owned by the Smithsonian Institute and in 2011 formed the basis of a celebrated exhibit at the National Museum of American History.[7] Jefferson's bible is significant not only for its famous original owner but also because of its distinctive production method, a literal cut-and-paste in which Jefferson used a razor to eliminate from his bible anything too supernatural for his rationalist taste and glue to compile a gospel narrative of Jesus without the Good News that the founding father deemed unbelievable. Jefferson's handmade bible is the definition of bespoke, made as it was principally for Jefferson's own use.[8] Its contents differ starkly from those of Turner's bible, both literally and figuratively. Turner's bible tells a story of his fight for freedom, hope for a miracle, while that of Jefferson, an enslaver, reveals that he had enough free time and material resources to free his bible from miracles so as to make biblical morality compatible with his vision of himself as a modern, rational man. The histories of these two personal bibles, especially in their differences, promise to complicate and enrich our discussions, narrations, and understandings of US history more broadly.

But what of *the Bible*? Can the bibles of Nat Turner and Thomas Jefferson tell us anything about *the Bible*? What of the bibles at the Museum of the American Indian whose ownership is murky and whose legacies are difficult? What of the unusual but very early Freer Codex with the unfamiliar words of Jesus? Can all of these bibles, and any others that have made their way over the years to "America's front lawn" – whether in protests, proselytizing efforts, or presidential inaugurations – be meaningfully classed together as "The Bible"? The short answer is no. The Bible does not exist. There are only bibles. For centuries, humans have made, circulated, and read bibles of many shapes and sizes, in differing languages, with varied lists of texts, with variant words, with particularized constraints on interpretation and practices of encounter. Those bibles each tell a story of a relationship between a textual object and a person or people. The more interesting answer, though, is "no, but . . ."

No, but . . . the Bible *does* exist in the realm of the imagination. The Bible exists as a social construct, a cultural icon, a conceptual category that can variously offer affiliation and designate boundaries, platform political aims, and provide ideological resources.[9] The Bible is continually made and remade, discursively.[10] In the chapters that follow, we will only refer to this cultural icon as "the Bible," while all particular bibles will not be capitalized. We do this to underscore that each of these bibles has its own history, distinct from other bibles, and is connected to, yet different from, the Bible as cultural icon.

There is a relatively new bible now on display among DC's institutions of national public memory: the one produced by the privately owned, aspirationally named Museum of the Bible. Founded, funded, and led by the Oklahoma-based Green family, the white evangelical owners of Hobby Lobby with a combined personal net worth of over $7 billion,[11] the Museum of the Bible (MOTB) opened in 2017 only a couple of blocks from the National Mall. Located among the Smithsonian museums, this 500-million-dollar institution purports to guide visitors through a selection of forty thousand Bible-related artifacts and a series of inter-active, immersive experiences intended to recreate the narratives, lands, and even foods of the Bible. Over 1 million people visited the MOTB in its first year of operation, its guest list including national and inter-national religious leaders and a host of government officials. This insti-tution has made waves in the national press, notably because of its material and financial connections to the Hobby Lobby antiquities smuggling scandals and revelations that some of the MOTB's most popular biblical artifacts are in reality modern forgeries.[12]

As in any museum, the visitor experience at the MOTB is impacted by the decisions of donors who have selected the institution for their contri-butions, of curators who have chosen which material to display, of design-ers who have created experiential opportunities to educate as well as entertain, of artists and content consultants who have fabricated visual and auditory materials, of educational programmers who plan and host events. We are interested in how these elements and more combine in the MOTB, as a privately funded endeavor in a public arena, to produce *the Bible.* There are a lot of bibles inside the MOTB. But the Museum of *the Bible,* in its very name, trades on the fantasy that there exists a single bible, The Bible. We find it analytically productive to approach the museum itself as a sort of bible, one you can walk through page by page. By design, the MOTB must cut and paste what it will include, like Jefferson did. With use, the MOTB's cover is wearing off as its bible, like Turner's, animates political discourse and advocacy. As with Codex Washingtonianus, the museum's bible has its own distinctive Jesus. And, like those bibles in the Museum of the American Indian, this museum's bible deserves analysis for whose interests it serves and protects.

The chapters that follow explore the contours of the museum's bible, not only what it says but also where it came from and how it works – and for whom. We argue that the MOTB produces and advertises a white

1. Exterior facade of the Museum of the Bible. Photo: the authors.

evangelical bible, one which authorizes white evangelical privilege in the United States, authenticates the usable pasts that animate white evangelical aspirations, and protects white evangelicals from critique. The museum's bible limits visitors' moral horizons in ways consistent with trends in white evangelicalism more broadly. Systems are obscured from view. Reckonings with racist pasts are made uncomplicated as this bible unburdens white Christian visitors from critically examining their tradition's complicity in and perpetration of harm. This museum's bible writes evangelical Christian insiderness into both country and cosmos. Further, we read the MOTB as an institution that not only produces and markets this particular bible but also claims ownership over the Bible as it collapses or obscures important conceptual distinctions between the museum's bible and the Bible as cultural icon.

The MOTB is housed in an old refrigerated warehouse built in the 1920s that later served as the Washington Design Center. The MOTB's renovations have transformed the building into a monument to its bible – conceived as the Bible – with multistoried golden "Gutenberg

Gates" welcoming visitors at the entrance. A large, elongated LED screen adorns the lobby's interior ceiling, supported by shiny pillars of polished white Jerusalem stone. The screen's rotating images of biblical art and stained glass windows make the museum feel a bit like a modern cathedral, or a tech-savvy megachurch sanctuary, sitting as it does alongside a Bible-themed coffee house and a gift shop. This first floor is where those visitors who pass security[13] purchase entrance tickets to the museum. Once free to enter, the MOTB now charges admission of between $9.99 and $24.99.[14] Floor 1 is likely not where most visitors spend the bulk of their time, as none of the permanent exhibits occupy this space. But the combination of opportunities on the first floor illustrates the particularities of this museum. One can wander from a room dedicated to a Vatican-sponsored special exhibit that features mostly replicas, to a virtual reality experience with spinning stools and headsets that take you to places in "biblical" Israel, to the MOTB's Bible-themed amusement arcade and playscape for the youngest of its visitors, and finally to the MOTB shop.

Let's, for a moment, envision a trio of activities available here that helps us highlight further the constructedness of the visitors' experience in the MOTB. The first of the three is inside the Vatican Museum-curated exhibit room. Here we find a replica of the fourth-century Codex Vaticanus encased in glass available for visitors' cursory inspection as they stand between art-covered walls that recall the Vatican's magisterial interiors. Codex Vaticanus is one of the three oldest biblical codices written in uncial (upper-case) characters. The manuscript is important to scholars interested in biblical textual criticism who endeavor to construct critical editions of the Septuagint (Greek translations of Hebrew scriptures) and the New Testament. Yet, unlike in the Sackler Gallery's "In the Beginning: Bibles before the Year 1,000" exhibit that featured Codex Washingtonianus, here the installation is not built around an actual artifact. Rather, it's a reproduction. The replica works to invoke the presence of a famous biblical artifact – likely for the purposes of respectability and the creation of an aura of antiquity and thus perceived authenticity – but does not produce the thing itself. A Bible Museum should, the logic would go, include a very old important witness to the biblical text.[15] And so here one has been fabricated, revealing the

2. Main lobby of Museum of the Bible. Photo: the authors.

curators' and designers' ability to transcend constraints that would have been created by limiting the museum's scope to its own collection of artifacts.[16]

Available nearby is our second activity worth reading in tandem, inside the children's experience called "Courageous Pages," which feels a bit like a Christian Chuck-E-Cheese.[17] Here museum guests both big and small can stand between two spring-loaded pillars for a memorable photo op, pretending to be a heroic Samson pushing the pillars apart with super strength. In the biblical story, found in Judges 13–16, Israelite judge Samson is a violent, vengeful, riddle-telling trickster whose antics finally lead him to capture by his enemies, the Philistines. He pushes the pillars apart in Judges 16:30: "Then Samson said, 'Let me die with the Philistines.' He strained with all his might; and the house fell on the lords and all the people who were in it. So those he killed at his death were more than those he had killed during his life" (NRSV). We emphasize here the gruesomeness of this bloody biblical murder-suicide to underscore the strangeness of including a reenactment of the moment in a playful children's exhibit. It makes sense, of course, when one considers that religious insiders regularly sanitize biblical stories to transform them into morality tales that are palatable and useful for teaching desired values. In this case, Samson is meant to teach the value of courage, no matter the consequences.

Our final stop on the first floor of the MOTB is the gift shop. Here, all visitors are also consumers – and potential owners. A great number of books are available for purchase, some bibles, some books about the Bible written by mainstream scholars, and several books authored by various members of the Green family. But the gift shop is not principally a bookstore. One could also buy a paperweight depicting a half-clothed Vashti from the story of Esther, a four-ounce glass jar of "biblical nuts in honey," expensive fine jewelry imported from Israel, a MOTB-branded fanny pack or tie, a replica of a Dead Sea Scroll, or one of many trendy home decor items bearing the words "God is love" that would look just as comfortable in a Hobby Lobby store.

We have thus moved from admiring a replica of Codex Vaticanus to imitating Samson in his moment of death to purchasing a bible-themed souvenir that is commodified, transportable, possessable. The combination illustrates well the point that the designers' and curators' choices in this museum were not dictated by actual artifacts – bibles – from the bottom up, but rather by a broader series of concerns involving effective storycraft, bids for respectability, and persuasive marketing.[18] The museum thus crafts a bible that feels natural to some populations of visitors while presenting itself as offering unmediated access to the Bible. We highlight and interrogate this unacknowledged role of the museum as producer of this bible in the chapters that follow.

Climbing the stairs one level, we find what the MOTB calls the Impact of the Bible floor, comprised of a threefold installation series: "Bible in America," "Bible in the World," and "Bible Now." A thrill ride named Washington Revelations completes the exhibit hall. Next up is the Stories of the Bible floor, with a special effects-filled Hebrew Bible/Old Testament experience, a "reconstructed" ancient Galilean village called "The World of Jesus of Nazareth," and a Hollywood-style theater featuring a film about the New Testament. The museum's fourth level is dubbed the History of the Bible floor and is advertised as using ancient artifacts and modern bibles to show how we got the Bible most visitors recognize and to track its worldwide distribution. Above that is a floor with a large Tabernacle-shaped theater. The opening ticketed show in this "World Stage Theater" was *Amazing Grace: The Musical*[19] and the theater serves as a daytime venue for the museum's regular "Public Readings of Scripture Experience."[20] Next door is a small installation curated by the Israel Antiquities Authority. On the museum's top floor is the MOTB's restaurant, called Manna, a Bible-themed garden, and a covered deck with spectacular views overlooking the US Capitol at one end and the Washington Monument at the other.

Yet the MOTB is more than its DC exhibits. The institution advertises a research arm and education initiatives.[21] It also originally had its own press imprint, through evangelical Christian publishing house Worthy Books, and it continues to put on a regular speaker series, develop a robust social media presence and online store, and host events in its for-rent event spaces ranging from film screenings to political organizing to podcast recordings to concerts. Social media posts reveal that evangelical film production and distribution company Pure Flix put on its first showing of *God's Not Dead: A Light in the Darkness* at the MOTB. A MOTB executive at that time, Tony Zeiss, appears in promotional material filmed inside the museum saying: "We are very, very pleased that this film was first screened at the Museum of the Bible. My take is it's gonna be wonderful affirmation for the faithful and it's going to bring hope to those who are a little less faithful."[22] Christian rock band Newsboys and then Vice President Mike Pence with Second Lady Karen Pence were in attendance as well. In January 2020, coinciding with that year's anti-abortion March for Life rally, the MOTB was host to an

"Evangelicals for Life" gathering, an evangelical antichoice conference put on in part by the Southern Baptist Convention's Ethics & Religious Liberty Commission.[23] Around the same time, the Christian Broadcasting Network filmed inside the MOTB to interview Fox News anchor and Liberty University graduate Shannon Bream about her book *Finding the Bright Side*.[24] That same month, Colorado Christian University's annual president's dinner[25] took place in a MOTB event space, an event in which Trump-appointed Secretary of Education Betsy DeVos made inflammatory comments comparing contemporary pro-choice policies to the proslavery movement during Abraham Lincoln's presidential tenure.[26] The Green family has also made use of the MOTB as a filming location, this time for a Bible study published by Lifeway, the publishing arm of the Southern Baptist Convention. The bible produced by the MOTB is constructed not only through its exhibits but also by the constellation of political and religious actors that fill its spaces, aligning their own policies, ideologies, actions, and money with *The Bible* by their very presence in the MOTB.

In its relatively short existence, the MOTB has changed its mission statement several times. In its first filing as a nonprofit in 2010, its mission statement struck a decidedly fundamentalist Christian tone: "To bring to life the living word of God, to tell its compelling story of preservation, and to inspire confidence in the absolute authority and reliability of the Bible." As Candida Moss and Joel Baden have documented, the original statement was changed two years later.[27] That updated mission – "to invite all people to engage with the Bible" – borrowed language from the American Bible Society (ABS), a large and long-standing Christian ministry of bible distribution. As evangelical scholar of American history John Fea has pointed out, the updated mission statement remained evangelistic in aim and practice without the obvious proselytizing of the original statement.[28] Though the 2012 mission statement reflected a public relations drive to present the MOTB as an educational resource and hub of research, it still demonstrated the evangelistic goals that led to the MOTB's founding. Since then, the museum has changed its mission statement once again, a fact that was revealed when the *Washington Post* reported that the MOTB threatened to sue the mayor of Washington DC.[29] Frustrated by the city's Covid-19 closures, the MOTB reportedly argued that the mayor's restrictions were a threat to religious freedom. Now presenting itself as a religious site rather than a nonreligious museum, the MOTB's current mission statement reads, "Museum of the Bible is a global, innovative, educational institution whose purpose is to invite all people to engage with the transformative power of the Bible."

Since the MOTB opened in November 2017, headlines have wondered whether the museum could move past widely reported controversies and scandals, in which artifacts in the museum's collection have been shown to be modern forgeries or illicitly acquired.[30] Reporting on the museum has further asked whether the institution could win over its critics, and, particularly, whether it could "overcome" the evangelicalism of its founding family to achieve its self-avowedly "nonsectarian" mission. Evidence suggests that under its current leadership the museum is pursuing a more evangelistic path. In the years just after the MOTB's opening, we were among a group of concerned biblical scholars who were interested in the question of the MOTB's relationship to evangelicalism, in part because of a felt desire for our academic field of inquiry not to be misrepresented or inaccurately appropriated in the public square. This museum exists in a prominent location, after all, and its proximity to public institutions lend it an air of authority. Additionally, its billionaire evangelical Christian funders were buying thousands of artifacts, controlling access to them, and asking members of our guild to become paid consultants or even de facto spokespeople (all while bound by nondisparagement clauses that limited academic freedom), in order to provide the MOTB with *ex post facto* academic credibility.[31] Museum of the Bible representatives attended our conferences as members of our guild gave papers pointing out perceived failings of the MOTB in its collection practices, the historical accuracy of its exhibits, and the degree to which non-Protestant traditions were misrepresented or marginalized. As many biblical scholars, including the two of us, continued to point out the evangelical "mistakes," museum representatives fired back that evangelical interests were at worst latent reminders of a previous vision for the institution.

Because of MOTB leadership's outreach to and sometimes conscription of professional biblical scholars into its project, it has been tempting for those of us primarily trained in the discipline of historical critical study of the Bible and also familiar with white Christianity in the United States to approach the museum's content with accuracy assessment in mind, that is, to examine its exhibits as experts on the history of biblical literature in order to make judgments about whether and how the exhibits have missed the mark. To do so, though, is to limit our methodological horizons to those most comfortable within the MOTB's own frame, to reproduce the assumption that historical critical study of bibles as libraries of ancient texts is somehow relevant to the transmedial, imaginary bible the MOTB makes scriptural. *Does Scripture Speak for Itself?* represents an evolution in our thinking about the significance of the MOTB. We approach it in this book not as a dialogue partner needing our advice and correction or as a target of ridicule but rather as an institutional object of analysis that gives us an opportunity to articulate and reflect on how contemporary white evangelicals are producing, consuming, and marketing a bible – and why that matters.[32]

In our research for this book, we visited the museum on multiple occasions to examine its exhibits, until September 2019, after which the Covid-19 pandemic made further visits unsafe. In the intervening time we have continued to follow updates on the museum and its exhibits through social media, press releases, and news stories. It is likely that the museum's exhibits will have evolved to some extent by the time this book is published. The analysis in what follows documents a period in the history of the museum's development as a material institution and thus will remain interesting even if, and as, the museum changes.

The analyses that we offer in the chapters that follow are neither journalistic nor ethnographic. We have learned much from journalistic work on the museum, which has been especially important in documenting the scandals that have dogged the museum's collection of artifacts. Much might also be learned in future studies that interview those involved in the museum's construction and operation, as well as those visitors who come to the museum, whether out of curiosity or a desire for a religious experience. Neither journalists nor ethnographers, we have analyzed the museum as a tangible institution, drawing on that which is visible to visitors, published by the museum and its press imprint, or said publicly by its employees and benefactors. We thus attend to the textual and the spatial while examining how both feature as elements within the larger institution of the MOTB.

In Chapter 1, we trace an important story of the production process of the MOTB's bible by interpreting the MOTB as the latest in a long line of institutions founded and funded by white evangelical business owners to advance their interests. Here we play a bit with the category of *provenance*, a word that has plagued the MOTB because of its donors' failures with illicit acquisitions of biblical artifacts. We reappropriate it, though, as a useful way of thinking about the origins of the bible produced by the MOTB. We suggest that the history we tell of white evangelicalism is essential for understanding the MOTB and the white evangelical bible it produces and advertises.

The next three chapters turn to the contents and contours of the MOTB's bible as constructed in the museum itself. Chapter 2, "Good Book," reveals that the bible produced by the MOTB is stridently benevolent, and further that that benevolence is particularly productive for white evangelicals who long for a national present and future in which the Bible holds as central a position in public life as they perceive it to have held in their nostalgic constructions of a Christian heritage for the United States. We demonstrate that through strategic negotiations of affiliation, the bible produced by the museum forges a path of redemption for white evangelicals that simultaneously works to excuse racist pasts, resist critique of the present, and ground a future in which white evangelicals can be moral authorities. Essential to our analysis is the recent work of Lauren R. Kerby, whose book *Saving History* outlines the nimbleness with which white evangelical Christians alternate between casting themselves as founders of the nation – insiders – and as marginalized, persecuted exiles–outsiders whose influence is under threat and needs defending.[33]

Chapter 3, "Reliable Bible," presses further into the distinctions of history and heritage as we show that the MOTB's bible transcends materiality even as the museum showcases material bibles of the past, present, and (envisioned) future. The MOTB's history provides a blueprint for evangelical aspirations of their bible's overcoming its particularity to become universal, which in turn authorizes their hegemony under cover of benevolence. Along the way, the museum's exhibits employ protective strategies that work to preserve its bible as a divine word from God that is easily accessible. Because of these protective strategies, the museum's bible is made doubly reliable, in its textual form and in the integrity of its content.

In Chapter 4, "Jesus, Israel, and a Christian America," we focus in particular on the transmedial nature of the MOTB's white evangelical bible. Here we make use of the work done by anthropologists of religion, such as James Bielo and Hillary Kaell, who study materialized bibles and recreations of biblical places. With sustained attention to the immersive and interactive, we articulate the narrative the MOTB's bible conscripts visitors into and consider how that narrative sacralizes landscapes that are special to contemporary white evangelical political interests. The museum's bible weaves a grand tapestry of theatrical experiences in which visitors become searchers for Jesus in a story of salvation and ultimately pilgrims to lands made sacred by Jesus, both the (imagined) holy land of Israel and the (perceived) promised land of America.

In our analyses, we retain the MOTB's names for its exhibits, including the three permanent exhibit floors – Impact of the Bible, Stories of the Bible, and History of the Bible – while redescribing them. The Impact of the Bible floor, we will show, is best seen as a series of installations celebrating white Christian heritage in the United States and advocating for and enacting Christian privilege.[34] The Stories of the Bible floor purports to be about biblical literacy but is better understood as a pilgrimage experience with Jesus at the center. The History of the Bible floor is actually a usable past for white evangelical dominion, conceived as divinely authorized.

Chapter 5 turns from the physical museum to its wealthy patrons, the Greens, who have fashioned themselves into the MOTB's "founding family" with a string of books, interviews, high profile speaking engagements, and other self-starting opportunities for Bible boosterism.[35] The Greens' philanthropic work with evangelical causes places them in a long history in the United States of evangelical business owners who have aligned their corporate projects with white evangelical interests through such activities as building institutions, funding missionary work, or sponsoring evangelical preachers. Yet in contrast to previous prominent examples, the Greens appear as vocal participants rather than anonymous funders. We argue in part that the MOTB functions to authorize the white evangelical Green family as Bible experts as the institution generates for them what we call "biblical capital." We analyze both how they generate this form of social capital through their myths of origins around the MOTB and how they are expending it to gain influence. Our close readings suggest that the bible the Greens commend as authoritative is capitalist, authoritarian and patriarchal, and white supremacist. Widespread acceptance of such a code would, in our judgment, result in retroactive acclaim for the Greens' accumulation of wealth, acquisition of artifacts, and Christian nationalist political action. In other words, their bible is one that works with them and for them.

Our use of the phrase "white evangelical," which we define more precisely in Chapter 1, is intended principally as description, not accusation. We have written this book not out of a need to fight a battle for intellectual territory or authority but out of the conviction that no mode of knowledge production and its institutional home(s) should be above analysis. As biblical scholars, we can assert that our guild is itself enmeshed within and shaped by white evangelicalism, Christian patriarchy and anti-Judaism, and colonialism. Inspired by the work of Vincent Wimbush, we are not interested in fighting over the "correct" reading of the Bible in its historical context, but rather in exploring the history of scriptures, "the psychology, the phenomenology, the sociology, the anthropology, the invention and uses, and the political consequences of the uses of the texts."[36] The MOTB's years-long success in involving – and alienating! – so many professional historical critics and archaeologists from a wide spectrum of religious and cultural affiliations shines another light on the centrality of white Protestant concerns and legacies in the guild of biblical studies. Many among us have a propensity to weigh in on "history" but not on ethics, to trace contexts without attention to the consequences.[37] It is important to us to confess at the outset of this book, then, that we are more than merely curious. We are stakeholders. We are critics. It is our hope that this mixing of American religious history with the cultural history of biblical literature will have something to say to our political present, particularly during a time in which our nation is wrestling with who belongs, who has access to resources, whose ideologies are normalized and celebrated, and whose are marginalized.

It is also a time in which some pockets of our academic field of origin, biblical studies – long shaped by the interests of white Christian men – is taking baby steps to reckon with its own whiteness, its own fantasy that *The Bible* exists, and the harmful consequences of both.

Like the bibles with which we opened this book – Nat Turner's, Thomas Jefferson's, Codex Washingtonianus, and the bibles in Indigenous languages – the Museum of the Bible teaches us less about *The Bible* than about a particular bible. In the end, our investigation of the MOTB is not focused on whether the institution gets *the Bible* right or wrong. But *good or bad* is fair game. So too is the question of why the MOTB constructs, performs, and sells the bible that it does. The white evangelical bible produced by the MOTB, in its privileging of whiteness, its desire for Christian hegemony, its imbrication with American neoliberal imperialism, is right for some more than others, and it is good for some and – to put it mildly – bad for others. We offer *Does Scripture Speak for Itself?* as a contribution to the growing body of literature cataloging and contextualizing white evangelical ideologies and practices as we also attend to the political and ethical stakes. White evangelical ways of knowing and understanding, ways of reading and thinking, have a history that runs deeper than the MOTB's exhibits. Central to that story are the ways white evangelical elites, rarely members of clergy, have built institutions to construct, reinforce, and amplify what evangelicals know of, say about, and ask of their bibles. Getting at these structures and practices of meaning requires an excavation of the ways white evangelicals have made and remade scriptural stories of their bibles and themselves over the course of US history.[38]

CHAPTER 1

Provenance

EVEN SINCE BEFORE IT OPENED, SCANDAL HAS DOGGED THE MOTB. Its collection, largely a result of the largesse of the Green family, has been plagued with fake and illicitly acquired objects. Scholars demonstrated that its Dead Sea Scrolls fragments were modern forgeries. Several of its manuscripts were stolen or purchased without the knowledge of their owners. A large number of items were seized by the US government or marked for repatriation. Many of these scandals can be grouped under one heading: provenance.[1]

Provenance is the data that accumulates around an object from the time of its creation to the present.[2] Where was it made? What was it made of? Where was it found? Who found it? Who owns it now and who has owned it in the past? Often bare bones information appears in small print on placards at museums, but museums generally keep larger records than those displayed in exhibits. They do this because the chain of custody of an object matters. It might help indicate the object's authenticity or adjudicate matters of legal ownership. International treaties governing the sale and purchase of certain kinds of objects come into play here too. Was the item looted from one country and imported into another? Was it stolen and then sold illegally? Studying an object's provenance, where it came from and how it got where it is, can have major implications for how we evaluate the significance of that object.[3] When the artifacts that would make up a large part of the MOTB's collection were being acquired by Hobby Lobby and the Green family, little attention was paid to the provenance of the objects that were purchased. Scrutiny from the academic community, federal law enforcement, the news media, and, in some cases, the MOTB's own curators have brought to light a criminal lack of attention to such matters. It remains to be seen how long it will take the museum to come to grips with its provenance problems.

The MOTB needs critical attention to questions of provenance to determine whether its artifacts are authentic and whether they have all been acquired legally – but that is not our project here. Scholars of provenance have noted that studying an object's provenance can be a window on to other interesting avenues of analysis. Research into provenance can shed light on the contexts in which an object was made and can "reveal an often-intricate network of relationships, patterns of activity, and motivations."[4] In this chapter we leverage the category of provenance to interrogate the origins and ownership histories of the bible produced by the MOTB, represented as "The Bible," digging beneath the placard that might be placed next to it if it were in a museum exhibit:

Museum of the Bible. 2017.
Brick, Steel, LED lights, Books.
A gift of the Green Family et al

Our story of the MOTB's provenance roots the institution's origins not solely in the particular interests of the Green family, about whom we will have much to say in Chapter 5, but further in the long history of white evangelicalism in the United States. The MOTB's bible, despite assumptions about timelessness and stability in the museum itself, is neither eternally preexistent nor beyond comprehension as a product of human history. There was a time when it was not. And there is a story to be told that lays bare where it came from, how it developed over time, whose interests shaped it along the way, and how people use it today (and to what ends). We here outline the historical, ideological, institutional, and sociocultural factors that have combined to make it possible for the Greens and their allies to have envisioned the construction of a billion-dollar institution near the National Mall that sustains, constructs, and sells a bible that "speaks for itself" and in support of their own interests – what we call a white evangelical bible.

As we will show, the MOTB belongs to a diffuse network built by white evangelical benefactors. The MOTB is the latest in a string of institutions, including schools, think tanks, political advocacy organizations, publishing houses, and ecclesiastical councils that have knit together white evangelicals by emulsifying, blending, and folding their sensibilities, presumptions, ideologies, and practices into a powerful assemblage of forces.[5]

WHITE EVANGELICALISM: AN INSTITUTIONAL APPROACH

White evangelicalism is a term used regularly by pundits and pollsters, most recently as a way of pointing to a sizable block of the coalition that elected Donald Trump president in 2016 and which has remained his most stable base.[6] This is not how we will use the term here. We particularly want to make it clear at the outset that we do not see white evangelicalism as either (a) a shorthand for racist white conservative Protestants, or (b) a shorthand for evangelicals more broadly. First, white evangelicals are not the only group of American Christians who have a complicated and dark history with race and racism. American Christianity of all kinds has yet to fully grapple with its entanglement with racism and whiteness.[7] Second, there are evangelicals who do not fit under our definition of white evangelicalism, and there are whites who identify as evangelical who likewise do not fit. Further, not all participants in white evangelicalism are themselves white. What we are pointing to is a group within evangelicalism defined just as much by its network of institutions as by its beliefs. "White" principally describes systems and institutions rather than demographics.[8] This may seem like a strange way of describing a religious group, comfortable as we are with defining religions by a shared set of beliefs.[9] Yet while sorting groups by beliefs may seem natural, it is far from simple. Beliefs are always only part of the story. White evangelicalism is most usefully construed as a sect within the larger history of American Christianity that built a durable coalition of institutions over the course of the late nineteenth and twentieth centuries to amplify a discrete set of theological, political, and economic beliefs and practices. While it has a longer history, white evangelicalism as we understand it crystallized in the middle of the last century and now operates as a significant force in American political life, notably as the base for the Republican Party.

WHAT IS AN EVANGELICAL? Evangelicalism, along with the study thereof, is messy. Evangelicals are hard to define, not least because many modern "evangelicals" don't use the term as a self-descriptor. The traditions that scholars define as evangelical represent a diversity of forms of early modern to modern Protestant Christianity, making it hard to mark clear boundaries around what the term covers. The dominant mode of defining evangelicalism has been through theological doctrine, what things they believe. A classic definition of evangelicalism is the quadrilateral developed by British historian David Bebbington: "*conversionism*, the belief that lives need to be changed; *activism*, the expression of the gospel in effort; *biblicism*, a particular regard for the Bible; and what may be called *crucicentrism*, a stress on the sacrifice of Christ on the cross. Together they form a quadrilateral of priorities that is the basis of Evangelicalism."[10] Bebbington's definition has been endorsed by the National Association of Evangelicals as both the proper way to mark evangelical identity and the method for identifying evangelicals for the purpose of research.[11] While it has been deeply influential in shaping scholarship on evangelicalism, it is important to note that Bebbington developed his quadrilateral as a way of describing evangelicals in early modern Britain. It is not necessarily helpful as a description of contemporary evangelicals in the United States. Further, while Bebbington's definition spurred research, its cooptation as a description of evangelicalism has turned it, as historian Timothy Gloege has argued, from a definition into a theological agenda.[12] If we press on the criteria Bebbington identifies, we can see the problem. Are evangelicals the only Christians who believe in religious conversion, care about the Bible, emphasize that Christian faith should manifest itself in action, or venerate the cross? Certainly not. As Gloege notes, presuming that "biblicism" is a unique attribute of evangelicals would be like "a political scientist defining Republicans as 'those who take the Constitution seriously.'"[13] One danger of defining evangelicals by broad theological categories is that such definitions end up doing theology rather than analysis.

A similar problem attends the theologically centered definition recently proffered by white evangelical scholar Thomas Kidd, a Baylor University professor who has been intimately connected with the MOTB: *"Evangelicals are born-again Protestants who cherish the Bible as the Word of God and who emphasize a personal relationship with Jesus Christ through the Holy Spirit."*[14] "This definition," Kidd writes, "hinges upon three aspects of what it means to be evangelical: being born again, the primacy of the Bible, and the divine presence of God the Son and God the Holy Spirit."[15] This theological definition of evangelicals allows Kidd to cast a wide net, drawing in the Puritans and the revivalists of the Great Awakening, anti-abolitionist and Social Gospel crusaders, and modern culture warriors of the Religious Right. Kidd's definition also makes space for Pentecostals in the evangelical tent and his accounting of who is in the movement places special emphasis on non-American evangelicals and Pentecostals. Kidd's definition suffers from the same problems as that of Bebbington. Lots of Protestants who would not identify as evangelical would evince connections to the Bible, Jesus, and the Holy Spirit. The focus on belief becomes a sharp tool to chip away heritages and practices now conceived as problematic. As American religious historian Kristin Kobes Du Mez has recently noted, theological similarities between evangelicals can be used to ignore racial differences that shape how shared theologies manifest in radically different politics and practices.[16] In interviews, Kidd has made clear that his definition is directed at contemporary theological and political issues, namely a frustration that white evangelicals like him have been identified as a key constituency in the Republican and Trumpist voting bloc.[17] Kidd's theological criteria cast evangelicalism as a big tent, multiethnic movement, which does the work of protecting the label of evangelical from what Kidd calls "white voters who call themselves evangelicals." Kidd's criteria, then, are designed to paint evangelicalism as multiethnic, while excluding white conservatives whom Kidd considers insufficiently evangelical.[18] At its core, we suggest, this definition is fundamentally border patrol born of defensiveness. In our judgment, Kidd's definition is ultimately a self-serving argument that protects his own evangelical respectability.

Theology as the primary indicator of identity functions as support for insider arguments. Definitions that rely solely on belief leverage theological markers of identity to make evangelicalism singular, while the tradition has always been multiple.[19] As evangelical scholar Mark Noll notes, the movement's "evangelical impulses have never by themselves yielded cohesive, institutionally compact, easily definable, well-coordinated, or clearly demarcated groups of Christians."[20] While a history of evangelicalism as a movement would need to pay attention to the decentralizing forces within the movement and treat it as a global phenomenon,[21] our project demands that we pay particular attention to a set of historical, institutional, and socio-logical developments within evangelicalism's big tent: the formation of the sect we call white evangelicalism, a sect that has created the conditions of possibility for the MOTB's bible. While traditional histories treat ideas as transcendent, our history situates them within systems, with particular attention to race, money, and politics.

White evangelicalism is a form of evangelicalism that is tied to a complex assemblage of institutions and forces that emerged in the wake of the Civil War but only fully crystallized after World War II. Its theological predilections were forged in the fire of post-Civil War socio-historical concerns during the tumult of Reconstruction and the Gilded Age. Its institutional supports were built by industrial patrons in the first half of the twentieth century. These institutions helped to spawn new networks and affiliations that made the sect into a political as well as ideological force, with figures like Billy Graham, Jerry Falwell, and Pat Robertson at the helm. At the same time, white evangelicals built a thriving consumer culture that tied their Christian identity to products that they bought and owned, from what music they listened to, what clothes they wore, or where they shopped.[22] While many white evangelicals do tend to believe in the theology articulated by Bebbington and Kidd, they share an additional set of theological beliefs that are likewise noteworthy and impactful: notions of divine chosenness, belief in a (semi-)imminent apocalypticism, and libertarian views on politics and economics. This form of evangelicalism was produced through the work of wealthy patrons, grassroots movements, and institutions. This material and historical assemblage has worked to make the theological beliefs of white evangelicals seem reasonable and self-evident, both to them and to those outside of the movement. (In fact, the movement has been so successful that evangelicals like Kidd can fear that their forms of evangelicalism have been excluded from broader social assumptions about who counts as an evangelical.)

In what follows we lay out a story of the sect we call white evangelicalism, taking seriously not just (dehistoricized) belief but also a set of institutions shaped by powerful donors that promote a particular theology, political orientation, consumptive practice, and economic philosophy. Our story in some places follows the mainstream account of the history of evangelicalism presented by scholars like Mark Noll, George Marsden, Grant Wacker, and others. This account often follows a trajectory from European pietistic movements to the Great Awakenings and then to Billy Graham. It is itself political and theological, in that it presumes that there is a stable and singular evangelical movement whose history can be traced and whose history is rooted in "respectable" theological and intellectual forebears, to whom errant modern evangelicals should harken.[23] Any history of evangelicalism is fictional since there has never been one evangelicalism; nor have all the actors who are claimed by evangelical history claimed the term for themselves. There are as many evangelicalisms as there are evangelicals. Our history of white evangelicalism is no less fictional; however, we offer it for heuristic purposes. We are not making claims to essence or completeness. Our story is crafted, rather, to help us to see white evangelical institutions that are missing from belief-centered histories. We highlight historical developments that shape and shaped the institutions and networks that, like the MOTB, have created, molded, and transmitted evangelical ideas. Our history is divided into four periods: the early evangelical movements in the eighteenth and early nineteenth centuries; the fusion of evangelical theology with dispensationalism in the post-Civil War period; the rise of the "fundamentalist" movement in the early twentieth century; and, finally, the construction of a robust network of institutions in which to house and promulgate fundamentalist theology.[24] It is with the building of this network and its subsequent activities that we see the emergence of what we will call white evangelicalism.

A BRIEF HISTORY OF WHITE EVANGELICALISM. Mainstream scholars of evangelicalism trace its origins to the early modern period and the emergence of pietistic revivalist movements in England and the

American colonies. By rooting the origins of evangelicalism in these movements, scholars can present evangelicalism as a big tent movement because, from the start, the movement cut across denominational lines and lacked a consistent theological outlook. Though we are skeptical of this myth of origins for evangelicalism, the metaphor of the big tent is suggestive not because it points to the singular origin of a diverse movement but because the tent, in the form of the tent revival, was an important institutional innovation in the early American religious landscape. Driven by charismatic, itinerant preachers who cultivated an accessible and emotional style of worship, tent revivals became wildly successful at spurring religious conversion in the eighteenth and nineteenth centuries, periods that modern scholars refer to as the First and Second Great Awakenings.[25] At the center of these revivals were charismatic preachers, like George Whitefield and Charles Grandison Finney, who eschewed the traditional theological expositions of the educated clergy in favor of direct appeals to the individual religious experiences of congregants shopping in the new religious marketplace of the early Republic that was made possible by the clearing of the American "frontier" for white settlers.[26] The revivals and their leaders drew strength from the gradual disestablishment of state churches in the years after the revolution.[27] As a result of the deregulation of the religious marketplace, religious seekers flocked to those who could thrill their emotions and speak to their hearts while also speaking in the language of the commonsense republicanism of the day. This commonsense republicanism fused Christian theology with liberalism, with its emphasis on individual freedom and voluntary choice.[28] The tent revivals that drew massive crowds crossed denominational lines, challenging the hierarchies of denominational structures and the expertise of religious professionals trained in the nation's seminaries.[29] In addition, these tent revivals marked an active time for Black conversion to Methodist and Baptist forms of Protestantism and the adoption, by Black Christian communities, of similar styles of worship to those offered by tent revivalists.[30] The "heart religion" fostered by tent revivals did not mean that early evangelicals completely embraced a free market of republican religion. Many evangelical elites in urban centers fretted about the instabilities introduced by the revivals and pushed for institutional interventions.[31]

Throughout this period, leading up to the Civil War, evangelical biblical interpretation tracked with a broader American appropriation of Enlightenment thought. In particular, the kind of Enlightenment rationality taken up by evangelicals presumed that correct interpretation was possible by each individual based on a rational assessment of the words on the page of scripture. Protestants had long emphasized the Reformation rallying cry of *sola scriptura* (by scripture alone) as an arbiter of Protestant orthodoxy. But this opened the door to a problem of hermeneutics: in the absence of sovereign decision-making, how would it be possible to determine what readings of scripture alone were correct?[32] In the early Republic, the freedom of individuals to read the Bible for themselves was shaped by a marriage of Christian and Enlightenment convictions: that the Bible was the arbiter of theological matters, that both religious and political authority required skepticism, that the United States possessed a unique covenantal relationship with God, and that understanding moral, theological, and political things was simple.[33] The confluence of these assumptions about religion and republicanism meant that "by the nineteenth century, it was an axiom of American public thought that free people should read, think, and reason for themselves,"[34] with the confidence that the Bible would speak plainly to each in the same way.[35]

This confidence in the "plain sense of Scripture" animated revivalist meetings of the Great Awakenings but also spurred the creation of Bible societies, the most famous being the American Bible Society, founded in 1816.[36] Like European Bible societies, the ABS sought to distribute bibles as widely as possible, under the conviction that their very ubiquity would have a unifying effect on the Republic. As biblical scholar Timothy Beal notes, the ABS's conviction that the Bible's interpretation was simple and universal can be seen in its mission statement: "to encourage a wider circulation of the Holy Scriptures without note or comment."[37] While this confidence in the Bible's transparency remained a common refrain, it was challenged by the lack of consensus among the early Republic's already diverse landscape of Christianities. If the Bible ought to be easily and universally interpretable and if God had made a covenant with the United States, why was there no agreement on the interpretation of scripture or the shape of the nation?[38]

The theological crisis of incongruous interpretations of the Bible stood at the heart of the debates between abolitionist and proslavery Christians in the lead up to the Civil War. Debates around the Bible's views on slavery began in earnest in the 1830s and soon led to widely divergent hermeneutics for interpreting the Bible.[39] No bible is short on passages that clearly condone, regulate, and assume the practice of slavery. This made the argument that the Bible was pro slavery more persuasive, in both the North and South, for those who relied on interpretation that privileged the "plain sense" of the text.[40] Abolitionist attacks on biblical support for slavery ended up relying on recourse to ethical principles and intuitive feelings that stood outside the plain wording of the text. The abolitionists rooted their critiques in the "self-evident truth" or the moral intuition that God intended all people to be free.[41] Thus, the abolitionist position was weak on textual evidence but was ultimately able to muster an argument rooted in a deeper set of principles that ran through the undercurrent of American religion.

While the question of slavery was resolved by the Union victory in the Civil War,[42] the resulting effects of the arguments around the Bible's relationship to slavery would have lasting consequences.[43] In the wake of the war, liberal Protestants built their own institutions that would allow them to dominate the religious landscape in the early twentieth century. Some of these Protestants would become associated with the Social Gospel movement, which took seriously the Bible's critiques of wealth and promotion of social justice in their bibles.[44] For many of the reformers tied to this movement, the Bible combined with a personal relationship with God offered a way to reform a society that had developed all manner of inequalities and vices as a result of the growth of cities during the Industrial Revolution.[45] At the same time, African Americans also left white churches, the effect not only of religious traditions and communities they had forged during their forced enslavement but also of the enforced segregation and white racism that characterized the Jim Crow South and the de facto segregation of the rest of the United States. With the departure of liberal whites and African Americans, evangelical churches solidified around a white theology of biblical literalism. This biblical literalism was embedded within what Anthea Butler has called the "Religion of the Lost Cause" that fused white southern resentment and racism with Christian theology.[46] The departure of African Americans from white evangelical churches and institutions marks the beginning of white evangelicalism as a distinct group among the various evangelical traditions.

Debates over slavery in the lead up to the Civil War accustomed white evangelicals to pointing to the literal words in their printed bibles as the primary interpretive move. "Open your Bibles to Deut 20:10–11, where we see that God plainly approves of enslaving one's enemies after battle." The end of the war had taken slavery off the table as a theological issue, which allowed white evangelicals in both the North and the South to forge new bonds around a biblical literalism that was not burdened by the defense of slavery.[47] Skeptical in the wake of abolitionist readings that appeared to them to run counter to the biblical text, white evangelicals turned away from social reform projects and turned inward, focusing on personal salvation and "redemption."[48]

White evangelicals soon found common cause with newly emerged corporate elites who shared white evangelicalism's skepticism around social reform – mostly because it would hurt their profits. Corporate evangelicals developed a new form of white evangelicalism that was safe for the respectable white middle class. An epicenter for this new branding of evangelicalism was the Moody Bible Institute in Chicago, under the leadership of Henry Crowell.[49] MBI's conservative evangelicalism merged business interests and newly developed strategies of consumer-based marketing with dispensational theology. Dispensational theology cast the Bible as a source for understanding history outside of the time periods narrated by the Bible itself.[50] Using methods of classification and cross-referencing developed by contemporary engineers and lawyers, dispensationalists used biblical prophecies to break all of human history into successive "dispensations," distinct time periods in which God worked with humanity in particular ways.[51] Dispensationalists tended to hang their chronologies around an eschatological expectation that the final judgment of God on the world was imminent. Thus there was no reason to work toward making society more just. They could remain as they were.

Dispensationalism imposed a "method" on biblical interpretation that required specialization and training to unlock the true meaning of the text. This method put limits on how meaning could be constructed by individual readers while also claiming to let the Bible speak for itself.[52] Dispensational theology blunted progressive arguments that society was and could continue to be improved through Christian social effort. It also attacked the social nature of Christian identity, asserting that the most important thing Christian institutions could do was to save souls that would be otherwise lost in the apocalypse, rather than wasting time ameliorating the effects or attacking the causes of economic inequality. Beyond the economic interests of many of its patrons, dispensationalism was an almost solely white theological project and dispensational theologians overlooked the violence used to oppress African Americans.[53] While pessimistic about progressive social engineering, this new dispensational evangelicalism gave corporate interests license to continue their business practices without ethical or theological limits.

The fights between conservative and progressive Christians soon gained new elements: Darwinism and evolution, German Higher Criticism and academic biblical studies, science and biblical miracles, and nationalism. The "modernists," as liberal Protestants came to be called, had built a robust network of church councils, seminaries, and missionary societies that would buttress the dominance of mainline Protestant denominations for the first half of the twentieth century. The conservative response turned to reelaborations of Christian "fundamentals," giving rise to the label "fundamentalism." Central to the articulation of the fundamentalist tradition was the "inerrancy" of the Bible, which framed the sacrality of the Bible in the language of scientific accuracy.[54]

With the financial support of western oil barons, the fundamentalists began to build their own institutions: dispensationalist Bible colleges on the model of MBI, missionary societies, and magazines that linked conservative evangelical clergy from different parts of the country for the first time.[55] In response to charges that they were insufficiently patriotic in the lead up to World War I, fundamentalists joined the modernists in accepting a role for nationalism in their theological identities.[56] Fundamentalist nationalism supported the resurgence of the Ku Klux Klan as an anti-immigrant project in the 1920s.[57] White evangelical institutions weathered the national embarrassment of the Scopes Monkey trial in 1925. While the trial has long been held up as the moment in which fundamentalists went into decline and retreated from American life, recent research has shown that it did not see fundamentalists withdraw from cultural engagement so much as push them to redefine themselves as a new breed of evangelical.[58]

Beginning in the 1930s and 1940s, corporate evangelicals began to build networks that brought together conservative evangelicals with business leaders. The repeal of prohibition was seen by white evangelicals as a shot across the bow from the Roosevelt administration. Despite having prominent voices on radio stations, white evangelicals had little political effect because they were not linked with the dominant forces resisting Roosevelt and the New Deal: major corporate interest groups like the National Association of Manufacturers.[59] The alliance between business leaders and conservative evangelicals was bridged by the formation of James Fifield's Spiritual Mobilization and the National Association of Evangelicals (NAE). These organizations used corporate funds to turn evangelical pastors against the New Deal and its "threat" to American free enterprise. In particular, they worked assiduously to align Christian theology with libertarian economic theory.[60] These networks would set the groundwork for the intensified conservative anti-Communism that would be the hallmark of the Cold War after World War II.[61] In this period, these same interests bankrolled conservative youth ministries (such as Youth for Christ, InterVarsity Christian Fellowship, and Campus Crusade for Christ) and helped launch *Christianity Today* as a mouthpiece for conservative interests.[62]

It was from these investments that new evangelicals emerged, represented by preachers like Billy Graham, who rebranded evangelicalism as individualistic, anti-Communist, and otherwise genially dispensationalist. Graham's brand of neo-evangelicalism was deeply connected to corporate interests that remained concerned about collectivism at home, even as they nominally supported the government's resistance to Communism abroad.[63] Collectivism at home was not only about fighting Communist sympathizers and the New Deal but also racialized fears of Black radicalism and the nascent Civil Rights movement.[64] Graham's ministry offered the perfect synthesis between pietistic religiosity and libertarian economics.[65] Neo-evangelicalism's success was made possible by huge demographic shifts, primarily in the Sun Belt. Migrations of conservative

Christians to the Sun Belt states created the potential for a radical realignment in the west, away from traditional mainline denominations to consumer-oriented megachurches and otherwise independent evangelical churches.[66] Mainline Protestant churches were able to dominate Christian political life in the first half of the twentieth century because they could act as gatekeepers to upwardly mobile professionals.[67] They also made use of church councils and federations, such as the National Council of Churches, that acted as organizing bases for political advocacy. Yet these structures did not keep up with demographic shifts in the west, making space for evangelical entrepreneurs to give the new transplants what they wanted: engaging and entertaining church services that focused on personal experience rather than collective responsibility.[68]

The neo-evangelicals made ample use of radio and television as media through which to spread their message. Graham's stadium-sized revival meetings riffed on the tent revivals that were so crucial to the origin myth of evangelicalism itself. They were made possible by networks of church and business partners.[69] Graham's preaching translated well as a consumer product in the expanding world of popular media. At the same time, other pioneers, like Charles Fuller and Bob Shuler, used radio to build evangelical coalitions around the fiction of "olde time religion."[70] The use of popular media allowed evangelicals to amplify their theological and political messages beyond the confines of the social networks that brought believers to individual churches.[71] These networks continued to expand into the 1970s and 1980s and eventually aligned with a wider assortment of conservative radio and television networks, such as a nationwide network of talk show radio hosts and Rupert Murdoch's publishing and television outlets.[72]

A final and important shift came with the attempts by activists within the Republican Party to align themselves with and recruit within evangelical churches. First, this shift followed the demographic realignments of the South during and after the Civil Rights movement. While the Republican and Democratic parties at mid-century each had liberal and conservative factions, Republicans saw potential for growth by drawing in conservative, white southern Democrats to their coalition. Over the course of the 1970s, the Republican Party was able to attract disaffected white conservatives to their party.[73] Key to this strategy was mobilizing white evangelicals. Evangelicals had debated the direction of their political leanings in the early 1970s, with some factions supporting a turn to social justice, racial reconciliation, and environmental stewardship.[74] Even when *Roe* v. *Wade* was handed down, it was initially supported by the Southern Baptist Convention and considered a "Catholic issue." Conservative evangelicals were drawn back into politics at the end of the 1970s when Supreme Court rulings began to threaten the tax-exempt status of white segregation academies run by evangelical churches.[75] The threat of government intervention in religious attempts to maintain segregation worried conservative evangelicals and brought them into the orbit of Republican organizers. Famously, conservative Catholic operative Paul Weyrich (among a handful of others) helped to shepherd evangelicals like Jerry Falwell and Pat Robertson into deeper political alignment with the Republican Party through institutions like the Committee for National Policy, Falwell's Moral Majority, and Ralph Reed's Christian Coalition.[76] Thus was born the coalition of white evangelicals that continues to be a major political force in the United States, particularly as supporters of the Republican party and Donald Trump.

The preceding narrative tells a story of how white evangelicals have become both a unique and identifiable sect within evangelicalism and a reliable voting bloc within the Republican coalition. In the wake of the Civil War, white evangelicals slowly built networks of churches, institutions, popular media outlets, and organizations that amplified white evangelical theology and galvanized a movement. White evangelical theology emerged from the Civil War with an attachment to the self-evident inerrancy of the Bible, a resistance to social reform, and an expectation of the imminent end of the world. Along the way these theological positions were fused with nationalism, libertarian economic thought, and racialized political stances. While the Civil War birthed the movement, the Civil Rights era was the catalyst that transformed white evangelicals into a Republican and then Trumpist bloc of white racial grievance. This was abetted by connections forged with business interests and conservative political leaders. The networks that built this movement have only expanded in recent decades, with the proliferation of conservative media, libertarian economic interests (connected to megadonors like the Koch and DeVos families), and the mobilization of white evangelicals around culture-war issues. Though we might be tempted to think of white evangelicalism as a recent phenomenon, the movement was built over a long period of time through huge investments in white evangelical infrastructure.

BUILDING WHITE EVANGELICAL INSTITUTIONS. The history of white evangelicalism is not simply a story about how a particular set of theological ideas spread over the course of the twentieth century. As Bruno Latour has aptly said, "An idea, even an idea of genius, even an idea that is to save millions of people, never moves of its own accord. It requires a force to fetch it, seize upon it for its own motives, move it, and often transform it."[77] White evangelical theology did not move of its own accord. It moved because of the work of powerful donors, educational institutions, churches, magazine distribution systems, radio and television stations, and political action committees.

Which brings us back to the Museum of the Bible. We interpret the MOTB as the latest in an extensive series of white evangelical institutions that have been paid for by wealthy corporate evangelical interests to amplify and project white evangelical theology and politics. The MOTB originated with the Greens, and Hobby Lobby and the Green family have been the principal funders of the museum's hefty price tag and the source of the bulk of the museum's collection of artifacts. Before they became famous as museum patrons, the Greens had engaged in a long-running campaign to advance white evangelical theology in the public square.[78] Hobby Lobby has regularly advertised its imbrication with evangelical identity in newspaper advertisements and in its practice of closing on Sundays.[79] The Green family also made national news in their successful fight against the Affordable Care Act's contraception mandate, culminating in the 2014 Supreme Court case known as *Burwell* v. *Hobby Lobby*. Given this track record, it makes sense to think of their institution, the MOTB, as one among many institutions built by white evangelical donors to amplify white evangelical theology. In what follows, we offer comparanda drawn from the early history of white evangelicalism that help illustrate how the Greens and their museum fit within this trajectory of institution building.

The Greens' philanthropic work with evangelical causes places them in a long history in the United States of evangelical business owners who have aligned their corporate projects with white evangelical interests through such activities as building institutions, funding missionary work, or sponsoring evangelical preachers. Alliances of wealthy business-men with Christian causes led to changes in both evangelical institutions, which became corporatized, and in businesses, which became infused with "Christian" precepts. Hobby Lobby was thus not the first corporation to attempt a fusion of Christian and capitalist principles. The early nineteenth century saw the creation of massive corporate evangelical enterprises devoted to distributing bibles and missiological texts. Run as massive print companies, institutions like the American Bible Society, the American Tract Society, and the American Sunday School Union modeled their practices on corporate techniques and relied on major corporate donors.[80] The American Tract Society's most important donor, for example, was Arthur Tappan, a silk merchant and one of the wealthiest people in New York at the time. In the early twentieth century, prominent Christian CEOs introduced to their businesses such practices as closing on the Sabbath and tithing corporate profits. This followed a model successfully publicized by Bruce Barton's famous *The Man Nobody Knows* (1925).[81] United States government policy acted as a stimulus for alliances between evangelicals and corporate interests, as corporations could channel money into evangelical causes and reap tax benefits as a result. Prominent families skirted inheritance taxes by using corporate profits to form nonprofit entities.[82]

The connections between evangelicals and business interests were not simply top-down. Some of the most famous evangelical preachers in the United States got their starts in retail. The famed evangelist D. L. Moody (1837–99) began his career as a shoe salesman, while Billy Graham (1918–2018) worked for the Fuller Brush Company before turning to Christian ministry. Once they became preachers, each drew on skills honed in the door-to-door marketplace to sell believers the value of Christianity. But neither did it on salesmanship alone. Behind each of them were powerful corporate sponsors that made their ministries possible. Moody's ministry in the 1860s was backed by prominent Chicago businessmen, for whom the pitch was that Moody's message would help form a new generation of Christian workers.[83] A generation later, Billy Sunday's revivals were supported by champions of industry, including the likes of John D. Rockefeller Jr. and S. S. Kresge.[84] Billy Graham's breakout crusade in Los Angeles in 1949 was funded by his corporate connections and rode the tide of Bible Belt migrations to the Sun Belt that was transforming California into a new hub for white evangelical theology.[85] From there, the evangelist built strong ties with western oil barons[86] and corporate executives,[87] from whom he received massive support for his ministry, later constituted as the Billy Graham Evangelistic Association.[88]

The Greens have joined this succession of white, wealthy evangelical donors who marry Christian and capitalistic interests with the building of evangelical institutions. Though the institutional framework of white evangelicalism has been constructed by many wealthy white Christians over time, the particular examples of Henry Crowell, Lyman Stewart, John D. Rockefeller Jr., J. Howard Pew, and Herbert Taylor help us further historicize their work and trace the provenance of the MOTB's bible. Each of these wealthy businessmen, with the exception of Rockefeller, put their capital to use in building institutions that amplified, directed, and shaped white evangelicalism. Crowell and Stewart built educational institutions while Pew and Taylor built networks between business interests and evangelicals.[89] The inclusion of Rockefeller in this list might be surprising since his philanthropic energies mostly benefited what are typically referred to as liberal, modernist, or progressive Christian causes. We include Rockefeller because the institutions he built served as models for institutions founded to counter his influence and because the fights that stemmed from that competition continue to shape the American religious landscape.[90]

In 1901, Henry Crowell joined the board of the Moody Bible Institute in Chicago, shortly after Moody's death. Crowell came to MBI after a successful career as the founder of the Quaker Oats Company, where he found great success "through the trifecta of trademark, package, and promotion," effectively employing what would become a model of consumer-focused branding.[91] As the institutional center of the MBI for the next several decades, Crowell embarked on a project of corporatizing MBI, instituting reforms of its bookkeeping, curriculum, publishing, and faculty.[92] He effectively used his business experience to turn MBI into a modern corporation. By the end of his tenure,

> MBI had a publishing wing that produced thousands of books, pamphlets, and flyers each year, all informed by modern methods of consumer marketing, standardization, and distribution. Thanks in no small part to Crowell, MBI was transformed into a multifaceted center for the promotion of a new kind of socially engaged conservative evangelicalism, one that would rely on big businessmen's influence to perpetually define and "revive" itself.[93]

While Crowell served as the institutional core of MBI during his tenure, he was careful in managing the institute's brand: an evangelicalism safe for middle-class consumption.[94] Crowell's MBI did not focus its attention on just any middle-class consumers; it aimed specifically at the white middle class.[95] It did this by supporting "respectable racism," which condemned practices like lynching but supported the Jim Crow order and resisted calls for racial justice.[96] Crowell's MBI was neither a seminary nor a church. It was instead a corporation that was organized around selling a branded product. Crowell's business experience and corporate perspective were folded into the Christian work of the MBI, creating a model that would be replicated in other white evangelical institutions. The MOTB in many ways resembles Crowell's MBI. As we explore further in subsequent chapters, it functions as an educational institution, a publisher, and an advocate for a respectable white evangelicalism that appeals to middle- and upper-class Americans.[97] The branding that accompanies the MOTB's various public relations campaigns harkens back to Crowell's tight control over the messaging that came out of MBI.

While Crowell was a businessman turned Christian administrator, Lyman Stewart spent his wealth, like the Greens have done, building institutions. His goal was to amplify his dispensationalist theology. Stewart was a California-based oilman who built Union Oil into a major force in the western oil market.[98] Raised a Presbyterian, he became a devotee of dispensationalism after attending the 1894 Niagara Bible Conference, a hub for early dispensationalist theology.[99] As Stewart's company became more established, he turned his attention and wealth to building institutions that would spread dispensational theology and resist the Social Gospel efforts of the Rockefellers, his ardent foes in both business and religion.[100] In 1891, he founded the Pacific Gospel Mission, now known as Union Rescue Mission, and helped pay for the building of the Church of the Open Door, both in Los Angeles. In 1908, he provided the funds for the creation of the Bible Institute of Los Angeles (known now as BIOLA University), which he hoped would be a training ground for Christian dispensationalists on the west coast as a counterweight to the modernist forces at eastern schools like Chicago Divinity School.[101] The current president of BIOLA, Barry H. Corey, serves on the board of the MOTB.[102] Stewart's philanthropic impulse was legendary, such that his desire to give away his money often put his business into danger.[103] But his most famous contribution to the movement, paradoxically, is his anonymous financial support, alongside that of his brother Milton, for *The Fundamentals*,[104] a twelve-volume defense of conservative, premillennial theology that would shape the course of white evangelical theology's course through the twentieth century.[105] Distributed at no cost to upwards of 300,000 people, *The Fundamentals* was Stewart's brainchild. Beyond bankrolling the project, he played a prominent role in the formation of its editorial board and in the scope and goals of the project.[106] Stewart envisioned the series as a platform for promoting dispensational theology and a kind of "spiritual muckraking" against liberal Christian theologians.[107] The editors of the series, led by Henry Crowell at MBI, saw *The Fundamentals* as an opportunity to sell a conservative orthodoxy to white middle-class Christians across denominations, creating a nationwide network of like-minded religious consumers. Not one of the articles in the series was written by an African American author, and only a few touched on the particular end-time fixations of dispensationalist thought. Instead, the topics covered included basic theological issues that explicitly did not attack distinctive positions of mainline Protestant denominations.[108] The mailing list that was put together to get *The Fundamentals* into readers' hands became one of the first national networks of conservative Protestants, and a prize that Stewart and his collaborators wrestled over. Ultimately, *The Fundamentals* helped to shape white evangelicalism into an imagined community, to use

Benedict Anderson's term, that saw itself as the embattled foe of theological and secular modernism defending "old-time religion."[109]

Like Christian philanthropists after him, including the Greens,
Stewart drew on the language of stewardship to frame his wealth.[110] He
also saw his business as part of what religious studies scholar B. M. Pietsch
calls an alchemical transmutation "of oil into money, of money into
theological education and missions projects, and of religious work into
the eternal salvation of human souls."[111] While Stewart's fundamentalist
views would later be tied to conservative political projects, during his
lifetime he supported progressive political and social activity, a fact which
shows that his activism occurred at a time before links between big
business, evangelicalism, and conservative politics had coalesced.[112]

Stewart's nemeses were the Rockefellers, the owners of the monopol-
istic Standard Oil. It was Standard's control of the oil market that pushed
Stewart west to California, where he could succeed in capturing crude
outside of Rockefeller's orbit. In the 1880s, Rockefeller Sr. began funnel-
ing his wealth into charitable organizations, notably Baptist missionary
societies and the University of Chicago, to which he would donate
$35 million over the course of several decades.[113] Rockefeller's charitable
giving was initially haphazard, much like Stewart's, until he hired
Frederick Gates, a Baptist pastor from Minneapolis, in 1892 to oversee
what would become the Rockefeller Foundation in 1913.[114] When John
D. Rockefeller Jr. took over the family's giving, he and Gates developed
a philanthropic empire of sorts, large enough to rival the family's oil
empire.

The Rockefeller support for Christian causes came at the same time
that the Social Gospel movement emerged as a response to the social and
economic problems of industrialization. Social Gospel theologians
articulated a Christian theology that pointed to biblical condemnations
of wealth and vice and directed believers to work toward the transformation of society's collective sins.[115] This ability to think systemically about
the intersection between social issues and theology led to the formation
of departments, commissions, and councils among progressive churches
to organize collective responses to urban poverty and vice. Rockefeller's
largesse spurred these developments, creating a host of institutions tied
to progressive interest in humanitarianism, social justice, and

ecumenism. Among the beneficiaries of Rockefeller's wealth were the Federal Council of Churches, later the National Council of Churches, Riverside Church in Manhattan, missionary societies, and new institutes promoting health, hygiene, and medical research. With progressive ministers and theologians like Harry Emerson Fosdick at Union Seminary, Rockefeller's philanthropy came to anchor what Darren Dochuk calls a "civil religion of crude," referring to the oil revenues that bankrolled it.[116] While Rockefeller's business pursuits emphasized rationalizing and managing the oil industry under the monopoly of Standard Oil, his philanthropic work aimed at reform that "propagated a social gospel that called on Christians to construct a better society by way of their economic and political clout."[117]

All of Rockefeller's philanthropic projects were resisted by Stewart, creating a competition that paralleled their corporate rivalry. But the vision of society offered by the Rockefeller Foundation and its investments would be countered a generation later by another dynastic oil family: the Pews, under the leadership of J. Howard Pew and a coterie of Pew family trusts.[118] J. Howard Pew was the scion of a prominent eastern oil family. He was raised Presbyterian, but his father, Joseph Newton Pew, ensured that J. Howard grew up sheltered from the Social Gospel turn that was happening across mainline churches.[119] He was educated in private schools and attended a Presbyterian college, Grove City College, whose curriculum was controlled by Joseph Newton Pew, the chair of the board of trustees. After a few courses at MIT, J. Howard went to work as an engineer at Sun Oil, his father's company, at the age of nineteen. When control of the family's oil interest passed to J. Howard, the threat of the Social Gospel movement had transformed into Roosevelt's New Deal, which was bitterly opposed by the corporate interests of industrialists like Pew. It was fear of the New Deal's threat to corporate and conservative interests, rather than the strident anti-Communism that would be at the forefront in the 1950s, that brought evangelicals into politics.[120] Roosevelt drew heavily on Social Gospel themes in selling the New Deal, and his efforts found support in the mainline churches that had been the recipients of Rockefeller's largesse.[121]

Like Rockefeller and Stewart, J. Howard stayed out of the fray directly, instead funding organizations that could bridge his libertarian economic philosophy with white evangelicalism.[122] Among the organizations that benefited from his money was James Fifield's Spiritual Mobilization, which spread Christian libertarianism from corporate boardrooms to evangelical pulpits.[123] When J. Howard soured on the project, he invested more money in Howard Kershner's Christian Freedom Foundation (CFF), which had a similar mission of sharing libertarian economics with Christian pastors.[124] CFF's magazine, *Christian Economics*, became a pet project of Pew's. He monitored each issue for signs of collectivism among its contributors. Pew also funded the formation in 1943 of the National Association of Evangelicals, which stood in opposition to Rockefeller's National Council of Churches.[125] The NAE served as a vehicle for rebranding fundamentalism, opposition to the New Deal, and resistance to Communism in favor of free-market libertarianism, and would become a hub for preachers like Billy Graham to work alongside prominent business leaders.[126] It also gave conservative clergy a venue for organizing their efforts, creating efficiencies in their overlapping missions and focus in their lobbying efforts.[127] These investments paid dividends by creating networks of Christian businessmen and evangelical clergy.

Pew also helped to fund conservative magazines like *National Review*, connected with the conservative Catholic William F. Buckley Jr. and *Christianity Today*.[128] The latter had deep ties to Billy Graham, whose father-in-law served as the editor, and to other major industrial donors who favored libertarian policies and hated unions and government regulation.[129] Pew was deeply involved behind the scenes in pushing his views on what *Christianity Today* should publish, and he occasionally penned articles for the magazine.[130] *Christianity Today* was able to do what Pew's earlier investments could not: convince evangelicals to distrust social reform. It did this not by critiquing progressive or liberal politics but rather by ruthlessly attacking the premise that the church should be involved in social reform at all.[131]

The founding of Fuller Seminary shows how the networks that Pew funded and moved through could produce new connections and institutions for the movement. In the 1940s Charles Fuller was a popular preacher in Long Beach, California, with a radio show called the *Old Fashioned Revival Hour*. Fuller used his financial success to found Fuller Theological Seminary in Pasadena in 1947. Harold Ockenga, the first president of the NAE, served as the first president of the seminary, which also attracted leading theologians like Wilbur Smith and future editor of *Christianity Today* Carl Henry.[132] When the financial strain of bankrolling the seminary became too much for Fuller's ministry to bear, he turned to oil prospecting to fund the school, forming Providential Oil and prospecting in California and Oklahoma.[133] While this business venture was going south, Pew invited Ockenga to a series of lectures directed at oil executives around the country. Through this working relationship, J. Howard was convinced to donate money to secure the seminary's finances. Fuller Seminary would go on to be an incubator of the neo-evangelicalism of leaders like Graham that sold a palatable white evangelicalism to the Sun Belt.[134] A generation later it would also incubate the New Apostolic Reformation, a neo-Pentecostal/Charismatic Christian movement, notably through seminars taught by C. Peter Wagner, that would go on to form a loose network of churches that have become some of the most visible supporters of Donald Trump.[135] The story of Fuller Seminary's creation as a white evangelical institution shows the utility of paying attention to networks of donors, radio stations, oil manufacturers, lobbying groups, and the organizations that tied them all together. The story of white evangelicalism is not one of ideas alone.

Pew's massive financial investments in the production of a libertarian Christian movement largely went nowhere, at least initially.[136] His brand of libertarianism was dogmatic and distrustful of institutional authority, which made it a hard sell for Christian clergy. It was also unclear how libertarianism could connect with Christian theology. While Pew convinced few Christians to take up the mantle of libertarianism, his money did fund the formation of mailing lists, magazines, and organizations that would create the platform upon which neo-evangelicals like Billy Graham would build. Through the 1950s, membership in mainline churches, staffed by liberally trained clergy, was a marker of solid, white middle-class respectability, a way to mark a family as trustworthy. By the 1960s, corporations looked to college education to determine whom they hired for increasingly professionalized labor, while the population growth in the Sun Belt outpaced the influence of mainline churches and their networks. Without the need for mainline respectability, the new white professional classes, particularly in the west, gravitated toward just the kind of churches that Pew had helped shape and Graham would come to champion: those with entertaining services that railed against big government and focused on the work of saving souls.[137]

Pew was one of a string of businessmen who became increasingly drawn to evangelicalism by the middle of the century because they saw in these groups allies in a fight against the threat of the New Deal.[138] Among this generation of Christian libertarian businessmen was Herbert J. Taylor. A Methodist and Rotarian in Chicago, Taylor made a name for himself by turning around Club Aluminum during the Great Depression.[139] He became famous for his "Four-Way Test" for corporate decision-making that would become one of the first templates for the popular genre of Christian business guidebooks.[140] Taylor's test became famous through his company's branded radio program *Club Time*, which gave Club Aluminum a chance to advertise its products while also selling Christians the benefits of merging Christian identity with capitalist ideology.[141] Taylor's business philosophy was explicitly Christian, rooted in his Christian theology of servant leadership.[142] Not only did it draw his Christian principles into managerial discourse; it also served as a model for Christian businessmen like Hobby Lobby founder David Green, who would also present their Christian principles as good for business.[143]

Like Pew, Taylor funneled his resources into creating new Christian networks to spread the gospel of Christian libertarianism, particularly to young people. Taylor founded the Christian Workers Foundation (CWF) in 1939. The CWF would help fund the expansion of Charles Fuller's *Old Fashioned Revival Hour* to a national audience in the early 1940s.[144] He later funneled Club Aluminum stock through CWF to finance the expansion of the InterVarsity Christian Fellowship and Young Life.[145] Taylor also gave financial support to Youth for Christ, which briefly used part of his house for meetings, and the Christian Business Men's Committee International (CBMCI).[146] The former was the springboard for Billy Graham's meteoric rise, while the latter was an all-white premillennialist network of businessmen that linked "evangelical identity and social authority to respectable manhood – especially white manhood – and the stilling power of the business elite."[147] Taylor's work made a huge impact on white evangelicalism. Evangelical business leaders, together, were now able to forge a more united influence bloc that amplified their power over policy, in both church and state. Further, because many of these business leaders worked in the defense industry, they were the bridges between the antistatist politics of evangelicals during the New Deal era and the anti-Communist politics of the military-industrial complex, which rejected big government outside of massive investments in the military. Finally, Taylor was among a vanguard of evangelical donors who saw the end of World War II as an opening for an American-backed evangelization of the world.[148] Taylor saw American imperial power as a tool that could be used to spread the gospel, along with capitalism, to new markets.

THE MUSEUM OF THE BIBLE WITHIN THE HISTORY OF WHITE EVANGELICAL INSTITUTION BUILDING. The history of white evangelicalism is a story of how a white conservative reaction to the Civil War spawned a movement that grew in scope and complexity throughout the twentieth century. Originating in white grievance, anti-Blackness, and a literal hermeneutic for reading the Bible, white evangelicalism soon folded in dispensational theology, antimodern skepticism, libertarian economic philosophy, and a resistance to social reform into its theological and political systems. This transformation was the result of material alliances that were forged between white evangelicals (with their churches) and emerging corporate business interests. Major donors, with their own causes and interests, seeded new networks and funded the formation of institutions and organizations that would, in turn, amplify white evangelical theology back over the network while continually folding in new allies. This was the network that carried evangelical ideas and gave a sense of fixity and stability to evangelical identity. The donors we have curated from this longer history made their biggest marks on the movement before it returned to the national spotlight alongside Billy Graham's telegenic smile in the 1960s and came to dominate the political landscape behind the Republican Party after the ascendancy of Ronald Reagan. In many ways, we would find similar figures in this time period: S. Truett Cathy, Sam Walton, Bill Hwang, the DeVos and Prince families, among others. The examples from this earlier period bring into focus the impact of Crowell, Stewart, Pew, and Taylor, less appreciated because they labored before evangelicalism had come into its own as a cohesive force.

How, then, does the Museum of the Bible fit into this history of white evangelicalism? Stewart, Pew, and the liberal Rockefellers transformed their oil empires into white, Christian empires, albeit competing ones. Each saw their extractive industries as transmutable machines: transforming money earned into saved souls. From these oil empires came schools, missionary societies, church councils, magazines, clergy and business networks, radio programs, and many other mechanisms for amplifying white Christian theology throughout US society and beyond. The Greens too sit atop an extractive empire, though one that transforms cheap labor and low-cost consumer products into capital for evangelization.[149] Like Taylor, the Greens see politics and economics as braided with theological causes. In particular, both see neoliberal political and economic power as vehicles for spreading the gospel, and vice versa.[150] Set near the US Capitol, at the heart of American power, the MOTB is a node within a network of white evangelicals that have long built institutions to connect their churches to political and economic power. The parade of politicians, interest groups, evangelical media, and tour groups to and through the MOTB makes it a meeting place similar to the business associations formed and patronized by men like Pew and Taylor.

This is not to say that these men would have been on board with all the particulars of the MOTB. Were they to have sat down together to talk politics and religion, J. Howard Pew and Lyman Stewart would likely not have seen eye to eye on every issue. Stewart was a fan of trust busting, after all. Yet the common threads that connect Stewart and Pew to the same history of white evangelicalism show that this is a movement that has developed over time as new alliances are forged and new institutions built. It is not uncommon, for example, for contemporary evangelicals to mourn the evangelicalism of their youth, now that the movement has changed, with the bulk of its constituents supportive of the Trumpist version of the Republican Party. By reading the MOTB as a white evangelical institution, we are not arguing that it is invested in precisely the same project as that of Pew, Stewart, or Crowell. We read the MOTB both as an amplifier and a transformer within the sound system of white evangelical culture. The MOTB magnifies theological and political themes common to the movement while also transforming them. The MOTB is an interested party among the other institutions that form the white evangelical network.

In the chapters that follow we analyze the museum as a machine that produces and publicizes a white evangelical bible for white evangelicals. We look at what themes it chooses to lift up and amplify and what it transforms. We look too at how the museum becomes useful to the Green family itself. By analyzing the museum and its donors as part of a larger history of white evangelical networks, we refuse to confine ourselves to assessing the MOTB's theology. Rather, following Pietsch's assessment of Lyman Stewart's benefactions, we think more expansive questions must be raised about the costs of this museum: the environmental and social costs of Hobby Lobby's supply chain, the political costs of the Greens' Christian Nationalism and Christian Zionism, the social costs of their philanthropic enterprises, and the costs of their ambitions for the dominance of a white evangelical bible.[151]

Studying the history of white evangelicalism and its institutions offers one way to get at the provenance of the MOTB and its bible. A different approach might be to read the MOTB as part of the colonial and imperial history of Euro-American museums, as in the recent work of Gregory Cuéllar.[152] Unlike its predecessors such as the British Museum, the MOTB is not a direct outgrowth of colonial regimes of conquest and capture; however, its origins and existence rely on neoliberal economic systems, such as the labor and supply chains that bring capital to Hobby Lobby, and on the economic inequalities and political instability that create the market for wealthy collectors to acquire artifacts. While a history of the MOTB among other museums would yield different and compelling insights, we see value and urgency in reading the museum as one among many similar attempts to create, distribute, and amplify the interests of white evangelicals and their bible. If we look at the museum from this angle, we can see in a new light the many institutional connections to other white evangelical groups that have begun to activate the MOTB as a white evangelical node. The MOTB currently has a number of exhibits sponsored by or produced in collaboration with white evangelical parachurch organizations such as the YouVersion Bible App, evangelical multimedia producers I Am Second and ColdWater Media, bible societies and missionary organizations such as IllumiNations Bible, Every Tribe, Every Nation, and the ABS, and so-called social reform ministries like Chuck Colson's Prison Fellowship. The museum has also partnered with evangelical institutions of scholarship and learning, from Tyndale House in Cambridge to evangelical colleges and universities in the United States. These connections have been facilitated in part by the Scholars Initiative, formerly the Green Scholars Initiative, which has contracted with these schools to do research on items in the museum's collection. As recently as 2019, the museum also brokered financial support for Christian Zionist tours of Israel.[153] Finally, the museum has had partnerships with evangelical book publishers, such as Worthy Books, which produced the MOTB BOOKS imprint, and Zondervan, which has published books by the Green family as the MOTB founders.

Another place to see the networks to which the MOTB is already connected is the donor wall that has been set up on the museum's first floor. Such walls are common in museums, offering a place to honor the benefactions of important donors. They tell us, among other things, about the social and professional networks that course through a museum. A cursory examination of the donor wall shows that the MOTB is tied to prominent white evangelical groups and business interests. Among the names listed are megachurch pastors Rick Warren and Joyce Meyer, megachurches like Gateway Church in Dallas/Fort Worth, Congressman Steven Pearce, and producer Mark Burnett, who was famously the architect of Donald Trump's rise as a TV personality on *The Apprentice*. Four different foundations linked to the DeVos family are listed,[154] along with major donors to conservative causes like Jack DeWitt, Ron Cameron (through his Mountaire Corporation), Sung Kook "Bill" Hwang (via his Grace and Mercy Foundation), and the Coors family. The Fellowship of Companies for Christ International is another benefactor. Founded in the late 1970s by an Atlanta businessman, the organization follows the pattern set by Taylor's CBMCI.[155] The MOTB is also listed as the recipient of $250,000 from the Thirteen

Foundation, a nonprofit funder of a whole host of conservative causes, from Koch network allies to anti-LGBT and anti-abortion groups to Christian nationalist groups like David Barton's Wallbuilders.[156] The nonprofit is run by Farris Wilks, a billionaire who, along with his brother Dan, made a fortune through fracking and has since become a major funder of right-wing groups.[157] Alongside these donors are several Christian ministries devoted to promoting money management or leadership training and representatives of major corporations: Coca-Cola, Interstate Batteries, Covington Aircraft, Jasco, Meguiars, and Coors Brewing. The names on MOTB's wall are not only a visible reminder of the conservative and business networks that made the museum possible but also a means of expanding the network itself. As Jon Sharpe, MOTB's chief relations officer, said in a recent interview:

> Getting high net worth individuals to hear or see others participating is a great way to cultivate them. In the museum we have a Wall of Stones, where some well-known business owners in America have their names displayed commemorating their investment in the mission to invite all people to engage with the transformational power of the Bible. I've observed other business owners standing at that wall and taking pictures of the names. Often people will ask us, "What does it take to get our name on that wall?" The wall becomes symbolic of being on a wall with other significant leaders across America who want to make a statement for generations to come.[158]

The donor wall at the museum is thus a reminder that capital, both real and symbolic, flows through the museum itself, a topic to which we will return in Chapter 5. These connections underscore the ways in which the MOTB was born from within a white evangelical network while also engaged in the work of expanding it, in ways similar to those of the early twentieth-century institutions we have explored in this chapter. In what follows we look at how the MOTB constructs and advertises a white evangelical bible that can speak to and resonate within this network.

CHAPTER 2

Good Book

THE MUSEUM OF THE BIBLE IS DESIGNED TO MAKE VISITORS feel good about the Bible. The visual experience is inviting, inspiring. Music ranging from serene to triumphant dominates a soundscape that recalls, at least for visitors with ears to hear, contemplative and joyful praise songs not unlike those frequently featured on the MOTB stage.[1] The feel-good vibes are consuming, even coercive, in their near relentless ubiquity and repetitive performance. The graces are amazing.

The MOTB does not draw visitors' attention to what many would say are bad or morally questionable parts of the Bible.[2] On the Stories of the Bible floor, for example, visitors reenact the Israelites' crossing of the Jordan River into Canaan – but without any dead bodies or other remnants of the violence portrayed in the book of Joshua. Hagar's pain (Genesis 16, 21) is unexplored. Jael's tent peg (Judges 4–5) is omitted. Biblical fantasies of sexual abuse (e.g. Ezekiel 23; Revelation 2) are absent. These Bible stories, usually passed over in sermons and Sunday school lessons, do not lend themselves well to entertaining museum exhibits for the masses. Selective storytelling in this context supports the MOTB's mission of being inviting and will likely strike observers as unsurprising. The MOTB's focus on the positive is worth noting, however, for the ways in which it sets this institution apart. Other Bible-themed attractions, such as the Ark Encounter and Creation Museum in Kentucky, capitalize on connecting the Bible to fear, warning visitors affectively of God's past violence in the flood and of dire consequences if they fail to obey God in the face of an impending apocalyptic judgment. Further, other museums have exhibited material that is difficult and even painful for visitors to encounter. One thinks, for example, of the United States Holocaust Memorial Museum just down the Mall from the MOTB. While the MOTB's presentation of the Bible as the Good Book is perhaps not unpredictable because of the institution's entanglements with evangelical Christianity, we must observe that it was also not inevitable based either on the actual contents of biblical literature or on the professional constraints of museum exhibition.

Good feelings in the MOTB are provoked and nourished by an organizing commitment, evident in the museum exhibits, to the goodness of the Bible itself. The Bible is conceived as fundamentally benevolent, inherently beneficial. Evangelical Christians are certainly not the only population group who think of the Bible in exceptionally positive ways. Its reputation as "the Good Book" extends beyond the particular religious sensibilities of the founders of the MOTB. As we turn now from contextualizing the museum as a white evangelical institution to describing the bible it constructs, we outline how the MOTB presents a bible that is exceptionally productive for white evangelical heritage-making in the United States and we interrogate the potential costs of this intellectual and affective project. The particular bible produced by the MOTB, we argue, is not merely good. It is good *for white evangelicals.*[3]

On the Impact of the Bible floor, MOTB exhibits ask us to appreciate – in both senses of the word, to acknowledge and to affirm – the Bible's foundational role in the nation's birth and other world-changing happenings, including such human necessities as hospitals, calendars, naming practices, and the songs of Elvis Presley. In the museum's "Bible in America" exhibit on the Impact floor, we encounter a vision of a national past in which the Bible served as a fundamental resource for Christian America's heroes: from the Pilgrims who landed on the shores of the New World to the fiery preachers of the Great Awakenings who inspired spiritual revival to the great figures of twentieth-century civil rights movements who fought for freedom for all. Progress is presented as dependent on the Bible, made possible by it and impossible without it.

At the MOTB, the Bible is an instrumental partner, an indispensable ally, and guiding light for positive change in history both in the United States and in the world.

This celebration of the Bible in history is a key ingredient in the MOTB's heritage-making for white evangelical Christians.[4] Dependent on a nostalgia for a past golden age in which the Bible has been central and authoritative, along with a simultaneous desire to see its centrality restored, this ideological system is rendered incoherent unless the Bible is conceived as inherently, and thus universally, beneficial. If the Bible is flawed, morally suspect, or even ambiguous, it cannot be commended for restoration in its perceived rightful place as authoritative guidebook. For the logic of white evangelical Christian heritage-making to work, the Bible *must* be good. Yet in a country largely defined by its history of racialized chattel slavery and plagued by such slavery's lingering effects, white evangelical Christians face an intellectual knot of how to untie the Bible from their ancestors' misdeeds. The Bible has not always been on the right side of history, in large part because history's sides only reveal their contours, and their rightness, in retrospect.[5] People have read (and indeed continue to read) their bibles to demand subservience to tyrannical regimes, abuses of or oppressive restrictions on women, deadly antisemitism, and a whole host of other positions that today appear obviously wrong to our moral sensibilities. Perhaps no case is more clear than the Atlantic slave trade and the institution of slavery in the New World.[6] Indeed, American chattel slavery is the most inconvenient historical reality for white evangelicals to reconcile with commitments to their own marginality and calls for the Bible to resume its rightfully authoritative position.

The MOTB engages in a series of creative negotiations to square a commitment to the Bible as the unassailable Good Book with historical realities that challenge this commitment. Such strategies include limiting chronological scope in beneficial ways, drawing distinctions between Bible devotees and Bible interpreters, selective history telling, distinguishing between "real" and hypocritical Christianity, and attributing positive change to divine providence while attributing negative change to human interference or disobedience. Particular attention to race and slavery in the museum helps us see how this institution creates a productive past for white evangelicals that can serve as a platform for advocating for a (re)centering of the Bible in US public life while at the same time defending against potential accusations that this version of the past fails to account for racial atrocities that could be presented as evidence against the Bible's inherent benevolence.[7] Ultimately, we show, the bible produced in the MOTB functions as a carefully constructed bridge over which white evangelicals can walk to reach the right side of victimhood in order to commend their moral authority in the nation.

BIBLICAL AUTHORITY AND RELIGIOUS LIBERTY IN AMERICA

Images of the *Mayflower* and a golden relief of its famous Compact greet visitors to the "Bible in America" corridor on the Museum's Impact of the Bible floor.[8] A multicolored tapestry lines the entire left side deep and wide. As viewers walk down the long hall, they pass a reproduction of the Liberty Bell, a rifle colloquially known as a Beecher's Bible, and, at one point, a feathered war bonnet belonging to the late Reverend Billy Graham.[9] Along the right side and through the middle are glass cases enclosing artifacts intended to illustrate the Bible's importance in the country's founding and the nation's subsequent journey towards abolition, women's suffrage, and the Civil Rights movement. Occupying over five thousand square feet in total, the exhibit covers a chronological span from 1492 to the 1980s, culminating in a guest survey soliciting feedback on how visitors normatively view the Bible in the United States today.[10] Persistent references to two values significant to modern evangelicals like the Greens – "biblical authority" and "religious liberty" – organize the exhibit. These are presented as intertwined ideals, markers of societal virtue that are necessary for individual and national flourishing. On the face of it, to outsiders these are two ideals that do not easily combine. On the whole, biblical literature, as much as one can generalize, demands allegiance to one god – and a specific god at that.[11] One invites cognitive dissonance in commending the Bible as an authoritative determiner of behavior for all and at the same time insisting that everyone should be able to behave in whatever ways they wish based on a variety of religious commitments. This potential logical fault line is not apparent in the MOTB exhibits, though. The exhibits unfold without tension.

Helpful to explain this phenomenon is the observation that "religious freedom," as Tisa Wenger has shown, is not a stable, democratizing ideal that advances the interests of all; rather, such rhetoric has been historically mobilized to benefit "dominant voices" who "linked racial whiteness, Protestant Christianity, and American national identity not only to freedom in general but often to [religious] freedom in particular."[12] The MOTB's invocation of this rhetoric draws on a larger discursive framework that privileges white actors and allies with Christian nationalist sentiments. The MOTB's uneasy alliance of "biblical authority" and "religious freedom" is also usefully examined alongside Lauren Kerby's observation that white evangelicals can move smoothly between understanding themselves, on the one hand, as the nation's founders and therefore rightful insiders to power and, on the other, as victims of marginalization in the nation's public square.[13] Kerby writes:

> [W]hen they speak as founders, white evangelicals argue that their Christian values are normative in American society and should be reflected in American laws. As victims, in contrast, they deplore their mistreatment by those in power and demand equal protection. White evangelicals move fluidly among these roles, as each offers a different position from which to claim moral authority. They are political shapeshifters, playing whichever part grants them the most power in a given situation.[14]

White evangelicals' self-casting and recasting that shifts between insider and outsider helps us reconcile the two themes of the MOTB's "Bible in America" exhibit. Biblical authority dominates because (and when) they align themselves with insiders, while appeals for religious freedom occur when they align themselves with outsiders. Consistent with Kerby's observation about white evangelicals on Christian heritage tours, the MOTB exhibit's combination of these themes offers two different platforms from which to sanction their own morality.

It is significant, we observe, that the "Bible in America" exhibit ends at a period in time that allows the museum not to weigh in on recent issues related to social justice that are more controversial among (or condemned by) many white evangelicals, including LGBTQ+ rights, immigration justice, and the Black Lives Matter movement. By skipping

3. Depictions of Rev. Billy Graham and Rev. Dr. Martin Luther King Jr. in the Museum of the Bible. Photo: the authors.

from the 1980s to today, the museum celebrates the Bible's perceived role in progressive issues that virtually everyone agrees in retrospect constituted good societal change and thereby avoids the risk of any visitor associating the Bible with progressive change that evangelicals would likely see as antithetical to biblical authority.

In addition to limiting its chronological scope to include only "settled" issues, the exhibit protects the Bible from blame for bad things by making a distinction between what the Bible does and what people do with the Bible, or between the Good Book and bad people. As Margaret M. Mitchell has pointed out in a trenchant critique of the "Bible in America" exhibit, the museum deploys a strategy of diminution to distract from what might be considered negative effects of the Bible, framed by the exhibit not as impact but as human interference in what otherwise would be positive – if the Bible would just be left alone to do its work.[15] We find this ideological distinction, between the Bible's good agency, on the one hand, and bad human intervention, on the other, in the placard that frames the entire "Bible in America" installation:

> Over time, the Bible helped inspire the country's ideas about democracy and the belief that religious liberty was essential to its success. It influenced many national debates, including the abolition of slavery and campaigns for civil rights. Frequently, people on opposing sides of an issue appealed to the Bible to support their cause. The impact of the Bible still resonates throughout American culture.

In its telling of American history, the exhibit consistently aligns the Bible on the side of historical social change considered positive.[16]

Further, the Bible is associated strategically with heroes of white evangelicalism whose racism is ignored or downplayed. Take, for example, the MOTB's presentation of George Whitefield (1714–70), an Anglican preacher who became an influential evangelist and popular orator of the so-called Great Awakening. The exhibit section devoted to him is about a quarter of the way down the wide hallway stretching ahead, but we can hear his voice upon taking our first step in the "Bible in America" corridor. "Be converted!" the voice enthusiastically shouts, reenacting Whitefield's impassioned plea derived from Matthew 18:3. As we make our way from 1492 to the eighteenth century, we are invited to sit and view on a massive curved screen a stylized visual presentation treating Whitefield's preaching career.[17] A recreation of his collapsible field pulpit lines the opposite wall.[18] Whitefield is unconditionally celebrated by the museum. Take this tweet from November 2019, for example: "#GeorgeWhitefield was an English Anglican priest. Throughout the colonies, he shared about personal salvation through Jesus, as he saw revealed in the Bible. Whitefield & other revivalists made an impact on their listeners. Learn about #TheGreatAwakening on the #ImpactFloor." What one would not suspect from the MOTB materials is that Whitefield owned other humans. Or that he argued in favor of slavery. Whitefield has often been lauded as one of the most popular preachers of the Great Awakening, in much the same way that he is lauded by the museum. In some of his earlier writings, he pressed for better treatment of slaves, but he did not question the institution itself. Later in his career he advocated for the expansion of legal slavery in the colonies and started a plantation in South Carolina to support his ministry.[19] Whitefield's writings on the proper treatment of slaves subsequently became instrumental in accommodating later evangelicals to the slave system as it developed from the colonial to the republican period.[20] Rather than being an early example of Christian compassion eventually leading toward support for abolition, Whitefield actually ended up prolonging the enslavement of Africans in the United States. Whitefield leaves a complicated legacy that the MOTB simplifies into a white evangelical heritage that is easy to embrace.[21] He is memorialized as someone who shared the gospel and made "an impact," the key term used by the museum for the Bible's role in history. Similarly, the MOTB exhibit includes a laudatory presentation of Billy Graham, perhaps the most beloved preacher in recent history among white evangelical Christians. While Graham's legacy in the Civil Rights movement is complex at best, the MOTB's "Bible in America" installation presents him, counterfactually,[22] as an early and essential champion of civil rights and ally of Rev. Martin Luther King Jr. The result is that both Whitefield and Graham are excused from their racist legacies, in a move that might be called vindication by omission. Their goodness, like that of the museum's bible itself, is shielded from critique.

The same sanitizing is not made available to other bible readers in US history. The MOTB's "Bible in America" exhibit does not overlook the historical fact that people read their bibles as permissive or supportive of the institution of slavery. (Indeed, to do so would be to invite immediate dismissal for inaccuracy.) It is instructive to follow the rhetorical cues in the MOTB installation in order to articulate who or what is implicated in the wrongdoing.

DEVOTEES, INTERPRETERS, AND OTHER HYPOCRITES

One prominent rhetorical distinction that the MOTB exhibit develops is between Bible devotees and Bible interpreters. Under the organizational benchmark entitled "Religious Freedom, A New Awakening," intended to represent the 1770s to the 1860s, we read this summary: "In the 1790s, a surge of evangelical revivals led to increased church membership and renewed devotion to the Bible. This religious vitality also opened the door to social change and ignited a campaign to abolish slavery in the United States. Southern slaveholders, however – some of them also involved in the revivals – interpreted the Bible as affirming slavery." Two human enterprises feature here in opposition to one another – devotion to the Bible, on the one hand, and interpretation of the Bible on the other. The word "devotion," associated with those whose "religious vitality" sparked the abolitionist movement, conjures notions of fidelity or deference to the Bible. Devotees, the reasoning goes, rejected slavery. To tease out the rest of the logic: if allegiance to the Bible leads to opposing slavery, then the Bible itself must oppose slavery. The Bible is thus protected from complicity in slavery in the United States, a task further accomplished with the deployment of the second human enterprise here. Interpretation is an activity attached only to proslavery readers. Those who love the Bible do what it says (= oppose slavery) and those who don't love what the Bible says interpret it to say something else (= affirm slavery). While both sets of people are in fact equally viable candidates to be described as devoted interpreters, only the abolitionists are here allowed to be *devoted* and only the proslavery readers are represented as engaging in *interpretation*.

A complementary technique on the museum's part to protect the Bible from complicity constructs a division between authentic and inauthentic Christianity. On a floor placard entitled "The fight to end slavery," appearing beneath a giant depiction of the busts of John Brown and Frederick Douglass, we are told that the latter "often cited the Bible in his speeches and writings." "But he also," the sign continues, "strongly rebuked the hypocrisy of organized Christianity that enabled and promoted slavery." This sign exculpates the Bible by putting it on Douglass's antislavery side and placing blame for slavery on "the hypocrisy of organized Christianity." Implied is that slavery could only be supported by *hypocritical* Christianity, which suggests that true, authentic, Bible-citing Christianity – like that of Douglass – cannot be proslavery.[23] The narrative underlying this distinction resonates with Protestant anti-Catholic polemic and repeats, though less explicitly, the framing of antislavery readers as devotees of the Bible and proslavery readers as faulty interpreters. If they were *authentically* listening to the *real* message of the Bible, we might conclude, they would have sided with the abolitionists. These exculpatory moves form part of a larger pattern on the Impact floor that shifts blame away from the Good Book and toward "bad" readers, as Mitchell has documented. The MOTB, she writes, "deflects responsibility for negative effects (social, political, ethical, theological) away from the Bible itself, and onto faulty *interpreters*."[24]

A related rhetorical technique has been frequently deployed by MOTB representatives to preserve the fundamental goodness of the Bible in the face of evils: a distinction between "use" or "impact," on the one hand, and "misuse" of the sacred text on the other. Moss and Baden noticed this pattern well before the MOTB opened its doors, in their interviews with members of the Green family and others involved in the museum's design and execution.[25] "When the Bible was used to oppose slavery," they paraphrase in the most germane example, "the Bible was speaking; when it was used to support slavery, the Bible was being misused."[26] Mitchell's close analysis of the Impact of the Bible floor reveals that this rhetorical strategy is thoroughgoing in the MOTB presentation. She summarizes: "Where 'the Bible' has done good things, it did them on its own through its clear and unambiguous message; where it has appeared to side with racism or political domination or resistance to scientific discovery, that has involved 'interpretations' that can be questioned."[27]

Museum signage on this issue might at first glance appear to be balanced, with admissions that the Bible could be invoked for both antislavery and proslavery arguments. They stack the deck, though, so as to lead visitors toward the conclusion that the Bible isn't proslavery. About halfway down the American history corridor, set along a wall just opposite a massive reproduction of William Lloyd Garrison's *The Liberator*, is a collection of artifacts and placards in a glass case meant to address the issue of "The Bible and Slavery." On the largest sign within the case, we read this summary statement:

> In the decades leading to the Civil War, the national controversy over slavery intensified. Each side invoked the authority of the Bible. The abolitionists, who pressed for an end to slavery, cited broad principles of justice and equality and specific biblical prohibitions against "man-stealing" (Deuteronomy 24:7). Proslavery factions, with equal fervor, turned to

specific passages in the Bible that condoned the practice in ancient Israel and seemed to sanction it in the New Testament.

This sign is designed with the assumption in mind that the (Christian) Bible does not *really* condone slavery.[28] Implied here is that any proslavery content in the Old Testament can be dismissed as antiquated, overshadowed by a new dispensation, and any New Testament content that could be construed to support slavery merely *seems* to sanction it.[29] Only the abolitionist side is given the luxury of a specific quotation, despite the fact that taking direct quotations from the Bible is a strategy that best serves the proslavery position.[30]

QUOTATION MARKS, PESKY EPISCOPALIANS, AND A STEAMBOAT EXPLOSION

Two constellations of artifacts flank this "The Bible and Slavery" sign, which divides artifacts purportedly according to whether their authors/creators supported or opposed slavery. The material appears selected and organized in such a way as to lead visitors away from the conclusion that it was (is) possible to read the Bible well and support slavery. The artifacts chosen to illustrate the Bible among proslavery readers give the impression that the proslavery side was weak or wrong, and the placards continue to shift blame away from the Bible to something else.

Alongside an 1850 book entitled *A Brief Examination of Scripture Testimony on The Institution of Slavery*, by Thornton Stringfellow, a Baptist pastor in Virginia,[31] we find an artifact from a decade later: an 1860 book entitled *Cotton is King and Pro-Slavery Arguments*, edited by E. N. Elliott.[32] "This collection of pro-slavery arguments," the sign reads, " . . . argued that slavery was not only essential to Southerners' wealth and the cotton economy, but it was also consistent with biblical teachings."[33] Visitors are then given a summary of how precisely these authors saw slavery as "consistent with" the Bible: "Faithful Christians, they asserted, could practice slavery if they obeyed 'humanitarian' guidelines found in the Bible." One would not know from the display itself that the word "humanitarian" never appears in *Cotton is King and Pro-Slavery Arguments*, since it is given in quotation marks. Our search through the text of this work found that the word is absent. The quotation marks encircling it on the sign, then, are actually scare quotes. The punctuation conveys that while the authors might have *thought* their principles were humanitarian, *we* know they really weren't. That is, the punctuation invites doubt on the part of the visitor that such guidelines could be accurately derived from the Bible.

Next is a book by John Henry Hopkins from 1864 entitled *A Scriptural, Ecclesiastical and Historical View of Slavery, from the Days of the Patriarch Abraham, to the Nineteenth Century* (New York: W. I. Pooley).[34] The accompanying placard reads: "John Henry Hopkins, an Episcopal bishop in Vermont, wrote this pamphlet justifying slavery based on passages from the New Testament. His arguments gave stark evidence of the Episcopal Church's involvement in slavery." Here, as elsewhere in the museum, the verb "justifying" is attached to the position that is now unpalatable. The language is manufactured to create space for the judgment that Hopkins was wrong. Further, even if the first half of this placard's content gestures toward the notion that the New Testament could be used to support slavery, its second half undoes it: the following sentence indicates that we are to take Hopkins's Bible reading not as "stark evidence" of the Bible's complicity in slavery but rather as evidence "of the Episcopal Church's involvement in slavery." As before, we have wiggle room to blame people or even organized (hypocritical?) religion – but not the Bible.

A careful read of Hopkins's work, not possible in the museum itself, reveals a possibility unaddressed in the MOTB: it was feasible to read the Bible as a devoted Christian, observe that the text does not condemn slavery, and entertain the idea that slavery was bad for other reasons. A read through his *A Scriptural, Ecclesiastical and Historical View of Slavery* reveals this personal admission, remarkable even if deployed for rhetorical effect:

> If it were a matter to be determined by my personal sympathies, tastes, or feelings, I should be as ready as any man to condemn the institution of slavery; for all my prejudices of education, habit, and social position stand entirely opposed to it. But as a Christian, I am solemnly warned not to be "wise in my own conceit," and not to "lean to my own understanding." As a Christian, I am compelled to submit my weak and erring intellect to the authority of the Almighty. (6)

He cannot make the Bible say something it does not say. He then goes on to argue through very careful textual analysis that the Bible cannot be said to condemn slavery as a moral wrong. And Hopkins is unwilling to throw out the Bible on account of its not squaring with his preference:

> And who are we, that in our modern wisdom presume to set aside the Word of God, and scorn the example of the divine Redeemer, and spurn the preaching and the conduct of his apostles, and invent for ourselves a "higher law" than those holy Scriptures which are given to us as "a light to our feet and a lamp to our paths," in the darkness of a sinful and a polluted world? ... Who are we that we are ready to trample on the doctrine of the Bible ... ?

Even so, the MOTB's framing of Hopkins blames the Episcopal Church rather than the Bible.

Rounding out this collection intended to illustrate the proslavery side of the Bible tug-of-war is a letter, we are told, penned by Charles Hodge (1797–

4. Exhibit treating the Bible and slavery in the Museum of the Bible. Photo: the authors.

1878), a Presbyterian theologian at Princeton Theological Seminary, and addressed to a Reverend J. Potts. The placard summarizes the position of the letter's author: Hodge "believed the Bible permitted slavery, but he also supported abolition and the policies of President Abraham Lincoln."[35] This is a weak articulation of a proslavery reading of the Bible. This example portrays the proslavery side as prime for undermining (the Bible merely permits slavery) or even ambivalent (since Hodge also supported abolition). It is a position, we might conclude, doomed to lose.

The illustration goes from weak to nonexistent when we examine the content of the letter on display. Only one side of the artifact is visible through the display case. It is unlikely that visitors expend the time and effort required to read its content, given how difficult the handwriting is to decipher, how small the text is, and how many other artifacts and displays are easily available nearby. If one were capable and curious enough to piece together what it says, a read-through of the document would leave one puzzled about its inclusion in this exhibit. A hand-scrawled date of March 5, 1850, at the top, gives way to the salutation "My dear sir" and then a personal message that reports the receipt of some money that the addressee had sent to the author. Our letter writer offers an explanation for why the money has not yet reached its final intended recipient: that unfortunate soul has sustained injuries from a steamboat explosion the previous week. His nose, mouth, and throat were scalded by steam, we read. His hand was wounded when he broke through a glass window on board. He "fainted several times from exhaustion." And that's the letter. There is no mention of slavery, no mention of the Bible. The proslavery side, as presented by the museum, is difficult to empathize with, difficult to take seriously. Its supporters are dismissed as wrong, or as fake, or as vacuous. The two sides – proslavery and antislavery – are thus not presented as equally viable.

THE SLAVE BIBLE

The nexus of slavery and the Bible's goodness was on full display in a temporary exhibit at MOTB that sought to uncover the dark history of how the Bible was made into a tool for supporting slavery: "The Slave Bible: Let the Story Be Told."[36] By taking a deep dive into the museum's exhibit, we can see how the presumption of the Bible's goodness precludes the ability to interrogate the complicated ways in which biblical writings and white Christian racism intertwined to support the slave system in the Antebellum South. On display from November 2018 through September 2019, the exhibit was heavily promoted on the museum's website. According to a press release, MOTB partnered with Fisk University, from whom the artifact was on loan, and the Center for the Study of African American Religious Life at the National Museum of African American History and Culture.[37] Steve Green publicly praised the exhibit, commenting on its consistency with his family's affection for the Bible and its strategic value for reaching a more diverse crowd.[38] It drew widespread media attention.

Published in London in 1807 (and again in 1808) on behalf of the Society for the Conversion of Negro Slaves, this book bears the title *Select Parts of the Holy Bible for the Use of the Negro Slaves in the British West-India Islands*. A promotional email from August 2018 summarized the MOTB's interpretation of the artifact. Bearing the subject line "A Bible that was manipulated to emphasize themes of submission and subservience," the message featured a photograph of the book against a dark background. Superimposed in large white letters was the phrase "The edited Bible." A bright red × went through the word "edited," resulting in a sleek visual – "The edited Bible" – with an obvious message: this is the Good Book gone bad. The body of the email read:

> There is neither Jew nor Greek, there is neither slave nor free, there is no male and female, for you are all one in Christ Jesus. (Galatians 3:28, ESV)
>
> Imagine a Bible that starts with creation but then jumps right to Joseph being sold into slavery and makes a point of how imprisonment benefited him! An edited Bible, where the Exodus story of God rescuing his people from slavery in Egypt is removed, together with every reference to freedom, such as the above passage from Galatians. A Bible that is manipulated to emphasize themes of submission and subservience. Does this sound like the Bible you know?
>
> In the early 1800s, Rev. Beilby Porteus, bishop of London, instructed a group of missionaries to create such a book.

"Prepare a short form of public prayers ... together with the select portions of Scripture ... particularly those which relate to the duties of slaves towards their masters."

In a twenty-first-century society that rejects slavery and racial oppression (at least in name), this book's title alone is enough to make us cringe. With its reminders of colonialism, racism, and the capture, exile, and dehumanization of millions of African people by white Europeans who settled the "New World," this artifact is unsettling. It is likely to prompt rage or guilt or both, depending on how one finds oneself situated within the legacy of slavery in the Americas. Yet the exhibit and the MOTB promotional material conceive of the primary harm as one perpetrated not against people but against the Bible. Ken McKenzie, then CEO of the MOTB, articulated such a perspective in an on-screen interview in April 2019 in response to NBC *Nightly News*'s Geoff Bennett, who asked the museum official: "When people encounter this exhibit, what lasting impression do you want them to leave with?"[39] McKenzie replied, "Well, we want to pass the message on that 'may this never happen again.'" While one might expect his "this" to refer to the enslavement of human beings, he instead continued, "The Bible itself is a, is a *whole* book; it's not one that you get to carve up and use this piece or that piece." As one placard in the exhibit read, "Its publishers deliberately removed portions of the biblical text, such as the exodus story, that could inspire hope for liberation." The image we end up with is a wounded bible – one that has been cut and left in fragments. It bears lacerations, unhealed scars, missing members. It limps – afflicted, constrained, hacked to pieces. And if the Bible is a (co)victim, it can't be a (co)perpetrator.

McKenzie's language about this artifact's production process mirrors the picture we get in the museum exhibit and promotional materials: the book's producers are represented as starting with a "complete" Bible and calculatedly suppressing its liberative content through excision of freedom-related passages. This assessment, however, is not entirely consistent with what is actually in the so-named "Slave Bible." If the publishers were weaponizing the Bible in the cause of slavery, they did not realize their goal to maximum effect. Several texts that support slavery as an institution (Exodus 21:2–11; Deuteronomy 15:12–18) and a long discussion of how the enslavement of non-Israelites was acceptable to Israel's god (Leviticus 25:39–46) were not included. Passages from the Pauline corpus supportive of slavery do not make an appearance either (1 Corinthians 7:21–24; Colossians 3:22–4:1; Philemon). Most significantly, the oft-repeated claim that the Exodus is absent is only partially true.[40] God's redemption of the Israelites from slavery in Egypt is recalled repeatedly. Consider this series of verses included that *do* appear in the book:[41]

> I am the LORD your God, who brought you out of the land of Egypt, out of the house of slavery (Deuteronomy 5:6).[42]
>
> Remember that you were a slave in the land of Egypt, and the LORD your God brought you out from there with a mighty hand and an outstretched arm; therefore the LORD your God commanded you to keep the sabbath day (Deuteronomy 5:15).
>
> ... take care that you do not forget the LORD, who brought you out of the land of Egypt, out of the house of slavery (Deuteronomy 6:12).
>
> When your children ask you in time to come, "What is the meaning of the decrees and the statutes and the ordinances that the LORD our God has commanded you?" then you shall say to your children, "We were Pharaoh's slaves in Egypt, but the LORD brought us out of Egypt with a mighty hand ..." (Deuteronomy 6:20–21).
>
> ... then do not exalt yourself, forgetting the LORD your God, who brought you out of the land of Egypt, out of the house of slavery ... (Deuteronomy 8:14).

Neither is eschatological hope absent from the "Slave Bible." While the artifact does not include the book of Revelation, it *does* include both 1 Corinthians 15 and 1 Thessalonians 4–5, two important New Testament passages with expectations for a redemptive future.

Further, in exhibit signage and promotional messages, the museum has truncated a nineteenth-century quotation to make it appear compatible with the exhibit's storytelling. On one wall appeared an 1808 quotation attributed to Rev. Beilby Porteus, identified as Bishop of London and

Founder of the Society for the Conversion and Religious Instruction and Education of the Negro Slaves. Mirroring its form in the email quoted above, it read: "Prepare a short form of public prayers for them . . . **together with select portions of Scripture** . . . particularly those which relate to the **duties of slaves towards their masters**" (bold original). The quotation is excerpted from a letter to "the Governors, Legislatures, and Proprietors of Plantations, in The British West-India Islands."[43] Porteus's aim is to convince these readers to allow enslaved Africans time and resources to receive Christian religious instruction.[44] Porteus envisions a labor-free Sunday so that the enslaved can gather and be formed into Christian slaves.[45] He speculates that local clergy would be willing to prepare

> a short form of public prayers for them [the enslaved], consisting of a number of the best Collects of the Liturgy, the Creed, the Lord's Prayer, and the Ten Commandments, together with select portions of Scripture, taken principally from the Psalms and Proverbs, the Gospels, and the plainest and most practical parts of the Epistles, particularly those which relate to the duties of slaves towards their masters.

The museum exhibit has taken Porteus's quotation out of its context and edited it to make it say something it does not say. When we read the unabridged statement, we find that he was not issuing a command, and specifically that he was not issuing a command to produce a bible. Porteus envisioned a collection that expanded beyond biblical texts and included liturgy for public worship. Such an anthology would have been similar to other compilations of biblical and religious texts intended for liturgical or devotional use, examples of which can be found displayed with appreciative tone at the museum.[46] Notice too that Porteus's proposed production process is one of building from the ground up. He wants the clergy to curate biblical passages deemed most relevant and situate them among other kinds of religiously useful texts. Since *Select Parts of the Holy Bible* includes only biblical texts, this artifact does not precisely embody what Porteus was commending. But if we think of the Porteus quotation as a lens through which to understand how *Select Parts of the Holy Bible* came to exist, as the museum invites us to do, it turns out that we must shift our thinking from cutting to curating – not a bible carved to pieces but a blank canvas ready to be filled. The full context of Porteus's statement gives us a clue as to what his criteria for inclusion of material would have been. Museum curators have excised a significant segment of Porteus's statement that makes the phrase "particularly those which relate to the duties of slaves towards their masters" appear to refer to all of scripture, when it actually refers to "the plainest and most practical parts of the Epistles" – a phrase which shows that Porteus was motivated principally by a desire to offer enslaved readers texts deemed easily digestible and relevant to their experiences. He was not playing seek and hide with freedom-themed Bible verses.

The book he imagines is not very different from other compilations of biblical passages aimed at making a bible accessible or relevant for a particular population of people with similar circumstances or shared interests. The MOTB has published examples of such tailored books of biblical content, available for purchase in the museum store.[47] It also holds historical analogues in its collection, such as a 1786 book entitled *The Holy Bible, Abridged,* published by Isaiah Thomas, described positively as "a very rare instructional and devotional work for children with appealing woodcut illustrations."[48] The museum's social media and web page advertise a facsimile reprint of "The Souldier's Pocket Bible," said to be originally issued for Oliver Cromwell's army and then reissued for American soldiers during World War I. It bears a longer title that explains the reason for its abridgement down to about one hundred verses that all deal with how to behave during war: this pocket-sized book was intended to "supply the want of the whole Bible, which a souldier cannot conveniently carry about him." Something is better than nothing, the logic goes. And the something is envisioned as particularly helpful for the intended population of readers. The producers' motivations were more mercenary than monstrous.[49]

A final example from the museum's social media presence illustrates the stark contrast between the negative representation of the "Slave Bible" and the positive representation of analogues. A marked shift in tone attended two Facebook posts shared three days apart, in February 2018. The first, appearing with the hashtag #BlackHistoryMonth, repeated the by now familiar narrative about the "Slave Bible": "This volume is called 'Holy,'" the post read, "but it is deeply manipulative."[50] Days later the museum posted a photo of Barack and Michelle Obama (unnamed) with heads bowed alongside a caption about the National Prayer Breakfast, held each year in Washington DC. The text focused on the American Bible Society's distribution of partial bibles to attendees. Rather than decrying the ABS's action as a mutilation of "the Bible," the caption is eager and exultant in tone, with an acclamatory exclamation mark standing at attention: "At the 2017 gathering, the American Bible Society distributed printed portions of the Gospels and Book of Acts to all leaders in attendance!"[51]

Partial bibles are not uniformly condemned by the museum. The difference between what's acceptable and what's not is not based on the act of curation itself. Tailoring is not inherently evil. Abridgement is not necessarily manipulative. Why, then, is such activity represented as the main problem in the "Slave Bible" exhibit? Why present tailoring and abridgement *in this case* as a stark moral issue? The answer has to do with saving the Bible: slavery is nearly universally condemned in our twenty-first-century collective American conscience, and the MOTB protects "the whole Bible" (and thus *the Bible*) from blame for such a moral evil by aligning this artifact, represented as a partial bible, with devious manipulation. By representing the act of cutting up the Bible into *Select Parts of the Holy Bible* as an evil act, the museum effectively situates the alternative – the *whole Bible* – on the other side of a moral binary that successfully (if illogically) exculpates the Bible from complicity in slavery.

We must pay attention to what is lost when biblical literature is framed in this way. The museum's demonization of the distribution of this partial bible leads visitors to champion an alternative scenario in which enslaved Africans should have been given access to a "complete" Bible – the ones that the white enslavers and their allies were using. This apparent solution to the problem, as the museum has framed it, implies that enslaved Africans depended on literacy to discover and use the Bible, when in fact they didn't.[52] One suspects that this desire on the part of white visitors actually reproduces the paternalism inherent to the legacy of white missionaries working among enslaved Africans.

The exhibit forecloses the possibility that cutting up a bible could be faithful and freeing. In *Jesus and the Disinherited*, Howard Thurman famously tells a story of his formerly enslaved grandmother's relationship to the Bible.[53] As a child, Thurman says, he read a bible aloud to her frequently since she did not read or write. "I was deeply impressed," he shares, "by the fact that she was most particular about the choice of Scripture." She apparently cherished some Psalms and parts of Isaiah but relished hearing the Gospels most of all. "But the Pauline epistles," he writes, "never." (Except for, it turns out, the apostle's famous hymn to love in 1 Corinthians 13). Thurman did not dare to satisfy his curiosity about his grandmother's rejection of Paul until he was much older, in college: "With a feeling of great temerity I asked her one day why it was that she would not let me read any of the Pauline letters. What she told me I shall never forget." He reports that his grandmother recounted this experience during her enslavement:

> "During the days of slavery," she said, "the master's minister would occasionally hold services for the slaves. Old McGhee was so mean that he would not let a Negro minister preach to his slaves. Always the white minister used as his text something from Paul. At least three or four times a year he used as a text: 'Slaves, be obedient to them that are your masters ... as unto Christ.' Then he would go on to show how it was God's will that we were slaves and how, if we were good and happy slaves, God would bless us. I promised my Maker that if I ever learned to read and if freedom ever came, I would not read that part of the Bible."

She refused to listen to "that part of the Bible" that experience taught her was oppressive. For her, being "particular about the choice of Scripture" was the only way to make her encounter with the Bible liberative. In this case, cutting up the Bible became a strategy to make it the Good Book. Any assertion that the solution to the problem introduced by the existence of "Slave Bible" was to distribute the "whole" Bible to enslaved Africans ignores actual historical ways that enslaved and formerly enslaved Africans made meaning out of biblical materials, thereby risking recentering whiteness.

Moreover, the museum's portrayal suggests that a bible would have to be tampered with in order for it to support slavery.[54] A casual flip through this artifact would provide all the counterevidence one needs to see that this claim cannot be sustained. So would a casual flip through any Christian bible. In the struggle over slavery through scripture, antislavery and abolitionist writers had to do far more hermeneutical work than did proslavery readers to make their bibles work in their favor.[55] The museum's "Slave Bible" exhibit obscures that it is actually easier to use a (whole) bible to make an argument in favor of slavery than against. Take, for example, a dominating interpretive visual display, adjacent to the artifact, which offered visitors a summary of the book's contents. On two catty-corner walls that met at a right angle appeared two hefty rectangular signboards. Contrasting headers in complementary script read "Passages excluded from the Slave Bible" and "Passages included in the Slave Bible," respectively. Smaller rectangles populated each sign, with scripture references or quotations arranged haphazardly into what functioned as two columns of collected biblical verses. These columns were useful insofar as they accurately conveyed some of the select parts that constitute *Select Parts*.

Yet an additional sentence on each sign introduced a logical mistake. The museum interprets the selection process as indicative of what texts were being used in contemporary Christian debates over slavery itself. Between the heading "Passages excluded from the Slave Bible" and the blocks of biblical material appeared the claim "Many who opposed slavery cited these and other verses to justify their position." Likewise, on the "Passages included in the Slave Bible" side was a similar claim: "Many who supported slavery cited these and other verses to justify their position." (The exhibit is silent on the tension this visual raises for the museum's presentation of the Bible as fundamentally liberative.) It is indeed the case that both abolitionists and anti-abolitionists appealed to their bibles as they argued for their side of the debate.[56] But the museum exhibit here leads us to an incoherent process of imagining how biblical materials entered debates about slavery. Rather than trace uses of bible passages in the historical record to identify which verses each side employed as scriptural warrant for their arguments, the exhibit assumes that whatever bible passages appeared in *Select Parts* must have been used by anti-abolitionists and that whatever bible passages were not included must have been used by abolitionists. This conclusion is not tenable – the Book of Psalms appears in the *Excluded* column but was not a fundamental resource for antislavery arguments,[57] and Daniel 1–9 and the Book of Acts appear on the *Included* column without figuring prominently among anti-abolitionists.[58]

More significant, however, is the impression this visual display offers visitors about the *way* in which biblical materials were mobilized in slavery debates. The exhibit suggests that abolitionists and anti-abolitionists had equally tenable materials to support their positions, that the debate was waged as a war of biblical words lying in wait to be picked up and thrown at each other. Yet proslavery and antislavery arguments often wrestled over the meaning of *the same verse.* For example, even Paul's famous statement "there is no longer ... slave nor free ... " in Galatians 3:28, which the museum featured in its promotional email as emblematic of the Bible's liberative promise, was deployed in different ways on both sides of the moral debate. While antislavery authors could mobilize Paul's statement (within a constellation of texts) in an attempt to neutralize the Pauline injunctions for slaves to obey their masters, proslavery authors argued that the rest of the apostle's words in Galatians 3:28 – the ones about male and female – provide proof that Paul did not mean "no longer slave nor free" literally but rather metaphorically since the apostle did not abolish gender literally.[59] There is no longer slave nor free *in Christ Jesus.*

The antislavery cause struggled in an effort to counter a "flat reading" of the biblical text. As biblical scholar J. Albert Harrill has shown, the range of abolitionist interpretive strategies – and, usually, their failures to prove coherent or persuasive – ultimately played a part in "a major paradigm shift away from literalism" in the nineteenth-century United States, one that paved the way for the acceptance of higher biblical criticism.[60] Interestingly, antislavery exegetical strategies also transformed the way that many viewed the Bible itself, whether the Bible could be considered ultimately authoritative or not. As Harrill argues, the "moral imperative" of rejecting slavery "fostered an interpretive approach that found conscience to be a more reliable guide to Christian morality than biblical authority."[61] That is a possibility the MOTB cannot entertain.

Plenty of people with "whole" bibles read their bibles and concluded that they supported slavery. Even though the missionaries who produced *Select Parts of the Holy Bible* were not manipulating a bible with malintent, they *were* engaged in other activities that we are likely to find abhorrent today. Lest Porteus be exculpated in the discussion so far, we must note that racism and paternalism fueled his commendation of Christian education for the enslaved. In his letter, Porteus portrays converted slaves as feathers in the caps of their enslavers, calling them a "pleasing and interesting spectacle, of a new and most numerous race of Christians 'plucked as a brand out of the fire,' rescued from the horrors and superstitions of Paganism." Yet if conversion was intended to rescue enslaved Africans from horrors, it was not horrors in the here and now. Porteus reasons that Christian slaves work harder and are more compliant than those who do not convert. He argues that plantation owners should allow their slaves to receive Christian religious education so that their sexual activity can be controlled with the hope of producing more offspring. More enslaved babies, more slaves, more labor, more profit.[62]

An opening placard in the exhibit attempted to acknowledge the relationship between the "Slave Bible" and missionary efforts to convert the enslaved. Conversion and education efforts were not lumped together with the missionaries' perceived Bible blunder: "These missionaries aimed to do more with the Slave Bible than convert and educate enslaved Africans. They edited the Slave Bible in a way that would instill obedience and preserve the system of slavery in the colonies." This framing implies that conversion and education are not activities that deserve interrogation. The curators suggest that these activities are innocent. A line is crossed, it seems, when the missionaries went further, when they messed with the Bible in order to oppress enslaved Africans into peaceful servitude to white colonist plantation owners. The logic is made explicit in the text overlaying the virtual tour of the exhibit on the museum's YouTube channel: "A British missionary organization created the Slave Bible. They hoped to convert enslaved Africans but also reinforce the colonial slave system." The adversative *but* invites the viewer to weigh these activities in opposition to each other. Converting, good. Reinforcing slavery, bad. As New Testament scholar Allen Dwight Callahan has observed in his analysis of a similar historical train of thought, "Slavery backhandedly facilitated the conversion of Africans, dragging them bound and shackled into the light of the Christian Gospel."[63]

Converting and educating slaves were not innocuous activities occurring in an ideological vacuum. The exhibit's sole focus on the use of the Bible in missionary efforts encourages visitors merely to question what was happening with the Bible rather than inviting them to question the larger framework in which the Bible was implicated.[64] The "Slave Bible" exhibit leaves no room for visitors to question how biblical texts shaped Christians who supported the racialized system of enslavement. Their Christianity, informed by their "whole Bible," allowed for racism, paternalism, oppression, and acceptance of the enslavement of other human beings. Rather than asking what these missionaries did to the Bible, perhaps we should be asking what their bibles did to them.

In one noteworthy quotation on display in the "Slave Bible" exhibit, Brad Braxton, the director of the Center for the Study of African American Religious Life at the NMAAHC, pushed past the false equivalencies animating the MOTB's overall presentation with this challenge: "In our interpretations of the Bible, is the end result domination or liberation?" The moral compass here is distinct from that of the rest of the exhibit in an important way: Braxton's question subjects the use of the Bible to a moral imperative that he does not claim, circularly, to be the right, true, self-evident message in the Bible. It opens up an intriguing possibility so far unimagined in the exhibit: that bibles aren't good by themselves. It's what readers do with their bibles that is good or bad.

But as soon as such a possibility was opened, the museum exhibit forcefully shut it down. At the exhibit's exit, visitors were invited to respond to what they had seen in an interactive crowd-sourced reflection. Visitors were to write answers to prompts and then add them to the previous responses on the wall.[65] "Would you," one of the questions asked, "call the Slave Bible the 'Good Book'?" Guests divided over whether the answer was yes or no. "No," one anonymous visitor wrote, "the good book is the whole Bible not excluding anything we don't want to hear in the moment. The Bible is there to tell us what we need to hear, not what we want to hear." This claim, interestingly, bears striking resemblance to Hopkins's expression of dismay that the Bible does not condemn slavery; it is not what he wanted to hear but he needed to follow it anyway.

Another visitor offered more casual disapproval ("Nah") with a similar rationale about the necessary fullness of the Bible: "It's part of the good book, but not without the full book can it be considered to be the Good book." A third example called out the issue of slavery specifically, contrasting the artifact on display with a *real* Bible: "I would not call the Slave Bible the good book because it only talked about slavery and did not discuss the real/true things that were in the real bible." One visitor wrote "yes and no" because "it was a book designed to oppress a people, but you cannot remove the bible's message of hope without removing the bible." Another commented affirmatively with a creative rhetorical contrast: "I call it a good book but not the best book. At least it contains part of the word. So in that way, it has good parts, but overall is not what God intended." By asking a yes or no question formulated in such a way that one cannot answer it without assenting to the premise that the Bible *is supposed to be* the Good Book, the museum ensures that regardless of whether visitors answer in the affirmative or the negative, they must accept the intended goodness of the Bible. It is difficult, perhaps even impossible, to resist the premise of this question.[66]

MOTB severely limited the choices for how people today can make meaning out of the existence of this historical artifact. The exhibit's ideological commitment to the inherent goodness of the Bible distracts us from the suffering of enslaved Africans and also invites us to ignore harrowing present-day stories narrated by those who have endured abuse from (often well-meaning) Bible-believing folk and who have experienced first hand that the Bible is not good for them.[67] The white evangelical bible produced by the MOTB demands devotion. It can do no wrong – no matter what anyone else says.

CONCLUSION: FROM VILLAINS TO VICTIMS TO HEROES

While Kerby is right that white evangelicals "must first save history in order to save the nation,"[68] we have shown that they must likewise save the Bible. By aligning themselves with Bible "devotees" rather than faulty interpreters, white evangelicals can find salvation from the sins of the past by shifting their group affinity to join the victims rather than the villains of history. As we've seen, the MOTB Impact floor exhibits forge such a path of redemption for white evangelical Christians and their Bible through the very framing of the question of the Bible and slavery.

Further, by presenting the Bible as the (co)victim in the "Slave Bible" exhibit, the MOTB provides a pathway for white evangelicals to see themselves too as victims, their cause as shared with the actual victims. It must be so, for otherwise white evangelicals would lose the moral authority by which they define the bounds of proper "biblical" behavior for others.

We have certainly not exhausted the examples that could be levied to demonstrate that the bible produced in MOTB is conceived as inherently beneficial, often in ways that benefit white Americans. They abound. In closing, we offer one further example in which the stakes are higher than those of others in our present political moment: the "Justice" display in the "Bible in the World" exhibit. Visitors are invited into a simulated prison cell complete with tall white vertical bars and a sliding grated door.

Overhead is an illuminated sign bearing the word "JUSTICE" amid neat rows of what could best be described as professional head shots of (mostly nonwhite) men in prison uniforms. We hear some of their stories as we take in videos of their studying the Bible while incarcerated. One documentary details the Bible College at the Louisiana State Penitentiary in Angola, a program run in partnership with New Orleans Baptist Theological Seminary. The MOTB background information explains of this exhibit: "Western concepts of both retributive and restorative justice are strongly rooted in the Bible. Here, a prison cell encapsulates stories of people in the prison system who are being impacted positively by the Bible."[69]

A photo of the simulated prison cell appeared on the MOTB's Facebook feed on February 23, 2018. Writers used the occasion of the death of famed white evangelist Billy Graham to advertise the "Justice" exhibit. The accompanying text read:

> Billy Graham, who passed away on Wednesday, will be buried in a casket built by inmates at the Louisiana State Penitentiary at Angola. Researchers at Angola have found that attending both Bible college and religious services helps inmates experience a profound identity transformation. The time wasted on crime, deviance, and addiction is recast as an imperative to help others avoid the same missteps.
>
> Learn more about Angola and Darrington Unit, a facility with a similar program, on the museum's Impact of the Bible Floor.

5. Simulated prison cell inside the Museum of the Bible. Photo: James Bielo.

One of these "researchers at Angola" is Byron R. Johnson, a professor at Baptist-affiliated Baylor University who served as an advisor for the exhibits on the Impact floor and who has authored several books including one entitled *More God, Less Crime*.[70] Johnson presented his research in the MOTB Speaker Series in an event called "The Role of the Bible in Prison Transformation," during which he called the MOTB his "second home away from home over the last five years."[71] As part of his talk he referred to the Bible as a "magic ingredient that keeps people out of trouble, protects them and insulates them, and also helps them do the right thing."[72] In this context, "the right thing" is technically not what's biblical, of course, but what's consistent with American law.

Only those visitors with previous knowledge of the institutions and actors involved might know enough to be made uneasy about the scenario being celebrated here: a school affiliated with the Southern Baptist Convention, whose origins lie in the white supremacist proslavery movement in the nineteenth century, is teaching the Bible to a literally captive audience in a prison located on the site of a former slave plantation and that is now imbricated in an American criminal justice system plagued by systemic racism in which nonwhite people are incarcerated at much higher rates. An ideological commitment to the Bible's inherent goodness constricts the moral imagination, distracts from systemic injustice. If the MOTB still exists in a hundred and fifty years, it is possible that the basement exhibit will be "The Prison Bible." But in the meantime, the white evangelical bible at the MOTB, good to its core, shields its producers from critique through a bit of white men's magic.

While the supernatural surrounding the MOTB's bible works on the museum's Impact floor to authorize white American evangelical privilege, we also find the miraculous on the MOTB's History of the Bible floor. There, as we will see in the next chapter, we turn from the goodness of the content of the white evangelical bible to its trustworthiness and its divine origin.

CHAPTER 3

Reliable Bible

We both know the Bible *is* historical. The Bible *is* archeological.
The Bible *is* cultural. The Bible is figurative. The Bible is true.
  And, the Bible is *transforming*.
                              Fundraising email from MOTB, July 15, 2020

With its relatively higher concentration of old things to look at, the
MOTB's History of the Bible floor feels the most traditionally
"historical" of the permanent exhibits. Visitors advance through the
installation chronologically in time from antiquity forward,
encountering the bulk of ancient artifacts, manuscripts, and replicas
on display in permanent exhibits. One can wander from cuneiform
tablets to the Dead Sea Scrolls display to a feature on the Aleppo
Codex to a series of early printed bibles to a Torah scribe who copies
the text live. Popular parlance about the MOTB suggests that it
materializes a bible that is "historically accurate" and "literally
true."[1] In reality, though, the museum is the product of a fusion of
the Greens' evangelical impulses with cost constraints, aspirations of
respectability, and the input of design firms and (some) biblical
scholars. As a result, the museum's exhibits on its History of the
Bible floor tell a different story – a more complex story, a less
obvious story. We show in this chapter that the Museum of the
Bible's History floor only coheres if "the Bible" is viewed as
a divinely derived Word made text, relying along the way on
providential developments of communication and preservation
technologies. Further, the MOTB uses a number of strategies, likely

invisible to non-expert visitors, to protect this story of the Bible from critique.

The MOTB's History of the Bible must resist critique because the exhibit is as much about the future as it is about the past. Or, rather, it produces a history useful for white evangelical Christian assumptions about and aspirations for the Bible. The exhibit floor's ultimate destination is the oval-shaped illumiNations hall, a kaleidoscopic display of modern bible translations intended for worldwide distribution. Curved overhead screens contribute to a busy, futuristic feel reminiscent of the *Wall-E* cruise ship in outer space. A digital calendar tracks time-to-translation for translation projects in progress. We encounter larger-than-life photographs of black and brown people with grateful smiles on their faces and bibles in their hands. Shelves that encircle visitors are lined from top to bottom with hundreds of bibles and bibles-in-waiting in a color-coded schema. Brown spines appear on bibles that currently exist in a particular language, while orange spines indicate bible translations in production and yellow spines symbolize translations yet to be started. The blank pages inside each yellow book appear as a need to be filled. A sign explains that illumiNations is "an alliance of the world's largest Bible agencies" who are "coordinating efforts" to "make the Bible available to everyone in the world – in their heart language and in a form they can use." Felt need for bible translation/distribution is rhetorically created (or enhanced) with the very naming of the goal as "eradicating Bible poverty."[2] (As elsewhere in the exhibit, there is no consideration that things might fall apart.)

In an interview with *Outreach Magazine* published in 2019, Steve Green's brother Mart describes his formative role in illumiNations and tells a story about how it came to be featured in the MOTB.[3] Having seen that early plans for the museum included over two hundred computer screens, Mart reports, he approached his brother Steve and made a pitch for how to use one of them:

"Man, is there any way I could get one of those computer screens, because I can tell what's going to happen is you're going to get people excited about the Bible. I want them to go out a little bit depressed that somebody doesn't have it. I want them to at least know that. I want them to say, "I've got the Bible and someone else doesn't. Is that right?"

Mart reports that younger brother Steve made him sweat a couple days but then exceeded his expectations: "we're going to give you 2,600 square feet of the museum." It's possible that Mart's story is apocryphal. But it's still instructive. Regardless of the accuracy of Mart's memory of the

6. illumiNations installation in the Museum of the Bible. Photo: the authors.

details, his perception of how his idea came to fruition, or the degree to which the anecdote's contours are shaped to be inspirational, the story is provocative for what it reveals about the function of the illumiNations exhibit. It suggests, first, that the rest of the museum would give visitors good feelings about the Bible and, second, that the Green family recognizes that those positive vibes are not ends in themselves. They can be corralled and directed toward action.

This MOTB floor tells a story about the past that can ground evangelical hopes that one day all people, unto the ends of the earth, will have a bible that speaks plainly to them. But the exhibit is not really about bibles. It is about "the Bible" – a conceptual category that transcends materiality. The History floor purports to trace the Bible's "Path to Universal Access." The exhibit's opening placard signals this progression:

> Long ago, before the Bible was gathered into one book, it began as a collection of oral traditions and writings accessible only to a few people. Embraced by many communities with different traditions, the Bible moved from handwritten scrolls to manuscript codices, to printed books to mobile devices. Today the Bible thrives worldwide. How did it grow and spread?

The museum exhibit will guide us from the past to the present, from the few to the many, from yellow spines to brown. As we will show, the museum's History is simultaneously, and ultimately, tracing a divine Word from God to humanity. None of the signage makes such an argument explicit, but as we will show in this chapter, the exhibit's themes of technology and transmission only cohere if the History told is not of "the Bible" made global but a Word – *the* Word – made stable, replicable, and accessible.

THE WORD MADE TEXT

The language of "access" typically attends resources or services considered to be necessary for human life or flourishing that are unevenly available to some people or population groups. Think of water, for example. Or education, or healthcare, or justice. Those advocating for "universal access" to such material or structural resources assume that the resource will benefit everyone and that barriers to equal distribution must be identified and eliminated. Yet, here the resource – "the Bible" – is imaginary. MOTB signage treats the Bible as a single, stable thing, separate from the forms "it" has taken materially through history. The MOTB's History makes most sense interpreted as a white evangelical account of a pretextual divine Word that transcends the particularity of any physical form even as it required, and still requires, human technological innovation to transmit it. Each new technology brings with it both benefits and risks, new problems to be solved.

IN THE BEGINNING: STABILIZING THE MESSAGE IN WRITING. After taking in the "Path to Universal Access" proclamation, visitors proceed through double glass doors to the beginning of the museum's History. Suggestively titled "IN THE BEGINNING," this opening section could have begun in a variety of ways.[4] To follow most mainstream biblical studies text books and syllabi would likely mean beginning with either the emergence of Israel in the land of Canaan (*circa* 1200 BCE) or with the composite nature of the Pentateuch, which many scholars hypothesize started taking shape in the sixth century BCE, as a window into Israelite history and historical writing. The former is how the exhibit of artifacts from the Israel Antiquities Authority on the MOTB's fifth floor opens. Entitled "The People of the Land: History and Archaeology of Ancient Israel," this exhibit uses archaeological materials to tell the history of ancient Israel from the Canaanite period to the Bar Kokhba revolt (second millennium BCE to second century CE) with artifacts curated from Israeli excavations.

Another option would have been to begin at Sinai, the biblical setting for God's giving the law to the Israelites through Moses. Many traditional religious adherents, including the Green family, for example, believe the revelation depicted in Exodus and Deuteronomy to have marked the origins of the texts that would become biblical. A book released under the MOTB's press imprint, entitled *The World's Greatest Book*, begins here.[5] Alternatively, the MOTB could have followed the lead of Answers in Genesis's Creation Museum in Kentucky, which goes even further back in the biblical narrative to the very creation of the world by God as depicted in the opening chapters of Genesis. The Creation Museum's history begins with God's creation of the world and Adam and Eve in the Garden of Eden. While mainstream biblical scholars do not read Genesis 1–3 as a historical record but rather as something more akin to ancient stories that ground ancient Israelite practice and offer narrative space for their speculations about the nature of their god and of humanity, the Creation Museum presents the Garden of Eden as a historical place – the literal beginning of time, the world, and humanity.[6]

The MOTB's History exhibit begins instead with "The Origins of Writing" in human history, assigned a date of 3200 BCE. Visitors are here invited to view ancient cuneiform writing on stone. As biblical scholars whose interests were initially sparked by analyzing how the museum presents biblical origins, we puzzled over the curators' choice here, given that the people who produced biblical writings did not originate writing and that no biblical literature can be persuasively dated as early as the invention of writing. A MOTB-produced video entitled "The History of Writing,"[7] posted online over a year prior to the museum's opening, connects the origins of cuneiform in Mesopotamia to the biblical character of Abraham. The narrator states, "If Abraham and other biblical patriarchs wrote, they might have used this method [cuneiform] or hieratic, Egypt's writing system." While this video suggests the historicity of Abraham and other mythic patriarchs, the museum exhibit in its current form does not make the connection between the origins of writing and the Bible explicit. The curiosity of this choice is worth dwelling on: Why start with cuneiform tablets that do not contain biblical texts or even precursors to biblical texts, that were not produced by the people group who wrote the literature now in the Bible – or even by their contemporary neighbors? Why have visitors engage with cuneiform tablets whose relationship to the Bible is not self-evident or addressed in signage?

This move can only be understood once one has moved through the entire History floor and noticed that technologies of textual transmission reign supreme as organizing features. The MOTB exhibit starts with the invention of writing in human history because writing is the first technology necessary for putting a divine message ("the Bible") into a textual form, which is more stable, and therefore replicable and reliable, than oral transmission. Writing is necessary for God's pretextual message to humans to become stable enough to be communicated and disseminated. As the signage indicates, writing changed the world: "Ancient Mesopotamians used reeds to mark signs on soft clay tablets. At first, they created only lists and receipts. Soon, however, scribes recorded everything from letters to literature. Writing gradually spread through the Fertile Crescent, changing the world forever." From the signs marked on clay tablets come more writing systems. Because the biblical writings' original languages are Hebrew, Aramaic, and Greek, the MOTB History's focus shifts to those. The placard entitled "Egyptian Writing: The beginning of the alphabet" reads: "Along with trade goods, ancient Near Eastern peoples shared many ideas and technologies. The Egyptian system of writing had a major impact in the region. | The world's first alphabet emerged from this cultural exchange. The descendants of this alphabet were used to write Hebrew, Aramaic, and Greek – the original languages of the Bible." The MOTB has here made Mesopotamians and Egyptians the unwitting inventors of biblical textuality, demonstrating a dismissive colonialist optic to ancient civilizations. Ancient societies invented writing, so the story suggests, without knowing that their technology would be used by God in a divine textual project. As professor of English and medievalist Jana Mathews notes, "The story of the ancient world is thus one of autonomous production and unconscious collaboration."[8]

This technology is featured because of its necessity for the message's reliability. Without the invention of writing, God's Word would be subject to generations of the telephone game, in which each retelling changes the original. Writing is a stabilizer. In later signage discussing "Voices of the Past," we read that scribes played a central role in overcoming the problem of orality: "Across the ancient Near East, writing was an elite skill. Passing on key traditions through speech and song was more prominent than it is today. Literary features of some passages in the Hebrew Bible suggest that ancient scribes wrote down stories and poems that previous generations had passed down through spoken words." But the MOTB exhibit simultaneously betrays anxiety about the durability of the *materials* that the ancient Israelites and Judahites wrote *on*. In a placard accompanying the rise of the Israelite monarchy, we read that "the people of Israel and Judah passed on stories, songs, and poetry by word of mouth and through writing. But they wrote on fragile materials, and no copies of biblical texts older than the 3rd century BC survive." Both oral tradition and fragile writing materials are here presented as problems: neither is durable. Oral tradition is precarious, but so is writing, which is subject to the fragility of the papyrus upon which it is inked. The MOTB contrasts this fragility with durable "stone monuments" used by "nearby cultures" that have survived. Writing is insufficient by itself. For the MOTB's History, new technologies are needed that can render the written Word more durable. We find one solution to the perceived problem in the next exhibit section.

COLLECTION AND THE CODEX: FROM JEWS TO CHRISTIANS. The next focus on the History floor is collection. Collecting writings offers otherwise fragile biblical texts a chance to survive and endure through the intentional practice of gathering, combining, and securing. Together with writing, collecting is a stabilizing technology. Analysis of MOTB signage reveals that collection as a description of the development of the Bible refers to an intentional process of acquisition, curation, and preservation that moves biblical texts in a safe space of care among Jewish communities. The Word's textual risks are ameliorated by the work of Jews. As visitors enter into the Second Temple period section of the History floor, a period of time initiated by the rebuilding of the Jerusalem Temple at the end of the Babylonian captivity, we are told that biblical writings were collected and organized by Jewish communities. In a banner describing "Hebrew Scripture" we read that this period is marked by "preserving traditions and shaping identity": "During the Second Temple period from the late 6th century BC to 1st century AD, fuller collections of Jewish Scripture took shape. They assumed a central role in Jewish religion and culture." Collection emerges here for the first time as a shift in how the Word becomes text. The adjective "fuller" shows that there is a teleology at work: we are moving along the path toward the emergence of a "full" bible, vocabulary likewise featured in the illumiNations exhibit to describe a Christian bible containing both Old and New Testaments.

The MOTB virtually ignores that recent historical work on the Second Temple period of Jewish history emphasizes the rich diversity of thinking and practice represented in a wide swath of Jewish scriptures, only some of which eventually became "biblical." We do not make this observation principally to suggest that the MOTB "made a mistake"; rather, we point this out because lacunae, gaps, and omissions are places where we can see how museum curation selectivity works and what stories such curation can create. Acknowledging variety in Second Temple Judaism could destabilize the History floor's teleology. Thus the museum's History interprets the destruction of the Second Jerusalem Temple by the Romans in 70 CE as a watershed event only in so much as it impacted the formation of the (Christian) bible. According to the MOTB signage, the Temple's destruction forced Jewish communities to organize and standardize collections of biblical texts. In an exhibit that visualizes the three different parts of the Tanakh (the Law, Prophets, and Writings) we find a placard entitled "Under Greek and Roman Rule: Diversity leads to stability." The placard reads:

> From the late-4th century BC, Jews lived under first Hellenistic, then Roman, rule. Under these new influences, their communities became more diverse. Nevertheless, along with the Torah, Jerusalem and its temple, remained the center of Judaism. During the Jewish Revolt of AD 66–74, the temple in Jerusalem was destroyed. The Romans killed many Jews, driving many more from the region. In response, leaders in the surviving Jewish communities worked to stabilize their scriptural traditions.

The Temple's destruction is tied to a push to "stabilize" the Bible as a monolithic response to trauma.

On an adjoining sign, we find out how this History conceives the stabilization process to have worked in practice: "Before their rebellion against the Romans, most Jews regarded the writings referred to as Torah and the Prophets as sacred. But some still questioned which other texts were of the same quality and importance. After the loss of the temple in Jerusalem, a consensus emerged among Jewish communities." This consensus was the threefold organization of the Tanakh. What started out as merely the collection of scriptural writings has now taken on a clear organization and a bounded limit. The signage's invocation of a mysterious *some* who *still* questioned what should be in the Bible shows how the history being told here is one that continues the inexorable march from precarity to stability, from partial to full. A developing technology of collection is what ensures that the Word can become the Bible.

The next major technological shift comes as the now constituted Tanakh is taken up and transformed into the full bible by the inclusion of the Christian New Testament. This textual revolution occurs through the introduction of a new material technology: the codex. It is with the codex that the Bible becomes a book, the Book of Books – but only when it is made so by Christians. In a side alcove off the main thoroughfare of the floor, which feels a bit like a detour, is an exhibit section that explains the transition from scroll to codex, with examples of each for visitors to touch and manipulate. Scrolls were writings on papyrus or parchment that were rolled up, making them harder to reference and store. A codex was an innovation that allowed multiple texts to be bound together in a book, similar to how modern print books are bound today. This textual technology transforms the Word into a book:

> The title "The Bible" comes from the Greek words "Τὰ Βιβλία" for "The Books." This reflects the fact that the Bible is actually a compilation of many texts. For centuries, biblical writings appeared on separate scrolls. Starting around the 2nd century AD, use of the new codex – bound book – format allowed multiple texts to be assembled in a single volume. But not everyone agreed on which books should be included in collections of scripture. Therefore, different collections of what came to be known as "The Bible" began to appear. Today, different religious traditions that use the Bible still do not agree on exactly which books it contains.

The Word has now become a book, a collection of what used to be scrolls, bound together for the first time. What continues to haunt the Book here, however, is the fact that it has not yet become fully stable in its table of contents. The written word is *still* debated. The repeated word "still" invokes a judgment of deviance and reveals an anxiety about destabilization. We find it once again under signage reflecting on the Bible's new ability to have a fixed canonical list:

> By the late 1st century AD, the Jewish community had reached final consensus on the contents of its Bible. ... For centuries, there was

debate among Christians over the exact contents of the emerging "New Testament." By the late 4th century, most groups agreed on the same 27 books. A few traditions still accept different numbers of books.

Along a wall are cases containing modern bibles with different tables of contents: Hebrew, Samaritan, Catholic, Protestant, Eastern Orthodox, Oriental Orthodox, and Assyrian (from left to right). Entitled "Book of Books," this exhibit section puts a Protestant bible in the center, flanked by the versions that "still" don't agree with this bible's full and fixed form. Though chronologically the visitor at this point is still in the second century CE, these bibles are all modern editions. Since these are examples of bibles used by contemporary communities, we should wonder why they are presented here in the past and not at some point later on the floor. Read alongside the signage, this exhibit marks the stability of the Bible's contents as a problem that challenges the promise of the codex form. It will take a few more technological innovations before the Bible can overcome the perceived threat of heterogeneity.

TRANSLATING THE BIBLE, TRANSMITTING THE MESSAGE. The next major technology in the museum's History is translation. While the codex holds promise as a vehicle for the spread of the Word, it can only realize its potential through translation, which allows for texts to circulate across borders. We have to go backwards a few centuries to see where this starts. Immediately to the right of the introduction of the Tanakh's tripartite structure is a large banner marking a chronological shift (250 BC–AD 500): "During the Greek and Roman periods, Jews continued to gather their sacred writings. In the 3rd century BC, they began translating these sacred texts from Hebrew into Greek. Christians later inherited these translations and added new books. Biblical writings soon spread throughout the Mediterranean world and beyond." Translation is here linked to the spread of the Bible. It is a requisite condition for it to become universally accessible.

Yet, in the logic of this exhibit, for the Bible to spread it has to be decoupled successively from Hebrew and from Jews. First, the MOTB's History tells us, ancient Jews translate the Tanakh from Hebrew into

Greek. A placard describing the resulting body of Greek translations, called the Septuagint, notes that the translation of the Tanakh into Greek "served the growing number of Jews around the Mediterranean who understood Greek better than Hebrew." Translation here spreads the Bible by following Jews who move around the Mediterranean. But then Christians move in. The museum's emphasis on translation is paired here with the language of inheritance: Christians *inherit* the Greek translations of the Bible from Jews. This language is repeated elsewhere in the exhibit, as, for example, in a placard describing the origin of the phrase "Old Testament": "This title affirmed the sacred status of the collection of writings [Christians] inherited from Jews. Meanwhile, it distinguished them from the new Christian writings." Inheritance is a crucial component of how translation allows for the spread of the Bible. After the Bible was made accessible through translation into Greek, it had to be decoupled from Jews to reach others. As an inheritance, the Bible is here figured as an object of value that was legally transferred to Christians. We cannot help but observe that the legal transfer of an inheritance only occurs after the original owner has died.

Passing through the museum's exhibition of early Christian papyri, many of which are replicas and not ancient artifacts, visitors enter an exhibit that features early Christian codices in the context of Christian translation. Here we see the codex freed up to cross ethnic and linguistic boundaries. On display are several codices and leaves from codices with biblical texts. These artifacts are tied explicitly to translations that take the Bible to new groups of people, framed interestingly as markets. Signage reads: "New audiences need new translations. The Bible was composed in Hebrew, Aramaic, and Greek. As it was carried around the Mediterranean, and introduced to new cultures, the text was translated for the ears of new listeners. By AD 600, translations of the Bible existed in at least 10 additional languages." In some cases, we are told, it was these consumer needs that required the production of new written technology. Christians are credited with inventing the alphabets of Armenian, Georgian, and Gothic for the purpose of translating the Bible.[9] The creation of new alphabets here ties back to the invention of writing as a necessity to textualizing and spreading the Word. The process here continues, but now under Christian supervision.[10] From here on out, Jews and their bibles remain frozen in Hebrew.

The promise of the codex as a textual technology is revealed in this section. Once the door of translation is opened, the codex is able to move quickly to new markets. As the visitor moves from language to language in the exhibit, the only difficulty that is mentioned is the need for the occasional new alphabet. We learn nothing of the complexities of translation, of the messiness of moving between linguistic and cultural systems. Nor is there any mention of the multiplicity of versions of biblical texts as these materials proliferate into new contexts. The process unfolds within a narrative of simple information transfer: the Bible remains the same as it is translated from one language to the next. Communication, presumably from the divine to humanity, is unfettered. That is, until new problems emerge.

THE PROBLEM OF THE HANDMADE BIBLE. The exhibit suggests that the codex served well as a technology for biblical transmission, but we quickly learn that it was hampered by the problems that are associated with its own production. As a handmade object, it was both expensive and subject to copying errors. In signage marked "Translating the Bible (AD 200–AD 1500)" we are told about the problems that come with dissemination of the Bible by hand:

> As use of the Bible grew, new followers wanted to hear or read it in their own language. Jewish officials worked to preserve the word of God, resulting in precise rules for copying the Hebrew text. Christian leaders' desire for unity and accurate teaching also led to more consistent versions of their Bibles. New universities and groups of wandering friars created demand for portable Bibles. The growth of universities also renewed controversy over language and access. Meanwhile, manuscript decoration became a specialized art form.

Translation is still doing what it needs to do as a mechanism of transmission, but it has created a concern for whether these new copies are accurate. The text needs to be stabilized with precise rules for copying.

As the exhibit progresses through Late Antiquity and the Middle Ages, we find an increased concern in the signage around the stability of the biblical text as it is translated and copied. In Latin, Jerome and the Vulgate are presented as important stabilizers. In a sign focused on "Standardizing the Latin Text," we are presented with the problem of diversity leading to instability: "Unifying the Bible in the West. By the 4th century, Latin translations of the Christian Bible were widely used, but many variations occurred between different copies. This situation created demand for a more reliable edition." Here we see a contradiction at the heart of the museum's narrative. We have, on the one hand, widespread use of Latin bibles and, on the other, an apparent demand for a reliable, universal edition. With the need for bibles being met, who was it who demanded a reliable edition? This question is never addressed nor answered in signage, but the construction of such a demand coheres with the overall concern we have identified on this exhibit floor: Word made Text has to be consistent and stable through time.

Jerome's translation of the Bible into Latin is held up as the stabilizing force needed in the West. Signage marks it the "standard text in the Western church for 1,000 years." While the exhibit presents such standardization as the result of a gradual process, the actual messiness that attended the Vulgate's production and reception are not represented. Augustine, to take an example, questioned Jerome's choice of texts used in his translation, and Jerome's decision to use Hebrew manuscripts (except when translating the Psalms) was both controversial and an act of appropriation similar to the museum's own rhetoric of Christian "inheritance" of the Bible from Jews.[11]

The museum then turns to the Masoretes to emphasize how Jews played a role in preserving a stable biblical text. One sign reads: "The work of the Masoretes – a group of biblical scholars – ensured that all Jewish communities read accurate copies of the Hebrew Bible." In an interactive exhibit nearby, we are told that there were "strict rules" that were enforced by Jewish scribes: "If there were more than three mistakes in a manuscript, it had to be recopied." And yet another placard in this corner of the floor, which accompanies a Sephardic Torah scroll on display, suggests that a *different* Jewish practice could simultaneously threaten the accessibility of biblical texts: that of cere-monially burying decommissioned Torah scrolls in accordance with traditional Jewish law. The artifact in question is a Hebrew manuscript identified as originating in the 1200s in the Iberian Peninsula that has been put together with another manuscript originating in central Europe in the 1800s. The sign reads: "Because this extremely early Sephardic scroll was later joined together with a more recent Polish scroll, *it was saved* from being ceremonially buried or placed in a genizah" (italics added). As Moss and Baden have written, such language suggests that the Torah scrolls need to be rescued "not from deterioration, but from their traditional Jewish rites."[12] Even as the Masoretes are doing the desired work of standardizing, then, the MOTB represents other Jews as working against the text's accessibility because they buried material witnesses to the Word. An unwitting visitor could be forgiven for thinking that Jews were ultimately hazard-ous to the Bible's survival because they put it underground, out of reach.

Yet ultimately the notion of the text's "accuracy" prevails as the most significant theme in this section. Several interactive exhibits work to suggest that biblical copying cannot fail to reproduce an accurate text, despite the fact that copying by hand often actually produced variations between texts. Next to the displays of early Christian codices, a touch screen invites visitors to use a finger to play-act scribal practice by copying biblical words. The Greek word for "light" (*phos*) appears in Greek characters, and visitors are asked to "follow the arrow to copy the phrase below." A more apt description would be to "trace," as the exhibit does not allow the visitor to copy freehand. The Greek charac-ters are provided in light gray outline on a simulated scrap of paper. The visitor's touch fills them in with black "ink." Out of curiosity, we experimented with whether we could manipulate or mess up the text. The computer ignored our touch when we tried to start from the final letter and trace backwards, when we tried to write a different letter, when we tried frantically to write anything but what was already given to us. In the end, we "copied" the text perfectly. The consequence – intended or not – of this interactive exhibit is that the visitor has embodied an imaginary scribe with superhuman powers of accurate transmission. Yet there were no computers, no letters to trace with an electronic policing system. Scribes colored outside the lines. This exhibit erases the problem of textual variation by giving visitors a false sense of historical scribes' accuracy in transmitting the text by hand copying.

A similar message of textual stability is suggested in another interactive exhibit near Jerome and the Masoretes. Here visitors are given the opportunity to copy biblical text by hand with manual writing instruments. Visitors are provided sheets of paper that allow them to trace over Hebrew letters in ink. The effect is similar to that of the virtual interactive: it is hard to mess up. Both exhibits fail to reckon with the actual practices of copying manuscripts in antiquity, which involved either

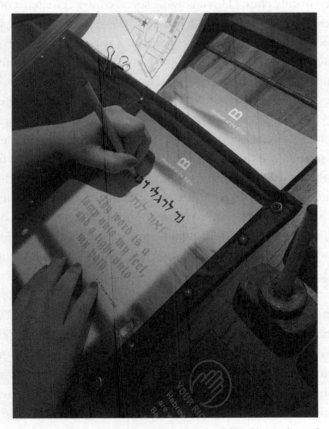

7. Interactive exhibit in the Museum of the Bible. Photo: the authors.

glancing back and forth between the copy and the original or writing by dictation. Why create interactive exhibits that do not match ancient copying practices? The museum has chosen to teach its audience that the hand-copying of ancient manuscripts did not lead to a loss of accuracy or stability in textual transmission.

Further concerns marked by the museum in the medieval period are perceived problems in the Bible's portability and accessibility. In an exhibit marked "Practical Groupings" that contains manuscripts from the ninth to tenth centuries, we learn that there was not yet a cost-effective technology for the Bible to be in one book: "Large manuscripts were expensive, so most Christian biblical codices did not include all the books of the Bible." Changes in the economy and the introduction of universities, we are told, increased the demand for bibles that were not just housed in churches: "This changing social context created a need for smaller, less expensive Bibles." The Bible's accessibility cannot be universal if bibles are too bulky and expensive. Cost has now emerged as a hindrance in the Bible's path to everyone. So too has the dominance of Jerome's Latin Vulgate. On a placard entitled "Bibles in Local Languages," we read that while Latin was "the universal language of learning," "growing numbers of the less educated clamored for access to the Bible in languages they understood." The signage further emphasizes that translations are needed in order to "increase understanding," a phrase that assumes that there is a message to be apprehended and comprehended rather than created or constructed. The problems, perceived or actual, of a shortfall of translations, the excessive cost of bible production, and the risks of hand-copying to textual stability, are resolved with perhaps the most important textual technology for the museum's story: the printing press.

AN AFFORDABLE, REPRODUCIBLE, READABLE BIBLE. The title of the next major exhibit section is "Revolutionary Words (1400–1650 CE)." Here we have a double entendre, pointing us toward the Protestant Reformation's democratization of bible reading through vernacular translation that accompanied the Protestant Reformation and the technological invention of the printing press, which made printed bibles less expensive to reproduce on a larger scale. The champions of

REVOLUTIONARY WORDS are Desiderius Erasmus, Martin Luther, and William Tyndale, who are all presented primarily as Bible translators (though this descriptor does not exhaust their actual activities). A placard entitled "THE GREAT TRANSLATORS" purports to offer a summary of "Bible scholarship during the Renaissance and Reformation" and reads: "Scholars, printers, reformers, politicians, and church leaders all influenced the development of the Bible during the 16th and 17th centuries. The work of three translators – Desiderius Erasmus, Martin Luther, and William Tyndale – had an immense impact."

Artifacts displayed nearby include Erasmus's Greek New Testament (1516) and Paraphrases of the Gospels and Acts (1524),[13] Luther's Pentateuch (1524)[14] and personal New Testament, and a fragment of Tyndale's English New Testament (1535)[15] and a copy of his 1552 New Testament.[16]

But the technological advancement that the MOTB celebrates here as the most important in the history of its bible is Gutenberg's printing press. Framing the transformations of the period with Protestant values, museum signage claims "the Bible" as "the center of the technological, intellectual, and social revolutions of the Renaissance," noting that it "was the first major book printed with movable type in Europe."[17] The printing industry is heralded as the technological means of making the (textual) Bible accessible to a wider audience. Gutenberg's press is the real star not only of this exhibit section but arguably of the MOTB as a whole.[18] The museum's facade is dominated by what the MOTB calls its "Gutenberg Gates," a huge reproduction of the plates used to produce Genesis 1 in the Gutenberg Bible. Prior to the opening of the MOTB in DC, these gates traveled around the country for public display and even had their own Twitter account.[19] A working replica of Gutenberg's press is featured on the Impact of the Bible floor. There the signage shows how important the press is to the MOTB's history of the Bible: "Copies of the Bible, once limited to scholars, clergy, and nobility, became widely available and affordable. Religious reform movements soon focused on printing the Bible in vernacular languages, allowing many more people to read it for themselves." For the MOTB, Gutenberg's press offers a huge new technological step forward in transmitting the Bible to the masses.

Mirroring the "Copy like a Scribe" activity we have already described is a complementary interactive for the Gutenberg Bible and the printing press on the History floor. "Print a phrase like Gutenberg!" the computer screen beckons. We read about the care with which the printer selected and moved each letter to the printing plate: "When setting type for the Gutenberg Bible, the printer carefully placed each piece letter by letter, and line by line, utilizing up to 2,600 pieces of type per page." We can try our hand at three different phrases from Genesis. Once one is selected, a row of movable plates appears across the lower portion of the screen with letters on each that the participant can select with a touch. Above is a template showing which letter should go where. Just as the scribal copying interactive policed visitors' touch to ensure accuracy, this computerized system likewise will not allow the participant to accidentally select a letter that should not come next. One cannot help but print the text perfectly.

And yet it is not the case that all bibles were thereby "accurately" produced. Two examples of famously "inaccurate" printings of the King James Version of the Bible are on display in the next section of the History, under a banner celebrating the KJV's literary qualities and wide appeal. One is a first edition of the KJV from 1611 nicknamed the "He" Bible because it uses the masculine rather than feminine pronoun in one place in chapter 3 of the book of Ruth (Ruth 3:15).[20] The second is the famous 1631 "Wicked Bible," so-called for a misprinting that reversed one of the Ten Commandments and endorsed rather than condemned extramarital sexual activity. "Thou shall commit adultery," its version of Exodus 20:14 reads.[21] The "Wicked Bible" on display at the museum has an additional page that was added post printing to correct the error. It's instructive to observe that the examples of "wrong" bibles here are ones that might be described as cute, quaint, or even laughable. They present mistakes in transmission as obvious and easily correctable.

So now the printing press has opened the door to the final stage of the Bible's history. By making bibles cheaper and easier to produce, the press allows the Bible to spread alongside the now central process of translation. But how to get it from Europe into the hands of people the world over?

(STABLE) BIBLES FOR EVERYONE! The next technology needed is a mechanism for the Bible's dissemination. The MOTB's answer to this logistical problem is European colonialism. The expansion of Europe's colonial holdings is seen as a blessing for the Bible and its Word. A key example of this phenomenon occurs on signage surrounding the King James Bible. The King James translation has had a huge effect on English literature, we are told, and it was able to achieve this influence through both government investment and Britain's colonial reach. Colonialism appears here as a good thing for its aid in bible dissemination: "Its literary qualities," we read, "along with the British Empire's world dominance, made the King James Bible the most influential and widely read Bible for the next 350 years." From the King James Bible to the work of European Bible societies, Europe's warships and trading vessels would take the Bible around the globe for the first time. The signage for this next phase of the museum's History ("Bibles for Everyone [AD 1750 – AD 2000]") likewise presents European colonialism as a positive mechanism for bible distribution. "Europeans expand the reach of the Bible," one placard announces. On top of an illuminated globe we see the continent of Africa with the assertion that "This migration of traders, explorers, missionaries, and others brought Judeo-Christian culture, traditions, and Bibles to many parts of the globe."[22] The large central header sign summarizes the themes that will occupy the remainder of this section:

> Growth in wealth, technology, and learning following the Industrial Revolution resulted in the transmission and translation of the Bible on a previously unimagined scale. More people than ever gained access to an increasing diversity of Bibles. But for some groups, the traditional form and language of the Bible have remained virtually unchanged.

This final sentence introduces an interesting adversative likely intended to explain why there is here a Torah scroll display alongside a Torah scribe (*sofer*). For the purposes of the museum's story of technological advancement, the most important piece of this placard is that European Bible societies are presented as central to the spread of the Bible in the age of European colonialism. These groups, the museum tells us, provided "Bibles for the world": "Missionaries carried Christianity around the world, creating unprecedented demand for the Christian Bible. In response, Bible societies were formed for the purpose of printing, distributing, and translating the Bible without financial gain." Once again we see the language of demand for bibles that requires translation. Thanks to advances in block printing, these bibles can now be supplied. Note that the description in the MOTB's *History* does not entertain ethical questions that could be raised about the spread of Christianity and its bibles via colonialism. Missing from the sign is any reflection on how the missionaries from Europe got to these new markets in the first place. Christian missionaries were only able to travel around the world with cheap bibles, we know, because they were parasitic on exploitative economic and militaristic networks that facilitated the capture, control, and exploitation of Asia, Africa, and the Americas.

As the colonial era gives way to the neoliberal world order, we return to translation. In a sign entitled "Continual translation: New languages and new ideas," we read: "New advances in biblical scholarship, the discovery of more ancient texts, and the desire to spread the Bible ensured a continual supply of new Bible translations. In the 20th century, the efforts of the American Bible Society, Wycliffe Bible Translators, and the Summer Institute of Linguistics made the United States the hub of translation activity." With an underlying premise that our world is in a state of constant need for bibles in translation, this sign outlines phenomena that have "ensured" the success of this project. The first – "new advances in biblical scholarship" – erases the possibility that professional research on biblical literature could challenge rather than support the enterprise of bible translation for purposes of distribution. Bible-boosting scholarship here eclipses critical scholarship, which is entirely removed from view for any visitor unfamiliar with the field of biblical studies (a point to which we return below). Utilizing "discovery" language that imputes a white imperial gaze,[23] the second phenomenon – "the discovery of more ancient texts" – recasts problems created by the proliferation of variant textual traditions and noncanonical literary works as actually useful for stabilizing a bible text through translation. The Bible now has everything it needs to spread its Word to the world. Under that celebratory note, visitors find themselves ready to approach the Word's telos in the illumiNations exhibit.

We pointed out above the variety of ways that a history of any bible could have started but that the MOTB does not employ. There is also an untold future on the MOTB's History floor that needs interrogating. Given that a major theme of the exhibit floor is, as we have shown, developing technologies of transmission, it might have made a fitting end to focus on the effects of the digital revolution on bible reading and distribution. After all, the Green family is involved with YouVersion, the biggest digital platform for disseminating biblical content everywhere via smartphones. Rather than capping off the MOTB's tracing of transmission technologies, though, this evangelical Christian digital platform is featured in the "Bible Now" display on the Impact floor. Why doesn't it fit in the History floor exhibit? Allow us to speculate: Digital bibles are fundamentally unstable.[24] Their inclusion here would risk challenging the narrative of inherent reliability of the Bible being produced in the MOTB. Bibles on smartphones do not have the same boundaries as a book. They pose a challenge to the traditional shape and contents of canon. And, as we will see in the next section, the MOTB History floor goes to great lengths to protect the reliability of the Word made text.

PROTECTIVE STRATEGIES: EVANGELICAL FENCES AROUND THE RELIABLE BIBLE

In an interview given on a podcast produced by an evangelical Christian men's ministry called Noble Warriors, MOTB Scholars Initiative director Daniel Stevens was asked about where the Bible comes from.[25] While noting that the Bible was written by many people in the past, the host pressed him, "But all under the inspiration of God, right?" Stevens confessed, "Yes. Yes, absolutely." When the host asked what makes the Bible special, Stevens replied in part, "It's from God." When pressed further about whether the bible that a reader has in their hands today can be trusted, Stevens responded, "I'm entirely confident that if you have a bible in your hands the original or initial reading is on the page. It might be in the footnotes sometimes ... but it's there. I haven't seen anything to cause me to question that." And, for Stevens, the purported reliability of manuscript evidence is because of divine intention and involvement in preservation. "We can trust," he commented, "that God ensures that what he wants to be known will be known and the words he wants to be known will be known." The host of the podcast reacted with appreciation that Stevens, as a representative of the MOTB, was as confident as he himself was. And at several points in the interview he commended the museum to his audience as a resource to help guests themselves become more confident in offering apologetic arguments for Christian faith.

In a telling moment following Stevens's somewhat complicated and detailed description of the textual trustworthiness of the Bible, the host responded after an awkward pause, "That's a lot of words and information." He then went on to affirm that everything Stevens had said supports his faith, the divine origins of the Bible, and its reliability. The History floor at the MOTB is also *a lot of words and information*. Much of it discretely accurate and interesting. There is a lot of "good history" presented to visitors. Both museum officials and our own discussions with colleagues in the guild of biblical studies have confirmed that well-qualified scholars had some input on the signage throughout the floor. The information available to take in is so extensive that visitors who are not already committed to a white evangelical bible likely feel like they are learning disinterested history. But just as the podcast host was able to assimilate the "words and information" into his epistemic schema that assumes the Bible is the Word of God, so white evangelical visitors on the History floor will encounter nothing that challenges the reliability of their bible or the narrative of its divine origins. And, in fact, we have shown so far in this chapter that the preexistence of the Word along with the need for it to be transmitted accurately and reliably through textual media is the interpretive key to understanding this floor at the museum. Central to the rhetorical success of this narrative is that it is not stated directly.

For the words and information to be even more potentially effective, though, protective strategies are necessary. A protective strategy is a phrase coined by some religious studies scholars, notably in the work of Wayne Proudfoot and Russell McCutcheon, to describe the choices, tools, frameworks, and assumptions that protect certain beliefs from scholarly analysis.[26] In what follows, we articulate the strategies deployed alongside the History floor's narrative that protect the

Word made Text from critical analysis.[27] Each of these strategies protects the history of the museum's white evangelical bible from disruption so that visitors can leave "knowing" that this bible has been reliably transmitted from God into text and can be safely sent to the ends of the earth.

INERRANCY AND HISTORICAL CONTEXT. The first protective strategy explains why the museum's narrative requires historicizing in the first place. Popular discourse around the museum paints its motivations as associated with an idea that the Bible can have no errors and must represent history as it happened. The MOTB's historicizing exhibits do not support this conclusion – but only because the museum encodes, as we will see, a different type of biblical inerrancy that can accommodate some methods and conclusions of biblical scholarship.

The museum exhibits are clear about the fact that the writings of the ancient Israelites that would eventually become biblical bear similarities to writings produced by surrounding cultures in the ancient Near East. In a sign entitled "Shared Traditions. Similar texts with distinct messages," we read: "Ancient texts from Israel's neighbors include many ideas, themes, and types of writings also found in the Bible. Similarities show how biblical traditions are rooted in the shared culture of the region. Differences offer clues about each group's distinct perspective." Dream interpretation, flood stories, treaties and covenants are examples of similar traditions found in ancient Israel's texts and those of other ancient Near Eastern cultures, each here illustrated with ancient objects and replicas. These moves could be read as counterevidence to our reading of the History floor. Are these not examples that the Bible is not unique and, therefore, not divinely inspired, not immune from contamination by other, human influences? But placing these exhibits in the context of white evangelical discourses of biblical inerrancy helps us see that the historicizing of the Bible's texts in their ancient Near Eastern context does not necessarily detract from a notion of the Bible's divine origins.

The idea that the Bible is the inspired Word of God has a long history within white evangelicalism. Often discussion of the Bible's sacredness is framed with the category of inerrancy. Inerrancy is the theological belief that the Bible, as God's Word, cannot be wrong, either in what it says about God, ethics, and theology, or in its historical details.[28] In his survey of the debates, biblical scholar Stephen Young has described two major streams of inerrantist thought within white evangelicalism: correspondence-truth inerrantists and genre inerrantists. We miss something important about the strategies at the MOTB if we collapse these distinctions or if we attribute to the museum the wrong type of inerrancy. Correspondence-truth inerrantists take a strict line on the Bible's lack of error. They "reject conceptions of inerrancy that allow for any affirmed errors, deliberate alterations of detail for theological purposes, or seemingly historical writing with little historical-referential content."[29] Genre inerrantists, by contrast, allow for biblical writers to take historically contingent license with how they wrote. They allow for certain kinds of socio-historical factors to have shaped the Bible. For genre inerrantists, "literary artistry, theological emphasis and exaggeration, and deliberate alterations of detail to make a point do not constitute inerrancy-invalidating errors – since the authors of those writings were not just trying to recount 'what really happened,' and their audiences knew and accepted these conventions."[30] That biblical authors drew on idioms, genres, and conventions common to their time would not, on this view, disrupt a conviction about the divinely inspired nature of the text. By creating exhibits that navigate white evangelical debates around inerrancy, the museum is able to present the Bible as a set of texts produced in (and speaking to) an ancient historical context without contradicting the idea that its stories are accurate, true, and divinely endorsed. Inerrancy, therefore, can be read quite comfortably out of the museum's History even as the museum does not make an argument that the Bible is "historically accurate" and "literally true" in the way that correspondence-truth inerrantists propose.

The historical approach offered in the exhibits that read biblical traditions and texts in their historical context actually works in tandem with the museum's unspoken narrative that the Bible is God's Word made text. Inerrantist scholars argue that their historical analyses are actually the only correct way of reading the Bible because they alone recognize the Bible's divine nature and take it into account. As Young notes, "At the root of what differentiates valid inerrantist scholarship from invalid inerrancy-denying scholarship is the failure of critics to approach the Bible 'on its own terms,' accepting its claims about God in relation to humanity and its own supernatural-inspiration and inerrancy."[31] In other words, the Bible is a special kind of historical object that can only be studied using tools appropriate to its nature. The Bible is simultaneously divine and historically contextual. To understand it on its own terms requires "inerrancy-modulated historical methods."[32]

This is precisely what the History floor offers to visitors: an inerrancy-modulated history of the Bible. White evangelicals who come to the MOTB with a belief in the Bible's inerrancy will find their views amplified by the History floor, while those lacking the context for the kind of history being produced will think that they are being presented with unmodulated historical scholarship. In either case, the white evangelical bible reigns.

THE TRANSLATOR'S INVISIBILITY. Another protective strategy at work on the History floor is the use of an instrumental model of translation. Translation is celebrated throughout the History floor as the mechanism by which the Bible is ultimately made accessible to all people.[33] The museum's use of translation as a technology of the Bible's transmission through time is also a protective strategy. Through all of its various invocations, translation is never seen as more than a simple linguistic equation: The Bible in language X is translated into the Bible in language Y. On both sides of the equation the Bible remains the same as the language changes. Translation as transmission allows the museum to suggest that the Bible's message has been conveyed transparently through time. It has been transmitted – not transformed – by translation.

The museum's concept of translation is built on an assumption that what happens in the process of moving from one language to another is simple transference, a model of translation that translation theorist and historian Lawrence Venuti has called the instrumental model of translation. The instrumental approach

> treats translation as the reproduction or transfer of an invariant that the
> source text contains or causes, typically described as its form, its meaning,

or its effect. ... In the instrumental mode, translation conveys an unchanging essence inherent in or produced by the source text, so that even if assimilated to the receiving language and culture that essence is transmitted intact.[34]

For instrumentalists, the language may change, but the message and the content stay the same.

We can see this model in operation in one of the interactive exhibits on the History floor that allows visitors to determine what kind of translator they are, based upon how they would translate a phrase from Hebrew into Greek, ostensibly mirroring the choices facing those who created the Septuagint in Jewish antiquity. There are only three possible outcomes: literalist, expressionist, and go-between. The literalist approach is defined as being a strict method that always translates the same word the same way, regardless of context. The expressionist approach is defined as one where the translator uses Greek expressions to translate Hebrew words/phrases so that Greek readers would be better able to understand. The go-between method is merely an inconsistent use of the first two approaches. For each of these approaches, the only issue that is raised is one of understanding; the literalist approach makes the translation harder to understand while the expressionist makes it easier. In neither case is there any reflection on whether the choices of the translator might affect the meaning of the text itself. Translation then conveys the same content unchanged, with the only variable being the level of difficulty of comprehension.[35] Translation can only be assessed here by the ease with which it makes the Bible's words accessible to readers.

What is hidden by the instrumentalist approach adopted by the museum is the violence that is done in the process of translation. As Venuti notes, in translation

the multiple contexts that constitute the source text, when translated, inevitably undergo various degrees of diminution and loss. The translator decontextualizes the source text by dismantling, disarranging, and abandoning features of its signifying process, starting from the very sounds of its words, extending to their connotations and intertextual relations, and including the meanings, values, and functions with which the source text is invested by readers and institutions in the source culture.[36]

In other words, translation is *not* transmission but transformation. A bible is not the same as it moves from language to language, edition to edition. The history of bible translation is not a story of how the Bible has spread to new cultures, but one in which diverse bibles have been transformed by conscious choices through contact with new cultural worlds.

One example, particularly germane to the work of the European and American Bible societies celebrated by the MOTB, is how bibles were translated and distributed in the context of colonialism. The work of Willie Jennings, a professor of systematic theology and African studies, treating the life of John Colenso, an Anglican missionary in South Africa in the mid nineteenth century, highlights how the colonial interests of the British in South Africa shaped both the missionary project and the translation of bibles into native languages.[37] Jennings shows how Colenso's missionary work presumed a universal message of the Bible that could be translated across culture, the fiction of which belied the actual result: the forced inscription of Africans into European problems, thought-worlds, and disciplinary control. Reflecting on Christian theorizing of translations that follow Venuti's instrumentalist model, Jennings notes:

> they cannot capture the simultaneity that constitutes the Christian world
> in new worlds. The multiple levels of translation, that is, of transference,
> transformation, transliteration of land, animals, space, language, and
> bodies, means that worlds overlap and in that overlap they are altered
> irrevocably, hybridized, and cross-pollinated. Equally important, new
> forms of racialized Being are coming into play and driving the
> performance of oral and written systems in new directions and in the
> service of new purposes.[38]

As bible translators rendered bibles into new languages, they initiated a messy process, marked as much by frustration and confusion as by liberation, that created new, overlapping, and cross-pollinated Christian worlds. The MOTB's celebration of translation cannot bear the complexities that attended and still attend translation on the ground.

One of the last exhibits before the visitor enters illumiNations is a bank of display cases showcasing a diverse array of modern print bibles aimed at varying populations of readers. There is a bible for environmentalists, for example, and one for Manga enthusiasts. This diversity is celebrated because it is presented as a boon to the spread of a stable message:

> Today people of all faiths have access to Bibles that represent their traditions and lifestyles. There is a wide variety of readability and format options tailored to appeal to specific communities, beliefs, and learning styles. Anyone looking to make a connection with the timeless words of the Bible can find an approach to illuminate their path.

The Bible and its words are presented as timeless while it is only the "extra-biblical" packaging and attendant commentary that is viewed as timely. Translation is not conceived to affect the stability of the Bible's *real* content.

Translation as transformation cannot be articulated on the History floor because it would destabilize the floor's underlying narrative that the Word made Text has been transmitted unchanging through time. The story of bible translation is better understood as a messy narrative of diversity rather than as one of miraculous stability. But the latter narrative is what the MOTB needs to convey to protect the white evangelical bible it constructs.[39]

FAKES, OBJECTS, AND ARCHAEOLOGICAL SCIENCE PROVE THE BIBLE. The next protective strategy has to do with the deployment of archaeology in the MOTB. In his survey of inerrantist scholarship on the Bible, Young notes that inerrantist historians "often deploy the rhetoric of science, criticism, or the legitimate-academic" as authorizing strategies in their writing.[40] This is also the case with the History floor, which trades on the notion that science supports the Bible. The particular science that is most often invoked is archaeology. While the MOTB exhibit does not advance obvious apologetics like those in the Creation Museum or Ark Encounter that would say unequivocally that we can dig up the remains of famous biblical characters or objects, the MOTB's use of archaeology does work to protect the idea of stable biblical text through time. Archaeology is represented as providing proof not for the notion that events narrated in biblical stories happened precisely how the Bible says but rather for the idea that the biblical text has remained accurate and stable from antiquity to the present. This latter claim, repeated in edutainment videos that populate the floor, functions as a protective strategy for the Word made Text: if you doubt that the Bible is the same today as it was when it was written, archaeology will reassure you. The MOTB can here satisfy critics who would roundly reject the idea that traces of the Garden of Eden or Noah's ark might one day be located while still recruiting archaeology as a support for its conception of the Bible as a divine Word.

A prominent example of this strategy can be viewed in the History floor's main theater.[41] With its own entrance separate from that of the main exhibit, the theater is most notable for its brightly colored foyer, equipped with a beat-up Jeep mounted on artificial rough terrain as a photo prop. The Jeep features in the short film inside, called *Drive Thru History* and hosted by Dave Stotts. Filled with the tropes of Hollywood action adventures, this video was commissioned by the MOTB from a partner production company that offers evangelical and Christian nationalist history documentaries.[42] The MOTB theater film, along with similar shorter segments that punctuate the exhibits on the History floor, provides a guiding narrative for the exhibit floor. Most importantly, the films use archaeology as a safeguard to the stability of the biblical text.

We meet Stotts as he arrives by helicopter at the archaeological excavations at Hazor. In the video, Stotts briefly lists what remains of Hazor from the biblical period and then reflects on what they mean:

> Archaeological sites like this allow us to connect the past to the present. Discoveries are being made every day that help us better understand the Bible. Many have said that the Bible is one of the most incredible stories in history. But there is another incredible story to be told. That is the astonishing history of the Bible's transmission and survival over the centuries. Despite war, burning, persecution, and pillaging, the Bible has pressed on to become the perennial bestseller of all time. The ruins at Hazor allow us to discover the world where the ancient Israelites lived. While residing in towns like these they passed down their stories, stories they recorded in biblical books such as Joshua, Kings, Samuel, and

Jeremiah. In time, accounts were written down, copied, and shared through the centuries.

Stotts's narration makes a number of assumptions that resonate with and amplify the History floor's narrative. He assumes that the Bible is a single story that has survived over time. He also calls it "incredible," relying on an unnamed "many" who have said this. His rhetoric suggests further that this single narrative has an almost anthropomorphic nature.[43] The Bible is both an object, a book that becomes a bestseller, and also an active agent that presses forward through persecution. It's a survivor. Archaeological research is then presented by Stotts as authorizing this narrative. Archaeological sites connect moderns to the biblical past, but not a past in which the complexities of lives lived in the Bronze Age are appreciated, but a past in which the Bible struggles to endure through the work of the Israelites.

As an example of how the Bible moved reliably through history, Stotts turns to the Dead Sea Scrolls (DSS) as evidence for the Bible's "careful transmission over time":

> In the last century, we uncovered the earliest biblical manuscripts ever found, remarkable evidence for the history of the written Bible. In 1946 on the northwest shore of the Dead Sea, Bedouin shepherds made one of the greatest manuscript discoveries of all time here in these caves: the Dead Sea Scrolls. They are comprised of the remains of hundreds of separate scrolls represented by tens of thousands of fragments. Based on various dating methods, we know that most of the Dead Sea Scrolls were originally produced between 200 BC and AD 70, making them collectively the oldest examples of the Hebrew Bible to survive anywhere in the world. Some of the biblical texts discovered here above Qumran are in substantial agreement with the Masoretic text, which is used as the basis for many translations of the Hebrew Bible we still read today. The Dead Sea Scrolls demonstrate their careful transmission over time.

There are many ways in which one might frame the DSS discoveries, and so it is useful to pay attention to what Stotts – and therefore the MOTB – includes and excludes.[44] He begins with their almost miraculous discovery and then turns to the rhetoric of science to date them. This dating is used to peg the manuscripts as the oldest examples of the Hebrew Bible and then to line them up with the later Masoretic text. This allows Stotts to conclude that the transmission of the Bible has been stable from the ancient past to the present.[45]

Occluded in Stotts's presentation are several facts: (1) not all the DSS were "biblical" texts (less than a quarter were); (2) other translations of the Hebrew scriptures proliferated around the Mediterranean at this same time, in Hebrew, Aramaic, and, crucially, Greek; (3) there was a community that preserved these documents at Qumran for their own purposes, which would have influenced the selection and use of these texts. (They did not have a future Christian Bible in mind.) These complexities could be backed up by similar assemblages of data, but they wouldn't allow Stotts to conclude that the Bible that is read today is remarkably, even miraculously, the same as the Bible read, copied, and preserved by ancient Jews.

Stotts conveys a fundamentally romantic view of what archaeology can say about the Bible. At the conclusion of the film, he comments:

> The Bible has been carefully transmitted through time, technology, and culture, from rare manuscripts to near universal accessibility. The Bible is continually being researched and more fully understood through new discoveries. Many people think that the further we progress from the ancient world of the Bible, the more disconnected we become from this old book. But actually, today's science is helping us better understand how carefully the Bible has been transmitted through time. The latest technologies . . . are now providing an even greater understanding of the history of the Bible.

Jewish scribes and Christian emperors, we are told, preserved the Bible and carefully transmitted it through time. Now science and archaeology have come along to authenticate this careful transmission. The MOTB *Drive Thru History* video transforms archaeology and an abstract notion of science into a protective strategy for the Bible's reliability.[46]

The invocation of the DSS as evidence that anchors and stabilizes the text of the Bible is not accidental. The DSS loom large in the imagination of evangelicals like the Greens because they have protected their bible from the onslaught of critical biblical scholarship that has emphasized the textual instability of biblical texts and bibles over time.[47] Dead Sea

Scrolls researcher Ludvik Kjeldsberg has recently shown how fragments of the DSS function as Protestant relics.[48] Invocations of the DSS or exhibitions of the fragments themselves are often attended by displays of devotion for the work that they do in anchoring the white evangelical bible's claims to textual stability.

It is arguably for this reason that the Green family and the MOTB purchased sixteen fragments of the DSS and originally displayed them in a special exhibit on the History floor.[49] Signage at the exhibit at the time of our most recent visit included an interpretive comment about the significance of the DSS that is just flat out not correct: "many discoveries show that the text of today's Hebrew Bible has remained consistent since at least the early 1st century BC." What's obscured here is the fact of textual plurality, that is that the same literary work existed in multiple versions simultaneously.[50] The exhibit resonates with the same arguments in Stotts's film. The subsequent publication of evidence that at least five of the sixteen MOTB fragments were modern forgeries caused the museum to remove the fragments from display[51] and eventually remodel the exhibit.[52] Well before that, as questions about the authenticity of the fragments swirled among academic biblical scholars, the museum added tags to the displayed fragments asking "Are these fragments real? Research continues."

The question of what is real and what is not hangs over the History floor in ways that might not be apparent to visitors who are accustomed to visiting museums where what they see are authentic historical objects. In fact, one of the most striking features of the History floor if one examines it very carefully is its use of reproductions of ancient artifacts. In some exhibits, particularly those treating earlier time periods, the bulk of the exhibits on display feature reproductions. For example, in an exhibit treating early Christian papyri, only two of the nine manuscripts on display are ancient. The rest are modern facsimiles.[53] Since the Green Collection is rumored to boast over 40,000 biblical manuscripts and artifacts, it is curious that so few of those objects are on display. News reports have indicated that many objects in the collection have been either seized or are slated for repatriation due to inappropriate acquisition on the part of Hobby

Lobby, the Greens, and their various agents.[54] But the question persists: Why the heavy reliance on reproductions? Jana Mathews argues that such reliance should be viewed as strategic on the part of the MOTB, in that it

> facilitates the converting of archaeological objects into religious relics. As representatives of the former, material artifacts function as types of physical evidence upon which belief is rooted; as forms of the latter, they promote belief, but are not essential requisites of it. Through flattening out archeology's authoritative privilege to the point that it is level with or arguably below that of devotional hermeneutics, the museum obscures the difference between real and fake artifacts, and, more importantly, conditions the visitor to not care.[55]

Mathews's observations point to how the rhetorics of archaeology, authenticity, and science work together to undergird the museum's narrative of the reliability of its bible. Because the MOTB invokes archaeology as a science that supports the Bible, visitors are primed to see the objects in the museum's exhibits as confirming what they already know. For this reason, there is little need for the objects on display to be real, since they are there not to advance knowledge but to promote belief. Whether real or facsimiles, the objects that visitors see are merely markers of a science that has already done the work of proving the Bible's miraculous stability through time. They are symbols rather than sites of encounter with the foreign, the surprising, or the new. These elements work together to protect the white evangelical bible and its divine origin and divinely ordained destiny.

TEXTUAL CRITICISM. The next protective strategy has to do with a subdiscipline within biblical scholarship called textual criticism, and it is likely the least visible to non-expert visitors. In fact, to best explain it we must first describe briefly how different camps of professional biblical scholars define and approach the tasks associated with this field of inquiry. Textual criticism is a specialized subfield within biblical studies that concerns itself with the editing, collating, and analyzing of extant, often fragmentary, biblical manuscripts.[56] Textual criticism originated among Renaissance and post-Reformation polymaths, like Erasmus, who began collating biblical manuscripts. However, it became a specific sub-field of biblical studies due to the expansion of European colonialism. Biblical scholars such as Gregory Cuéllar and Yii-Jan Lin have shown us in recent years, crucially, that textual criticism was made possible by the formation of colonial logics of classification and the acquisition of texts and artifacts through colonial conquest.[57] It likely comes as no surprise, given the MOTB's celebration of colonialism generally, that the museum represents the contours of textual criticism differently, and its project more optimistically. For most of its history, text criticism has focused on finding the original words of biblical texts. This quest for the original has made text criticism an important intellectual site for the production of white evangelical bibles. There are, for example, explicitly "evangelical" textual critics, several of whom have been employees of or contributors to the MOTB.[58] Another stream within textual criticism eschews the quest for the original text and focuses instead on a search for the earliest attainable form of each biblical text. This is done by dating, sorting, and comparing all the copies of biblical literature that survive from premodernity so as to build a composite text that can stand in for a hypothetical early version. This composite version does not represent any actually existing biblical manuscript but rather the constructive work of teams of modern scholars who decide what form the earliest attainable version of a given text might have looked like given the surviving manuscripts.

Textual criticism of the Bible has always been a contentious field within biblical studies, both because it has had a tendency to disrupt theological assumptions about a stable text and because the skills necessary to become a textual critic are hard to acquire and, thus, scholarship on text criticism is prone to obscurantism. In the field of New Testament textual criticism, scholars like Eldon Epp, David Parker, and Brent Nongbri have challenged many of the field's assumptions, rendering the quest for the original text of New Testament documents (called "autographs") obsolete, though that does not mean the quest for the original text has ever ended.[59]

Textual critics working with both sets of goals (the original versus the oldest attainable) regularly collaborate in their work and present at many of the same academic venues. Some of the results of this work are regularly published as critical editions of the Greek New Testament, which is formally called the Nestle-Aland Novum Testamentum Graece, and of the Hebrew Bible, called the Biblia Hebraica Stuttgartensia (BHS), though there are more critical editions than just these two produced by textual critics. We note the Nestle-Aland and the BHS because these are the editions from which modern translators and biblical scholars often work, meaning that the biblical translations produced in modernity are based not on some singular biblical text but on a hypothetical composite text produced by modern text critics. In either case, the end goal is to use real artifacts to reconstruct a hypothetical text useful for translation. The search is conditioned by a desire for what came prior to the object in one's hands. A different approach to manuscripts would be to study them not as witnesses to a prior text unseen but as material objects that in themselves deserve analysis not for how they can get us to an imagined past but for how they help us understand their particularized presents, that is, the conditions of their production. Each could be placed in time and space as valuable evidence of the people who produced it, who cared for it, and for whom it came to be significant.

If the MOTB had followed the last of these trends, its exhibits would have been built around the actual artifacts they had available to display, and thus had fewer replicas and rather less of a long narrative arc. Instead, the MOTB reproduces the instinct in biblical textual criticism that longs for an earlier text. Further, the sort of textual criticism that is most prominent in the MOTB is one that conceals rather than celebrates the plural nature of biblical literature's transmission.[60] Plurality is not a good fit for the narrative of the History floor at the MOTB since it is a discipline that acknowledges that multiple versions of biblical texts have circulated from antiquity until the not too distant past would imperil the case that the Bible has been miraculously transmitted from the past to the present.

The MOTB exhibits text-critical editions of the Bible at the very end of the story, as examples of how Bibles are translated. The signage that accompanies this exhibit ("In search of the earliest text") reads:

> Discoveries of ancient codices – such as Codex Sinaiticus in the mid-1800s – gave new focus to studying the text of the Septuagint and the New Testament.

> Scholars compared ancient Greek manuscripts to determine which words were the oldest, a process called "textual criticism." Many Greek editions resulted from their work. The standard Greek edition from which most New Testament translations are now made is the Nestle-Aland *Novum Testamentum Graece*. The original text of the Greek Old Testament (the Septuagint) is being published by a research project in Goettingen, Germany based on the known surviving manuscripts.

The description here of textual criticism neutralizes any threat the evolving discipline might present to the MOTB's narrative while affirming its fundamental premise that we should all be on the hunt for earlier texts. Here we learn that scholars determined the oldest words in ancient manuscripts and that the "original text" of the Septuagint is being published. The Nestle-Aland itself is presented as a basis for translation. The signage describes this scholarly work in terms that cohere with the white evangelical bible the History floor has constructed: the text has been stable over time and so the bible in our hands is reliable.

Evidence suggests that inspiring confidence in the white evangelical Bible was a key strategy of the marketing of the MOTB to Christian audiences.[61] Further, behind the scenes, white evangelical institutions like the MOTB, particularly through its Green Scholars Initiative, have quietly poured millions of dollars into training, supporting, and equipping evangelical text critics.[62] These evangelical actors are then able to publish academic work that engages in the same protective strategies surrounding access to a divine message through surviving textual witnesses to biblical texts.

The entanglements run deep but bubble to the surface frequently. To take one example: in December 2018, MOTB scholarly consultant Peter J. Williams, who is also warden of Tyndale House, in Cambridge, gave a public presentation in the museum's "Bible Research Lab" on the MOTB's History floor. After showing guests leaves from a MOTB artifact he has been engaged to research (the Codex Climaci Rescriptus), he summarized in his assuring British accent his most recent apologetic tract entitled *Can We Trust the Gospels?*[63] (His answer is yes.)[64] Williams is an active member and founding figure of the online collective Evangelical Textual Criticism (ETC). Formed in 2005, ETC is defined on its website as "a forum for people with knowledge of the Bible in its original languages to discuss its manuscripts and textual history from the perspective of historic evangelical theology." Most contributors are white presenting, and most are male presenting. Many of them, like Williams, have consulted for or have held an official position with the MOTB, including Michael W. Holmes, erstwhile executive director of the MOTB Scholars Initiative. Practitioners of ETC rely on premises that they do not defend, in part because faith is sufficient to make the premises so. In a post entitled "What this blog is about" (October 14, 2005), Williams writes: "[this forum] is not going to be embarrassed about believing that the Bible is true and that the Bible is made up of particular words which come from God." Two years later while considering the question "What's Special about Evangelical Textual Criticism?" (January 1, 2007), Williams offered this vision of their task: "An evangelical textual critic approaches the text with a sense of religious reverence. He understands his task as a basic exegetical step, establishing and confirming words which God, through human agents, provided for the guidance of the church." These assumptions shape the kind of text that can be reconstructed by the textual critic and the aims of such a project. But here lies an important contrast with the MOTB's own self-presentation: while Williams and other ETC practitioners articulate the epistemological constraints and theological commitments guiding their work, the MOTB History works to present them as natural.

For the logic of the museum's History to work, it cannot be otherwise. Potential sites of conflict for the reliability of the Bible, conceived ultimately as a divine message, must be smoothed over to pave the way for visitors to buy into what illumiNations is doing as necessary, unproblematic work. The museum's History shields visitors from textual diversity and plurality, from thorny questions about translation and colonial encounters, and from alternative ways of imagining how to handle manuscripts because it has to. To return to the MOTB's "universal access" language: If the museum's bible is to be made available to all as a fundamental resource, what is distributed must be accurate and the act of distribution must be good. One would not, for example, be satisfied giving contaminated water to people in a drought. In order for the water to be beneficial, it must be pure water. On this analogy, "the Bible" must be reliable. "The Bible" that is being constructed, and ultimately protected, on this floor is a message from God to humanity that could only be disseminated effectively and accurately via the medium of an evolving set of textual technologies. But to be successful this project also needs evangelical action, which, as Mart Green presciently observed in the interview we discussed above, the MOTB's History floor is primed to inspire.

CONCLUSION: WORD DOMINATION

The Museum of the Bible's History of the Bible floor is a productive past, one that is ultimately aspirational. It narrates a myth of origins for a reliable bible that white evangelicals can feel good about distributing to every race, place, and nation on earth. Returning to Mart Green's fascinating interview helps us see that a friendly white evangelical audience is buying it – literally. He is reported to have told the following story about the illumiNations exhibit:

> Earlier I mentioned the yellow Bibles. A guy goes to the museum (of the Bible) and his wife is getting ready to turn 60. He says, "Oh, I know what I want to get my wife for her 60th birthday!" I want to give you a million dollars for my wife's 60th birthday.
>
> So we gave him the yellow Bible – because it was turned to orange once it got started, right? And for his wife's birthday, she unwrapped a blank Bible with a people group's name on it. And he says, "Perfect. I know what my wife will do. She'll put it right by her bedside and start journaling in it and praying for that people group."

This anecdote captures a constellation of entitlement, missionary paternalism, othering, and devotional consumption. We can't help but notice a contradiction here too: the Bible resists stabilizing. The Bible here presents an opportunity for the wife to pair her own personal thoughts and experiences, through journaling, with her deepest desires for other people, through praying. This bible is now one that an American evangelical Christian will write.

Despite the MOTB History floor's obsession with the textualization of a divine message to humans via the Bible, the MOTB's bible transcends the textual. In the next chapter, we turn to the transmedial nature of the museum's white evangelical bible as we continue to articulate how this bible works.

114

CHAPTER 4

Jesus, Israel, and a Christian America

FEW VISITORS WOULD START THEIR TOUR OF THE MUSEUM of the Bible on the sixth-floor south-facing open-air roof deck. Its view cannot match the north side's impressive vista of DC, including the US Capitol. Further, it's exposed to the elements. Any comfort it might provide is subject to the vagaries of the weather. Cafeteria tables and outdoor couches provide overflow seating for Manna, the MOTB's Mediterranean-themed restaurant next door. The deck's northern facade is lined with water walls whose drips along glass panes pool at the bottom into a narrow pond. A small, delicate tree sits just in front of the pond. Banks of ornamental grasses and wildflowers line the western and southern ends. There is very little signage in the space, making it seem merely a decorative place to take one's lunch or get some fresh air. While this rooftop patio is likely where a tourist's day ends, or where they take a short break, it is a good place for us to start as we articulate an essential characteristic of the museum's bible: the MOTB's bible is transmedial.[1] We move from words on a page to experiences designed to engage all the senses.

Museum designers report having had grand visions for how the rooftop outdoor space opposite the Capitol viewing deck would function. It is actually a "biblical garden."[2] Promotional material invites visitors to "stroll through this rooftop garden to enjoy the natural environment and plant varieties mentioned throughout the Bible."[3] The banks of grasses and wildflowers point, according to landscape designer Doug

Hays, to the settings of Jesus's outdoor preaching.[4] Because of DC's climate, however, the designers had to get creative with the plants they chose, drawing from species native to nonbiblical contexts. The MOTB's biblical garden doesn't exude the typical sights and smells of the Mediterranean. There are no intricately knotted olive trees, no rosemary and coriander, no figs or palms.

The MOTB's garden was designed instead to evoke biblical imagery.[5] The tree near the water wall stands for the Tree of Life in the Garden of Eden (Genesis 3:22) and heavenly New Jerusalem (Revelation 22:2). The designers report choosing a weeping willow, not knowing or perhaps not caring that willows, unlike the mythical Tree of Life, do not produce fruit.[6] For Hays, gardens bookend the story of the Bible from Genesis to Revelation, making them places to inspire "desire to draw near to God" and sites for "the soul's yearning to be restored." The MOTB garden's biblicism is less in letting the visitor "smell what Jesus smelled" than in carefully cultivating a space for contemplation and prayer (alongside cafeteria food). Yet the MOTB garden is a reminder that this museum participates in a broader practice of performing the Bible via material spaces, what anthropologist James Bielo calls "materializing the Bible."[7] In ways far more sophisticated than the biblically themed roof garden, the major exhibits at the MOTB engage visitors through interactive features, haptic feedback, virtual and material simulations, sounds and sights, and cinematic storytelling. The museum gives flesh, lights, and sounds to the white evangelical bible. At the same time, the bodily inscription of visitors works to make trust in and devotion to this bible *feel* natural. The MOTB's major interactive and experiential exhibits transport the bodies of visitors into cinematic, simulated, and reconstructed environments that make the white evangelical bible feel real, tangible, and true.[8]

In previous chapters we focused on what the MOTB teaches through its exhibits, tracing the ideologies and assumptions embedded within the museum's pedagogy. But the museum also offers its visitors the opportunity to experience its bible in three dimensions. In order to understand how a white evangelical bible is produced at the MOTB, we have to resist the tyranny of the textual. Because we are so habituated to thinking of the Bible as a text, this may be a strange argument to some. But the reality is that scriptures are often heard and seen as much as they are read.[9] The transmedial bible constructed at the MOTB is not just ideological or theological, but felt and experienced by and through the bodies of visitors. The museum's bible is produced in part by performance.[10] In this chapter, we follow the sacred drama that enfolds museum visitors and then explore the stage on which that drama is set. While the plot revolves around the central character of Jesus, the setting is a pair of biblicized landscapes, Israel as "holy land" and America as "promised land." Both turn visitors into pilgrims. We will see that the immersive white evangelical bible produced by the MOTB is as political as it is pedagogical, as demanding of devotion as of curiosity.

WAITING FOR JESUS AT THE MUSEUM OF THE BIBLE

The most immersive series of the MOTB's permanent floors is on the Stories of the Bible floor, with its award-winning "Hebrew Bible" walk-through exhibit, its recreation of an ancient Galilean village, and its Hollywood-style "New Testament" movie theater complete with velvet curtains and biblical characters pitched as movie stars. Since the invention of the medium of film, the story of Jesus has appeared on it. Jesus films have told, like the canonical gospels themselves, different stories of Jesus, depending on the proclivities and choices of the writers, directors, and studios involved. In each case, the transition to celluloid is both a translation and a transformation, a new biblical story wrought with the captivating magic of film. Even when filmmakers attempt to "stick to the text" of the Bible, movement between two distinct forms of media (from print to film) requires a transformation not just of the story but also of the Bible itself. Each Bible movie is, itself, a new bible. The MOTB's immersive biblical exhibits also create a bible for its visitors, one in which they not only watch stories unfold on the silver screen but also wander and explore, touch and feel. These immersive experiences are pedagogical both in the content they present and in the ways that they conscript visitors' bodies into affective relationships with the subject matter. Visitors are meant to leave both having learned *and felt* something.

We can see this at work in the three immersive exhibits on the Stories of the Bible floor. Choices have to be made when taking a bible from text to screen, from text to recreated physical space. These choices – what to include, what to exclude, and how to represent what is included – are what shape the bible on the MOTB Stories floor. One of the most important choices that the designers on this floor made was to keep Jesus largely out of view. The MOTB, we argue below, capitalizes on Jesus's strategic absence. While some evangelical visitors have expressed chagrin at what appears to be a sore, perhaps even ironic, lack of Jesus in a Bible museum,[11] we suggest that interrogating Jesus's absence allows us, paradoxically, to see the contours of the bible presented to visitors on the floor. Often what is unsaid is as important as what is said. So too here. As Michel Foucault once wrote, silence is "an element that functions alongside the things said, with them and in relation to them within over-all strategies."[12] That which is unseen is still present in subtle and interesting ways. Jesus's absence allows for a narrative cohesion that is not readily apparent across the three exhibits on the floor.

These three exhibits comprise the sum total of installations on the floor and their spatial arrangement makes them easy to move between. Though each exhibit was produced by a different design team, they are presented on the floor as part of an interlinked whole that offers an accounting of the "narrative" of the Bible. We seek to articulate the questions the exhibits ask, answer, and leave unanswered. Where is Jesus? And where is he not? Our story unfolds in three parts: "Jesus Anticipated," "Jesus Deferred," and "Jesus Obscured." The absence of Jesus, paradoxically, shows his ubiquity in the museum, with consequences for how the MOTB produces its bible and how that constructed bible feels to visitors who, literally, walk within it.

JESUS ANTICIPATED. The Stories floor opens with a walking tour through a story of the Hebrew Bible, a thirty-minute ambulatory experience in which visitors are said to "encounter significant narratives from the Hebrew Bible, including the stories of Noah's ark, the burning bush, and the Passover!"[13] Significant for whom? A close reading of the Hebrew Bible exhibit demonstrates that the narrative of the Tanakh/Old Testament that visitors encounter is permeated with Christian theological presuppositions which are not native to the Hebrew Bible stories themselves.[14] From beginning to end, the metanarrative woven in this exhibit poses two questions: How will humanity's broken relationship to God be restored? And how will the chosen people find home? The exhibit closes having resolved the perceived need for Jews to return home while leaving unresolved the question of universal humanity's disrupted relationship to God. In this museum, this latter problem cannot be resolved by the Hebrew Bible/Old Testament alone.

Entering the exhibit, visitors watch creation unfold visually on a large LED screen. Light bursts onto the scene and then a narrator glosses the story for us. In the MOTB's Genesis, a double dilemma is understood to be introduced by the first humans' disruption of unity with God, a result of their misuse of the "gift of choice." Humankind is (1) separated from God and (2) separated from "home." We hear: "Humankind's once perfect unity with God, creation, and each other is broken. Their eyes are opened and they begin to understand: every choice has consequences. This is where our journey begins, the journey to rebuild their relationship with God and to find home again." At its beginning, this exhibit presents the Hebrew Bible's story as a universal story of all humanity. Adam and Eve's disobedience has consequences beyond those specific curses delimited in Genesis 3. Not only is "every choice" invoked as having "consequences," but all future humans are envisioned subsequently as being presented with a binary choice: "Throughout the journey every generation – every person – can choose to mend the relationship that was broken or perpetuate the divide between human-kind and God." The goal is to cross the divide. The language of home, which is the frame at work here more familiar to Jewish interpreters of this story, is temporarily dropped.[15]

Next a loud storm soundtrack welcomes visitors aboard Noah's Ark as they are invited into the next room. A dark winding hallway reminiscent of a cave whose walls are adorned with figural animals in illuminated yellow boxes gives way to a room of almost glaring bright light. The rainbow. Renewal. The world has been, according to the narrator, "washed."[16] But all is not well. The problem remains, the narrator tells us, this time framing the universal dilemma as "the gap between God and humankind." A wall depicting the generations of Noah to Abraham gets us quickly to another room in which the stories of Abraham through the Israelites' enslavement in Egypt will be glossed under the glitter of an artificial night sky filled with stars. The wall does not merely advance the story, however; it uses the term "genealogy," for the first time employing language we might associate with genetics, family, or ethnicity. For the first time, a category with particularity – one that intimates that this story might belong to a particular group of people – enters the storytelling.

Humanity's dilemma so conceived takes a new form – idolatry, not named as such – but then begins to be solved, we learn, in Abraham's tale: "rather than abandoning humanity, God reaches across the divide to an unlikely man, Abraham ... and his wife, Sarah." God makes the first move. He offers Abraham a covenant, "an unbreakable promise." Genesis 15:6 (though not explicitly cited) takes center stage here: Abraham's faithfulness, his "trust" in God, is emphasized. The narrator summarizes God's part of this covenant in terms of promise: "God promises a land and descendants as numerous as the stars in the sky and that through him all families will be blessed." The words "all families" are said in a tone of awe, signaling this as the pinnacle of the promise.

In truth, the narrator sounds like the apostle Paul. Our guide conflates different versions of God's covenantal promise with Abra(ha)m, notably Genesis 12:1–3, 15:5–6, and 22:17–18, giving a reading of the covenant consistent with that offered by Paul in his letters to the Galatians and Romans. Paul's reading of the Abrahamic covenant sees Abraham's righteousness in Genesis 15:6 as the mechanism by which gentiles become Abraham's descendants, heirs according to the promise (Galatians 3:6–9, 29). Paul reads God's promise to Abraham as a blessing that is available to anyone who believes. This is because the true offspring of Abraham is Christ (Galatians 3:16, 29), from whom all the nations inherit covenantal access to God through faith. This is how, for Christian readers, "all families" are blessed through the covenant.

Occluded in the Hebrew Bible exhibit are other aspects of the covenant that emerge in Genesis: the offer of land that belonged to other tribes (15:18–21); the particularity of the covenant's application to either Abra(ha)m's literal descendants (12:2; 15:5) or an undefined number of nations (17:1–8; 22:17–18); the alternative covenant with Ishmael (21:12–13); or the covenant's relationship to the keeping of God's law (either in the form of circumcision [17:9–14] or more generally [26:1–5]).[17] The narration does not allow for the possibility of seeing the covenant as solely tied to land, family, Jews, or the practice of the law, aspects of the covenant that are central to how Jewish readers have usually read Genesis. A similar universalizing move happens next in the quick transition from Abraham to Isaac to Jacob/Israel: "The family tree now has its name," the narrator celebrates. An assurance of worldwide reach, framed once more with emphasis on promise, quickly follows: "God promises to bless the world through his descendants." God's reaching across the gap is offered as comprehensive, limited not to a single family. The stars continue to sparkle.

Before we can get to Moses's story, the room goes dark. The Israelites have been enslaved. "Promise" language returns as the narrator reflects on the implications of the Israelites' enslavement for the larger story being spun: "The light of God's promise seems to have gone out." The next few moments cultivate anticipation in almost eerie silence as visitors sit in the darkness, waiting. Then, finally, a baby cries. The sound signals hope, redemption anticipated. Moses's (unnamed) mother is said to make a *choice* (to put Moses in the river), one that is celebrated as having salvific ripples for the entire people: "one mother, desperate to save her son, makes a choice that becomes the salvation of Israel." Such language recalls the opening scene of the exhibit in which the first humans are said to realize that all choices have consequences, thus discursively enveloping Moses's mother's action within this larger narrative of human choice and the relationship between God and humanity, even as the choice is marked as related to the fate of the Israelites.

Our way to the next room is lit as a bush appears and then appears to burn. Bright flashes of red and yellow accompany a booming polyvocal (male and female) voice. God beckons Moses to rescue God's people from Egypt: "Moses, I am the God of your ancestors, the God of Abraham, Isaac, and Jacob. I am sending you to rescue my people from Egypt." When God speaks next, the idea of a particular family is invoked. The Hebrews are claimed as God's "people." God will use Moses, we are told, to "challenge the gods of Egypt and bring the people home again." The theme of return to home resurfaces, having been introduced in the beginning as one of the two central dilemmas created by the first humans' choice but thus far having been eclipsed by the other – the disrepair in the relationship of God to humanity. The alternation between the particular and the universal produces tension around whom this story is ultimately for.

Next we are told to move – "quickly." It's the Exodus. The next room, entered through a doorway marked with illuminated red paint to mimic blood, plays an identity trick. Everyone who passes through the door is adopted into Israel. Indeed, the narrator invites us inside with English, "Step inside," glossed with the only modern Hebrew to appear in the exhibit: "b'vakasha." We hear the story of Moses's plea to Pharaoh, ten plagues, and Pharaoh's final relent. The music crescendos and the dramatic words "Let the Exodus begin!" are voiced as a new door opens up. Visitors reenact the escape through the parted waters of the Red Sea, represented by a large tunnel of vertical blue lights. Everyone is part of the story. "Quickly now. Keep moving forward. There is no time to waste." But narration disappears as visitors exit the Red Sea and then wind through a small room meant to signify Sinai. Only those who linger to write down the verse references (Exodus 19:4–6; 25:16; 24:12) on the wall placards – or have the books of Exodus and Deuteronomy memorized – are likely to realize that this room represents God's giving of the law to Israel. Moses, who in this exhibit is principally baby savior and exodus leader – not lawgiver – gives way to Joshua as participants amble over the Jordan River, complete with twelve gigantic stones bearing the names of the twelve tribes of Israel. In good Pauline fashion, the Abrahamic covenant – with its implications for universal humanity – is centered. By contrast, the Deuteronomic covenant – with its particularity to the relationship between God and Israel, which Christianity would come to reject – is passed over more quickly than the Israelites' blood-marked doors.

Visitors next walk through a dark, menacing hallway meant to represent the period of Israel's judges. Wall placards with a miniature Deborah, Gideon, and Samson mark the journey. Then comes a comparatively light-filled room dedicated to the story of Ruth. It is placed chronologically in the exhibit where the book of Ruth appears in the Christian, not the Jewish, canon.[18] We watch Ruth's story play out on stylized screens on the wall, which look a bit like stones strewn about. The narrator here imbues Ruth with a level of significance not accorded her by the writers of the Hebrew Bible: "In the days when the judges ruled, there was no king in Israel. The tribes struggled to work together to embrace Torah. ... But the quiet devotion of a foreign woman named Ruth shines like a beacon of hope." Drawing on the postbiblical trope of Ruth as a model convert, the exhibit highlights her foreignness as it relates her fidelity to family.[19] Ruth's *choice* to remain with her Israelite mother-in-law Naomi, go with her to Naomi's homeland, and cling to (Naomi's) God is celebrated as "a profound decision that will ripple through time."

A "beacon of hope" rippling through time. This exhibit has extremely high expectations for Ruth the Moabite and her enduring impact. Note that her "quiet devotion" is pitched as a positive step in contrast to the tribes' inability to keep the law. She is ultimately said to personify "the heart of God's Torah." This claim invites particular interrogation as a principal moment in which this exhibit constructs Jewish law. Framing Ruth's story as one that revolves around Torah is at first blush an odd choice – both in terms of the exhibit itself and in terms of what is actually in the biblical book. Up to this point in the Hebrew Bible experience, the word "Torah" has not been mentioned. Further, Torah is conspicuously absent from the book of Ruth.[20] What makes sense of this framing, though, is the implicit logic animating the presentation of material: the movement from the particular to the universal in the context of the exhibit's inaugural theological problem of the damaged relationship of God and humanity.[21] "Torah" here is equated with finding "refuge" in God, clinging to one's mother-in-law, and laboring to provide for a family member. This construction evacuates Torah of precisely the specific elements of Jewish legal code that Christians, fatefully following Paul, historically rejected as externally oriented and ultimately unnecessary. This is an understanding of Jewish law that is user-friendly for Christian supersessionism.

And, in fact, the meaning that the museum ultimately finds in Ruth's story is likewise ripe for Christian claims to Jewish tradition. As the narrator reports the marriage of Ruth to Boaz and their having a "family of their own," he concludes Ruth's story with a summative gloss uttered in a self-satisfied tone: "Abraham's family tree grows a new branch. And Ruth the Moabite becomes part of the promise." Incorporating Ruth into the "promise" makes sense within the logic of the present exhibit, given its emphasis on God's covenantal promises to

Abraham. The meaning of the phrase "new branch" is less immediately apparent. Why do we have here a new branch of Abraham's family tree? Strictly speaking, wouldn't any child born to an Israelite be a "new branch"? Why is this one marked and celebrated as something different? As we will see repeatedly on the Stories floor, what is left unsaid is key. This branch imagery, the sense of awe at some new thing happening, and the prominent place given to Ruth in the overall narrative are best explained by considering how Isaiah 11:1 figures in later Christian trad- ition as a prediction of Jesus as the prophesied branch from the stump of Jesse (see Ruth 4:17, in which Jesse is named as Ruth's grandson): "A shoot shall come out from the stump of Jesse, and a branch shall grow out of his roots" (Isaiah 11:1; cf. Matthew 1:5–6, in which Ruth, Boaz, and Jesse feature prominently in Jesus's genealogy).[22] In the MOTB, Ruth's story becomes a beacon of Jesus.

We then move into a new theater room with a screen enveloping the audience on three sides. The visuals are dramatic. The final four minutes of the story are framed with a reflection on ancient Israel's fights and failures: "It's been a long journey since God made the covenant with Abraham. God delivered the Torah through Moses, instructions to live as God's people. The tribes struggled to embrace it." Visitors then watch a swift journey through the transition from judges to monarchy, the Assyrian destruction of Israel, and the Babylonian destruction of Jerusalem, culminating in exile. The narrator laments: "Jerusalem, David's city, burned to the ground. Solomon's temple destroyed. The Israelites forced into exile. It seemed like the end." Then the music shifts toward the hopeful as the narrator tells of the Persian defeat of Babylonia and the prophets' promises of Israel's restoration. "And soon the exile was over," we hear. As Ezra is revealed to be our narrator, we imaginatively find ourselves among those who returned to the land to rebuild home: "Many Jews returned to rebuild the land and the temple. Families gathered and asked me, Ezra the scribe, to read from the Torah, to tell them again the covenant promise and the journey home."[23]

The front wall retracts slowly, revealing an encased Torah scroll that we walk past as we exit. And so visitors leave the Hebrew Bible experience with one of its two inaugural problems solved: the Jewish people have come home again. But universal humanity's rift with God remains. What of the promise to Abraham that God would bless all families? The story that the exhibit has sought to tell is only partially finished. There is more. And the stage has been set for a solution, anticipated by the "new branch" gloss in the museum's story of Ruth and the Pauline focus on the Abrahamic covenant. Even before we leave, we are primed to be waiting for Jesus.

Visitors leaving the Hebrew Bible journey and surveying their two choices of doors that remain on the Stories floor – Door 1 is "The World of Jesus of Nazareth," Door 2, predictably, "The New Testament" – might think that the wait will be short. The experience in both is more complicated, though. The waiting continues.

JESUS DEFERRED. The most natural door to pass through after exiting the Hebrew Bible experience belongs to an exhibit promising to deliver "The World of Jesus of Nazareth." Inside is a recreated Nazareth village, with stone structures, artificial trees, painted landscapes, a synagogue, a table set for eating, a construction site. Among the tourists milling about are actors playing Jewish inhabitants of ancient Nazareth – two or three at a time, in our experience. Pastoral sounds broadcast from hidden speakers in a sky that is perpetually an ethereal shade. Jesus's world feels a bit like a movie set, lacking verve. It's lying in anticipation. Or perhaps it has been deserted. The advertised purpose of including this attraction in the museum is to offer visitors an "accurate and authentic" experience of first-century Palestine.[24] Anyone looking to offer visitors an experience of what it meant to live in Palestine in the first century could consider presenting a section of Jerusalem, the cultic center of the region, or perhaps Caesarea, a bustling harbor town, or even one of the fishing villages on the shores of the Sea of Galilee. While Nazareth barely registers in the broader corpus of biblical literature, it is featured at MOTB because it is where Jesus grew up.

Yet Jesus himself is conspicuously absent. As visitors enter the attraction, a placard below an artificial olive tree sets expectations: "Jesus went through the cities and villages proclaiming the good news of the kingdom of God" (Luke 8:1). Jesus is not home. Why isn't Jesus here, we might wonder, and what does his absence do for visitors? In the MOTB village, we argue, Jesus's absence makes him paradoxically even more present. In fact, his presence through absence is everywhere if one looks

8. "The World of Jesus of Nazareth" exhibit in the Museum of the Bible. Photo: the authors.

carefully. The first doorway inside the village, located to the right of the entry, reveals a room structured around Jesus's teachings. The room contains artifacts chosen for their relevance to Jesus's parables. Ancient coins are displayed alongside a placard reading "Silver Coins. The Good Samaritan. Luke 10:25–37." A staff is glossed with "Shepherd's Staff. The Lost Sheep. Luke 15:1–7." Bread appears with "Loaves of Bread. The Friend at Midnight. Luke 11:5–13." The quick, repeated succession of object ("ancient people ate bread!"), Bible story ("hey, Jesus did stuff with bread!"), Bible reference ("this is where we can read that Jesus did stuff with bread") invites the visitor to think about the everyday objects around them as reminders of Jesus.[25] To push the point further, consider a possible alternative: One could imagine a recreated ancient village that teaches visitors how ancient bread was made, how it fit into the dietary practices of first-century Galileans, or what its cultural significance was.[26] The move to link bread to a parable in which a character asks a friend to borrow bread in the middle of the night stands out particularly for its having been shaped by a focus on Jesus.

Hebrew Bible/Old Testament verses also punctuate the exhibit. For example, a sign entitled "Light to Dispel Darkness" accompanies a selection of oil lamps and directs visitors to Psalm 18:28. The "Daily Life at Home" placard describes women's labor of keeping a home in antiquity, interestingly linking such work to Proverbs 31:27, part of a Bible chapter traditionally associated with ideal Christian womanhood in many circles of conservative evangelicalism.[27] Beyond bringing the Bible into a central interpretive frame, these signs do another kind of cumulative work: they point back to the exhibit we've just been through, the Hebrew Bible experience. Lest anyone think there has been a break in the story, these signs construct coherence for visitors, a through-line that progresses from the Hebrew Bible to Jesus's world (and, later, to the New Testament). The sign that does this most explicitly is one that reads "Hospitality." Citing the injunction to care for strangers found in Leviticus 19:33–34, the placard uses Boaz – from the book of Ruth – as its signal hero of hospitality. Visitors coming fresh from the Hebrew Bible experience will have just spent several minutes taking in the MOTB's reflection on the importance of the Ruth story and here experience its "ripple[s] through time."

Other signs label Nazareth as part of the "Promised Land" given by God, connecting visitors' present fictional setting to the promises of God evoked in the Hebrew Bible experience and to the "home" that features prominently in the Hebrew Bible exhibit's conclusion.[28] Our journey into Jesus's world, then, cannot be divorced from the story wrought by the museum's selective retelling of the Hebrew Bible/Old Testament.[29] We have here entered the home promised by God. But what of the unresolved problem of humanity's relationship with God? For its resolution, we need Jesus.

We don't find him yet, but he is on everyone's mind here in Nazareth. Following flexible scripts, the actors populating Nazareth begin by performing their specific role – rabbi, carpenter, and so on – and eventually find ways to talk about Jesus. They functionally mimic John the Baptist as portrayed in the canonical gospels as pointing to Jesus, paving the way, heightening expectation. Take, for example, the "rabbi" of the Nazareth synagogue during one of our visits, whose Torah reading for the day gave way to speculation about the local carpenter's son:[30]

So, by the way, Nazareth. Nazareth. You might know one of our sons from here who has become rather famous. His name is Yeshua. I think you say "Jesus." *Do you know this name?*

Jesus isn't here – but he haunts the place through the stories told about him. The rabbi-actor went on to describe Nazareth as the place where Jesus grew up, the buildings we see as places Jesus built with his own hands, and this very synagogue as the place where Jesus was taught Torah. The rabbi-actor expressed dismay at Jesus's apparently recent behavior at this very synagogue:

Well, we're very worried about [Jesus]. Can I share with you why we're worried? Well, you know he grew up here, yes? ... Well now he's a man of thirty years old and he has come in here on a recent Shabbat and read from the Scroll of Isaiah. Well, you know this passage: "the Spirit of the Lord God is upon me, for the Lord has ... has anointed me to preach good news to the afflicted." Then he sat down where he always used to sit and astounded us. Do you know what he said after reading that passage? He said, "Today in your hearing this scripture is fulfilled!" WHAT? It's just Jesus from our village. You see why we're worried? Well, we got angry with him ... because he was claiming to be God. So we drove him out of the village to throw him off the edge. And he got away from us. Now, we understand, he's down in Galilee preaching in synagogues like this about the kingdom of God.

So that is where Jesus is. Jesus isn't here – but he's on everyone's lips. He's now on our minds. The rabbi's voice became quieter as he adopted a tone of incredulity, of hesitant admiration:

But I tell you the things we heard. We've heard he's given sight to a man born blind. We ... We've heard that he has walked across the Sea of Galilee?! We've heard that he's fed thousands of people with scraps of fish and bread with baskets of leftovers! So now, I tell you. I leave you with this question that we're starting to ask ourselves. You know after all we've seen and heard, we're asking ourselves this: Who is this Jesus, really? You see, we thought we knew! But now we're not so sure. So this is the question, isn't it? Who is this Jesus?

"Who is this Jesus?" indeed. Everyone is thinking about the Jesus who isn't here anymore.

9. Actor portraying a rabbi in the Museum of the Bible. Photo: the authors.

This script appears to be derived from Luke 4:16–30 (and pointedly not the parallel versions in Matthew 13:54–58 and Mark 6:1–6). The folksy rabbi repeats Luke's story in which the Nazarenes attempt to throw Jesus off a cliff. He does so in such a way that the audience laughs out loud at the attempted murder of a local boy about whom people are "worried." The rabbi also follows Luke in reporting that Jesus read from Isaiah in the synagogue. Significantly, in none of the synoptic gospels is it assumed that Jesus there claims to be "God." In fact, the title that Jesus uses for himself is "prophet" (Matthew 13:57, Mark 6:4, and Luke 4:24–27). Our rabbi-actor inserts a later Christian theological claim about Jesus's deity into the mouth of a first-century rabbi.

The rabbi's speech highlights a potentially harmful consequence of how Jesus is portrayed here: Mirroring a similar problem that has plagued both professional biblical scholarship and Christian confession, Jesus's absence is here made into a statement of his difference from Jews and Jewishness.[31] The MOTB had a decision to make about whether (and how) to portray Jesus. Should they have an actor playing him? And if so, what kind of actor? How can one reconcile Jesus's Jewishness, as a nonnegotiable aspect of his humanity, with his purported divinity? Biblical scholar Adele Reinhartz has noted that this is a problem that plagues Jesus films.[32] A poignant and entertaining scene in the Coen Brothers' 2016 film *Hail Caesar!* dramatizes the problem well. We watch as a Roman Catholic priest, a Greek Orthodox priest, a Protestant minister, and a rabbi gather around a long boardroom table at a semi-fictional movie studio in mid-century Los Angeles to share their reactions to a new movie about Jesus the studio is filming. "Does the depiction of Christ Jesus cut the mustard?" protagonist Eddie Mannix wants to know. In a rapid-fire exchange, the religious leaders banter about the nature of Jesus of Nazareth. Depending on who's speaking, he is "a man," "part God," "not God," or "not not-God," as the Christians struggle to find explicable trinitarian language and the frustrated rabbi provokes them.[33] The "ancient" "rabbi" in the MOTB exhibit has a similar problem to solve. Notice the cognitive dissonance that the MOTB rabbi expresses: We (Jewish villagers) thought this Jesus was one of us, but maybe he isn't! Jesus is from this carefully curated world of Nazareth, a shaper of it even, but he does not really belong here. And his foreignness is what explains, in the logic of our ancient rabbi, his absence. Jesus is of this world but not in it.

We leave Nazareth wondering about where to find Jesus, whose absence is simultaneously a ubiquitous presence. Moving on from the village, we might think we'll find Jesus in the final exhibit on the Stories floor. But here too, it's complicated.

JESUS OBSCURED. The final stop on the Stories floor is "The New Testament Theater," described on the MOTB website as "a 210-degree panoramic screen [that] gradually reveals itself from behind a grand-draped curtain, providing a unique, dramatic environment for the story of the New Testament."[34] Here, the history of Jesus film analogues continues to prove instructive in illuminating Jesus's absence.

The MOTB's New Testament film is introduced by a narrator who informs the audience, "This twelve-minute cinematic odyssey paints an authentic portrait of these texts and the stories they tell. And now it's time to begin your journey into the New Testament." It is worth lingering on the phrase "authentic portrait." What is an authentic portrait of a text, or a body of texts? On the one hand, the phrase avoids claims to historical accuracy or objective truth. To be authentic is to be true to real life, to gesture toward the real that is only evoked by the digital images projected on the screen. Visitors are thus primed to experience a film that shows them what the New Testament really is. On the other hand, portraits are not usually commissioned for books, but rather for people. At its heart, the New Testament film is a portrait of Jesus. Significantly, though, Jesus is seen only fleetingly, just as in classic Hollywood films like *Ben Hur* and indeed in the fictional Jesus film in *Hail Caesar!* whose producers dared not portray Jesus with too much specificity. Up to this point on the Stories floor, Jesus has been anticipated and deferred. Now, when he is finally given his star turn in front of the camera, we find him obscured from view, seen only through the eyes of characters from early Christian literature.

In the MOTB's account of the New Testament, the disciple John narrates our story from the island of Patmos.[35] He begins with John 1:1, a text that describes a time period even prior to that invoked in the opening lines of Genesis: "In the beginning was the Word and the Word was with God and the Word was God." The story we are about to encounter is one that starts before the creation of the world. It extends, furthermore, all the way to the world's end as we move from the prologue of John to the New Jerusalem envisioned in Revelation 21. This universal history envelops the story that was told in the Hebrew Bible exhibit. In other words, we start the story over. The world is forged anew, no longer through the prism of tragedy but from the perspective

131

of God's redemptive work in Jesus, the preexistent Word. As John's prologue echoes through the theater, the screen projects stylized images of creation, the fruit of the tree of the knowledge of good and evil, and the serpent, all of which culminates in the veiled arrival of Jesus. We argued above that the Hebrew Bible exhibit leaves unresolved the issue of humanity's disrupted relationship with God. In the opening of the New Testament film, we find the MOTB's answer to how this problem is solved: Jesus.

And what kind of Jesus is revealed to be the answer? It is significant that the MOTB film skips Jesus's life and teaching prior to his final week. It begins instead at the Last Supper. The MOTB film's closest analogues in the history of Jesus films are the earliest ones, from the 1890s, which were in reality short passion plays, narratives that focused on Jesus's suffering and death rather than his life and ministry.[36] If, following Martin Kähler, the canonical gospels are passion narratives with extended introductions,[37] the MOTB film is a passion narrative with an extended conclusion. The MOTB movie cuts Jesus's birth, family life, and ministry from the story, much as Cecil B. DeMille's *The King of Kings* (1927) omits Jesus's birth or baptism by John, while harmonizing or assembling into new combinations other details from the gospels.[38] Even more significantly, like the Jesus films of the Production Code era, the museum's New Testament film shows Jesus only indirectly, focusing instead on how biblical characters react to Jesus.[39] In the MOTB movie, we only see the back of Jesus's head.

The story is told entirely from the perspective of observers of Jesus. Successive characters narrate their experiences of Jesus, a move that steps away from the content of the New Testament and toward a speculative psychology of its characters. The Roman centurion at the crucifixion of Jesus, for example, tells us: "The next day, I was there at Golgotha. At the moment of his death, after all we had done to him, he asked God to forgive us. Surely this man was the Son of God." The centurion's utterance that Jesus was the Son of God (Mark 15:39, Matthew 27:54) is given a psychological motivation by harmonizing Mark and Matthew with Luke, which is the only account in which Jesus says "Father, forgive them for they know not what they do" (23:34). The centurion, the lone representative of the Roman state in the film, is made to intone the

Christian theological idea that Jesus's death on the cross was an act that offered forgiveness for human sin.

In the canonical gospels, however, the centurion's utterance is not connected directly to Jesus's desire to forgive, but is rather framed as a reaction to the miraculous events that attend Jesus's death, including the darkening of the sun, the tearing of the Temple veil, an earthquake, the breaking open of tombs, and the dead coming back to life (depending on which version of the story one is reading; see Mark 15:33–39; Matthew 27:45–54; Luke 23:44–47). In the gospels, it is the terrifying miracles that accompany Jesus's death that show him to be the Son of God (or righteous, as in Luke's version), rather than his capacity to forgive. For the MOTB filmmakers, an authentic visualization of the centurion involves harmonizing, obscuring other motivations, and inserting theological conviction.

Following Jesus's death, we see resurrection appearances from the perspective of still more characters: Mary Magdalene, Thomas, and Paul (with additional excerpts of preaching about Jesus voiced by Peter, Matthew, and Stephen). Jesus is not seen directly. The focus of the camera is on these characters' reception of Jesus. This directorial choice mirrors Code-era Jesus films that shied away from placing him directly in front of the camera. Next, the MOTB's story shifts from encounters with the risen, yet off-screen, Jesus to the first preaching of the disciples and then to the conversion of Saul. Visitors watch as Jesus's disciples begin to fulfill the "great commission" of Matthew 28, in which Jesus commands his disciples to preach the Good News to the ends of the earth. Paul becomes the vessel for this, through brief images of his missionary work and eventual imprisonment. Paul's narration harmonizes a number of passages from the New Testament into a universalizing message, addressed to "rich and poor, male and female, Jew and Gentile," a play on Galatians 3:28 (slaves, present in this verse in the New Testament, have lost their place in Paul's missionary work in the film). Ultimately, the good news breaks out fully from its Judean origins and even from confinement in temporally bound human lives: "The message traveled from life to life, until it could no longer be contained."[40]

After Paul heads off to martyrdom, we return to John, who sits writing and stargazing in a candlelit cave on Patmos. He tells us that his "old teacher" came to him one last time to offer him a vision. John then quotes from Revelation 21:3–4, in which the New Jerusalem descends from heaven. In this new Jerusalem, God dwells with humanity, and suffering and death are no more.[41] The placidity with which John reflects on the New Jerusalem softens the actual tone of the New Testament book of Revelation, which is primarily a narrative of divine violence meted out against those who oppose Christ's followers as the end draws nigh. Finally, we find the answer to the question of how humanity's relationship with God will be restored. Jesus, whom the film renders as a universal savior god, will dwell with humanity again and the bond will be reforged. Jesus is the answer to the Hebrew Bible exhibit's unanswered question.

But there is more. As Paul's mission expands, we see him walk out into the world on an unfurling papyrus scroll. The outstretched scroll-road represents movement from Jerusalem out into the broader Mediterranean. By choosing a scroll as the metaphor for the spread of Christianity, the film builds on a larger argument that runs throughout the museum, namely that the story of the Bible itself is a journey towards universal access, from the particular to the universal.[42] The Hebrew Bible exhibit ends with Torah being preserved by the Israelites in their restored ancestral homeland and the stories told in the Nazareth village paint first-century Jewish life as intimately tied to biblical imagery, while the first-century Jews portrayed there are presented as confused, scripturally ignorant, and potentially violent. The New Testament film completes the narrative circuit by visualizing Christians as those who take the Bible from ancient Jews along the path to universal distribution.[43]

The film closes having answered the question left hanging over the entire Stories floor. The relationship between God and humanity will be restored in the future by Jesus, the son of God. This message has spread from the narrow confines of a particular people, confused villagers, and the old Jerusalem, to reach all of humanity through the writings of the earliest Christians. Jesus remains obscured, yes, but only because, as God, his time to dwell fully, to be seen directly, is still a way off. In a sense, we are still waiting for Jesus. The Stories of the Bible floor thereby protects Jesus's divinity – and the possibility of his resurrection and expected return.

Those who experience the exhibits on the Stories floor are immersed in a bible that they feel rather than read. They hear its soundtrack and see it in color. In Nazareth they can touch the story and even reenact it. The tactile experience of the MOTB's bible teaches through the mind and the body. Through such an experience, the visitor is offered a possibility. "What if all this were true? It could have happened. I felt what it would have been like." To walk through the Stories floor is to move through a carefully constructed series of worlds that are highly persuasive, partly because of the ways they skirt conscious thought and direct themselves to the body. The choreography gives visitors access to "the narrative" of the Bible, offering them the content necessary to understand, if they don't already, what is in the Bible itself. As with any digest, choices had to be made. Stories had to be cut. Sayings compressed. Whole scenes rewritten. The editing process for such things is always brutal. But what is produced is not the same thing as any printed bible from which it draws inspiration. The Stories floor is an imagining of biblical narrative, pared down so as to tell the stories that the MOTB thinks its visitors need to know. And what they need to know, as we have argued, is that Jesus is the answer to a perceived problem of God's relationship with humanity.

"Jesus is the answer" is perhaps not surprising as a message coming from an institution entangled with evangelical contributors. What we want to emphasize, though, is that the question itself (and its naturalization among Christians) deserves interrogation, both for its construction as canon and its attendant costs. The interpretive framework of seeing the world as fallen and in need of redemption, of a need for repairing a relationship between God and humanity through Jesus, is made scriptural through these exhibits. This move depends, we note, on a flattening of the diverse christologies preserved in the New Testament itself in addition to those belonging to Christian denominations outside of evangelicalism. Visitors to the MOTB are asked to understand – to *feel* – the Bible fundamentally as a story of Jesus's redemption of a fallen humanity, a narrative that sits at the core of this white evangelical bible.[44] Jews have their place in the story, but they are placeholders for what must come next. In this, the Stories floor is steeped in Christian traditions of supersessionism, the belief that Christianity replaces Judaism, that the Church is now the possessor of the covenant made between the God of Israel and Abraham. Jesus's centrality in this edutaining biblical narrative ultimately scripts Jews out of their role in their own story.[45] Why would we, after all, seek the living among the dead?

HOLY LAND AND PROMISED LAND: SACRED LANDSCAPES AT THE MOTB

Dramatic performances need settings, and the MOTB's bible cannot be understood without dwelling on the pair of places sacralized within and by this institution. If Jesus is made available primarily through absence at the MOTB, the landscapes of Israel and DC as sacred spaces are almost overwhelming in their conspicuous (re)production at this museum. While recreations of biblical Israel are common and Christian heritage tours of DC certainly predate the opening of the MOTB, this museum is significant for how it fuses these together. One can now visit "the Holy Land,"[46] defined as biblical Israel, by visiting the capital city of the United States. One can walk easily under one roof from the biblical garden to Jesus's hometown to a thrill ride that virtually flies visitors around DC – all without leaving the MOTB. In this section, we explore how the MOTB immerses visitors in these particular sacred landscapes. As is often the case in materialized performances of the Bible, the MOTB's immersive bible is intertwined with pilgrimage. As a site of pilgrimage, the MOTB transports visitors to sites that are "connected" to the Bible.

Pilgrims travel to holy sites for many reasons.[47] Some travel to mark devotion to a deity, others to find healing or help from a god or saint. Within the Christian tradition, not all pilgrims journey to the lands featured in the Bible. A variety of sacred landscapes are available to Christians, from the healing sanctuary at Lourdes in France to the shrine of the Virgin of Guadalupe, with countless others in between. With so many options, the choices that Christians make regarding what land-scapes and sites are sacred to them tell us something about their theology and their politics. The sites that feature in the MOTB show which places it wants visitors to see as biblical, as part of the story that is told within the pages of the Bible. By rendering certain sites and landscapes biblical, as we will see, the MOTB reveals its deep investment in Christian Zionist[48] and Christian nationalist theologies.[49]

HOLY LAND. Tucked away on the fifth floor of the MOTB is a worn stone, weighing roughly a ton. Unlike most museum exhibits, this one invites visitors to touch the rough surface of the ancient object on display.

The stone would be unremarkable but for what it was made to support: the terrace of the Second Jewish Temple in Jerusalem. On loan to the MOTB as part of an exhibit by the Israel Antiquities Authority called "The People of the Land: History and Archaeology of Ancient Israel," the stone once formed part of the Western Wall that supported Herod the Great's expansion of the temple complex.[50] As we touch this piece of the "Temple," we accept the MOTB's invitation to become pilgrims. As one evangelical news site put it, "It's an opportunity to get a glimpse of the Holy Land without visiting the Middle East."[51]

The MOTB makes an explicit connection between its exhibits and Christian pilgrimage. In fact, these experiences are marketed as substitutes for expensive travel to Israel/Palestine. On the first floor of the MOTB, viewers are offered a chance to buy a ticket to Explore! – a virtual reality tour of biblical sites in Israel. The MOTB's marketing video claims: "Years ago, a trip to see the lands of the Bible was available to only a few. Now, Museum of the Bible is bringing these breathtaking sites to EVERYONE!"[52] In addition to celebrating such democratization, the MOTB emphasizes that this pilgrimage can be had by those on a budget:

> Visit the lands of the Bible on a shoestring budget! This all-new virtual reality experience offers an exciting tour of 34 of the most famous biblical sites. This state-of-the-art attraction allows you to soar across the Sea of Galilee, climb the stairs to the Temple Mount, explore the path of the good Samaritan and visit the Church of the Holy Sepulchre during midnight services. If you've never been to these fascinating places or even if you've been 100 times, you won't want to miss this new attraction.[53]

The experience itself is something akin to tourism by drone. Visitors enter a large, unadorned room just off the main entry hall on the museum's first floor. They sit on swiveling chairs, set apart from one another, and are then handed a virtual reality headset. As the video rolls, the headset places the visitor into a series of sites in Israel/Palestine. They can swivel around 360 degrees using their chair, but the camera typically moves slowly forward, making it difficult to explore the spaces shown with the full advantage of all angles. Each site presented is approached through this slow procession of the camera before a quick cut takes viewers to another site. The virtual trip is accompanied by an orchestral score without any narration; however, the holy sites are textually marked with their name and a biblical reference, usually from the Christian New Testament. The sites are not arranged in geographic or chronological order, making it hard to delineate an obvious narrative. As Sarah Porter has argued, Explore! offers a Christianizing version of the Holy Land.[54] The bulk of the sites visited relate to New Testament events. Because the video lacks narration, the citation of biblical references without explication assumes that visitors will already know these verses. When the Western Wall is shown, for example, the image features a reference to Mark 13:1, which is Jesus's prophecy that the Temple will be destroyed. The Temple Mount is not figured for the viewer as a site sacred to Christians, Jews, and Muslims, but as a site for remembering a prophecy by Jesus. Explore! offers visitors an inexpensive alternative to pilgrimage to the Holy Land through a curated and directed experience of sacred sites in Israel/Palestine mostly connected with Christian sources.

We have already explored the immersive experience offered to visitors in "The World of Jesus of Nazareth," the recreation of a first-century Galilean village. There we focused on the stories that were told by the actors and the signage. But we can also read it as a site that promises, in the words of James Bielo, "to collapse the distance that separates the here and now from the scriptural there and then."[55] While the MOTB's leadership has framed the village as an authentic recreation in which visitors can learn about first-century life,[56] it can also be analyzed within the framework of simulated pilgrimage. This Nazareth village creates an embodied connection between the visitor and the Bible, Jesus, and the land of Israel.[57] The carefully constructed immersive experience that is being offered here is akin to what Bielo calls "simming," a now common form of heritage tourism that "excels at generating affective attachments to the past."[58] Because there is no prescribed route through the village, visitors make their own choices as they go. The voluntary nature of the experience allows visitors to imagine themselves as independent agents in this reconstructed past.[59] There is a connection, then, between imagination and religious experience. Recreations of biblical places, like Nazareth, create that space for imagining oneself in the world of the Bible and, in turn, render that world plausible. To understand the affective experience of visitors, we have to pay attention to how the landscape has been constructed for us. The village itself is a tranquil place, especially after the loud effects of the Hebrew Bible walking tour. The soundscape includes soft bird calls and flowing water. Knotty olive trees provide faux shade from the artificial lighting. Aspects of daily life (food, cooking implements, an olive press) are visible, but no work is performed. This is less a working village than a site of play. Visitors wander at their own pace and at their own direction. They can enter into conversations with the local rabbi or handle a Torah scroll in the synagogue. At the far end of the village, they can sit and take in a wall painted with a panoramic view of the Sea of Galilee.

Yet, all the while, this immersion is not *actually* open-ended but is constrained by the choices of the designers. As Porter has discussed, the designers of the exhibit based it on their experiences of visiting Israel, about which they spoke of as a kind of enlightenment:

> Again and again, team members enthuse that visiting Israel meant that they *got it*. They were transformed by a phenomenological encounter in which the entire sensorium was implicated. The "real" essence of the Land of Israel can be distilled from the natural landscape and shared with others. But note the parts of Israel that do not appear in the Museum or in team reports: people, politics, history after the first century CE.[60]

The designers envisioned an idealized Nazareth, shorn of the messy details of daily life. We are offered a sanitized and biblically inflected experience of ancient life. Visitors can walk away feeling like they have learned something without being confronted by the visceral smells of a premodern village, the shock of cultural and linguistic difference, or the violence of living under an occupying force.[61]

One way to understand the bodily effects of Nazareth's design is to distinguish between what Hillary Kaell, an expert on Christian pilgrimage, calls static and mobilized gazes. Walking through the village, choosing what to focus on or whom to talk to, touching objects and feeling artificial stones and trees, the visitor is engaging a mobilized gaze. As Kaell puts it, "The mobilized gaze is an embodied practice that creates a feeling of empathy so strong as to evoke presence – Jesus seems to travel along with us as we move along Holy Land roads."[62] Moving through

Nazareth collapses the past and the present, evokes the presence of Jesus and his world, and incites a connection through the body of the visitor. The mobilized gaze can be contrasted with the static gaze offered to those who sit and stare at the panoramic painting of the Sea of Galilee, or, as is more often the case, snap a selfie of themselves in front of it as if they were on the rim of the Grand Canyon. The static gaze of a panoramic view offers pilgrims a way of feeling connected to a landscape while avoiding the gritty particularities of life "down there." As Kaell notes of Holy Land pilgrims, "The Galilee serves a Fifth Gospel function: its physical tangibility is taken as proof that the biblical narrative (and Jesus' miracle) did literally take place here and, by extension, that God's response to the pilgrims' prayers is real."[63] American pilgrims often fear that "the land has changed so drastically since the time of Jesus that it contains no trace of his presence. This worry gestures at an essential theological conundrum: it is the Holy Land's imagined immutability that offers a tangible manifestation of biblical truths, and yet all material things and places, if one thinks theologically, are fleeting."[64] This means that it is essential for Holy Land tour guides to include panoramic vistas periodically: "The panoramic gaze miniaturizes the city [Nazareth] ... eliminating contemporary technology and noise, and disengaging its Arab inhabitants from their particular cultural and historical circumstances; all Holy Land people look picturesquely biblical from a distance."[65] The panoramic view in the Nazareth village lacks the destabilizing potential of a real cityscape. It is, after all, a painting of an idealized landscape. But this is what makes it an ideal pilgrimage site. It allows for an experience of a sacred landscape without the danger of modern disruption. It smooths out the process by which the past and the present collapse into a sacred experience.[66]

By the way in which it allows visitors to explore and reflect, to engage and experience, a curated ancient space, "The World of Jesus of Nazareth" functions like a pilgrimage site. As Porter has noted,

> In this micro-pilgrimage to a place that fractures, replicates, and dispenses the Land of Israel, the visitor's body is wooed into a false intimacy with a fictive Land of Israel that bears little resemblance to either the true Nazareth of the first century or the lived experience of the people who

have lived there since. One is tricked into thinking, "I've been there. I know that place."[67]

The intimacy that Nazareth inculcates in visitors is thus twofold. One leaves feeling connected to Jesus and his biblically inflected world while also feeling connected to an idealized form of Israel as space, place, and state.[68] All the while in Washington DC.

PROMISED LAND. Visitors are encouraged to see Washington DC as a sacred site alongside sites from Israel. Those who ride Washington Revelations, a theme-park-style ride that takes visitors on a virtual flight over DC, see monuments throughout the nation's capital inscribed with biblical verses. This renders Washington DC as a sacred "biblical" landscape in much the same way as Israel is rendered as such. One can experience the Bible and its god at the Washington monument just as at the Church of the Holy Sepulchre. This narrative teaches visitors to see the monuments and buildings in the capital through the lens of Christian nationalist heritage tourism, which views the United States as a Christian nation in need of restoration to its "biblical" roots.

The museum's website emphasizes the sensory thrills on offer in Washington Revelations: "In this 6-minute exhilarating experience, fly past iconic places like the Lincoln Memorial, through the US Capitol and over the Washington Monument as you discover biblical imagery and verses all around Washington DC!"[69] The promise of "revelations" hints at what is in store: the chance to catch glimpses of the divine in the physical landscape of the nation's capital. The ride itself is similar in genre to Explore!, offering a sequence of site visits in rapid succession. Instead of wearing virtual reality headsets, visitors stand while holding onto supports as they look at a large curved screen ahead that gives the impression of depth. As the camera flies between sites, the ride enhances the motion by adding wind and water spray effects. The content of the visuals follows a repeated formula: the camera sweeps across the landscape of DC and then zooms in on a building so that viewers can see a biblical inscription or image. In the Library of Congress, they see a statue of the apostle Paul and inscriptions of Micah 6:8 and Leviticus 19:18. At the Confederate Memorial in Arlington National Cemetery they see Isaiah 2:4. The ride culminates with a dramatic reveal of Laus Deo ("praise to god") carved on the Washington Monument. As they leave, visitors are reminded that there are many more revelations to be had in the capital: "You can search for the Bible by touring our capital city. You'll be amazed at what you find."

Washington Revelations offers visitors a condensed, virtual version of what has long been offered by Christian nationalist tour guides: a story of the sacred, Christian origins of the United States. In her recent work on white evangelical tour groups in DC, Lauren Kerby has shown that a whole industry has grown up to bring white evangelicals to tour the nation's capital.[70] In its fly-over tour of the capital, Washington Revelations offers a narrative that associates Christians with the nation's founding, inviting Christians in the audience to see themselves as "founders" of the nation, as quintessential insiders. By highlighting inscriptions on the nation's central institutions, the tour makes an implicit argument that this is a Christian nation. Kerby has documented similar rhetoric on Christian heritage tours: "One key task of Christian heritage tours is to activate ambient religious objects, making them visible to Christian tourists. ... Once activated, these objects asserted that Christianity was the founding faith of the nation and ought to play an outsize[d] role in American politics and the public square."[71] On the MOTB ride, we approach each monument as would any viewer, before the object is transformed by a shift in perspective to highlight its "biblical" character. The camera focuses in on a Christian image or a biblical citation, effectively activating the ambient Christianness of the object or site. Once this is activated, such Christianized sites become powerful affective incitements to a narrative of white Christian supremacy:

> [T]he sites and objects they came to see corroborated their claims about the central place of Christians and Christianity in the United States. The city is chock full of Christian iconography, biblical inscriptions, and statues of Christian leaders. Seeing this evidence of America's Christian heritage is tours' raison d'être, and it had the desired effect. Tourists felt a sense of ownership for the city and, by extension, the nation.[72]

While Washington Revelations does not dwell on other narratives common to Christian heritage tours, namely those that cast Christians as outsiders fighting to reclaim the nation from wicked, secular elites, the ride does present a narrative in which white Christians are the ultimate insiders, the founders of a Christian nation. The narrator's invitation to explore the city looking for more biblical citations is meant to incite further investigation of the Christian character of the capital, to empower visitors to activate other ambient Christian objects, to naturalize Christian insiderness. In so doing, Washington Revelations participates in a broader pilgrimage industry for white Christians while also offering a thrilling experience of Christian nationalism.

In sum: the MOTB transforms museum visitors into Christian pilgrims. These pilgrimage experiences are all virtual in their own ways, constructed by different design teams to offer visitors immersive, affective experiences of places outside the museum. The places that one can virtually visit are important to note: Israel and Washington DC. Biblical sites in Israel are tied together by being places "where Jesus walked." Other places associated with bibles – such as Italy, Greece, Turkey, Syria, Lebanon, Egypt – are not included. Given the MOTB's relationships with Christian Zionist groups, this focus on offering visitors an experience of spaces within the borders of the modern state of Israel and the Palestinian territories is political in nature.[73] Washington Revelations adds another spatial component. Though the objects featured on this virtual tour can be found in the neighborhood, the ride offers them something they can't get anywhere else: a thrilling air ride that activates the ambient Christian symbolism of these monuments before their very eyes in the context of a Bible museum.

CONCLUSION

There is another "biblical garden" of sorts at the MOTB, this time an oversized portrait in glass depicting the gospels' setting of Jesus's post-resurrection appearances. While Jesus is hard to find on the Stories floor, which we addressed above, the resurrected Jesus is prominently featured here in a visually arresting Tiffany stained glass window on the grand stairwell of the Impact floor. Entitled "Easter Morning," the piece dates from 1901, originally created for a church sanctuary in New Jersey. It was purchased by the MOTB in 2013. A brilliant Jesus with a bright halo and white robes stands in the Garden of Gethsemane, with Calvary's crosses in the distance adjacent to a stunning pink sunrise on the horizon.[74] Jesus's pale white face is made brighter when the light shines through, thanks to

Tiffany's innovative technique of combining single-layer and multilayered glass. This stained glass on display brings together the themes of this chapter: we have a white, divine Jesus depicted in a medium designed to incite worship (given the object's original liturgical context). He is standing in a garden in the "holy land" that is now accessible to museum visitors in DC. It is positioned to usher travelers into the "Bible in America" exhibit.

10. Louis Comfort Tiffany, "Easter Morning" (1909), stained glass window in the Museum of the Bible. Photo: the authors.

Visitors who find themselves caught up in the imaginative worlds constructed at the museum will leave the exhibits feeling connected to Jesus, a biblicized Israel, and a Christian US. By working through the bodies of visitors, these exhibits create affective bonds that short-circuit critical thought. Visitors play, feel thrills, see their senses overwhelmed or virtually bypassed. In so doing, they are enacting a white evangelical bible, its theology, and its politics, that they will carry back home with them after they leave. This is not to say that these embodied experiences will have the same effects on each visitor. Some visitors will skip the exhibits that require extra costs, particularly now that the MOTB charges an entrance fee, in contrast to the federal museums in the neighborhood. Some will take in exhibits in different orders than we have presented here, perhaps making it harder to see the connections we have described. And still others will have little frame of reference due to less experience with printed bibles or knowledge of geopolitical histories of the United States and Israel. For those with as little as a passing interest in the Bible, however, these exhibits will constrain their imaginations in ways that they might not be equipped to discern, limiting their ability to counter claims offered by white evangelicals in the public square as to what The Bible says. For white evangelicals, whose devotion to the Bible may spur them to pay extra for biblical thrills or guided tours, wait in longer lines, or visit repeatedly, the bible that is constructed for them by the museum will resonate and amplify what they already think they know about the Bible. The MOTB and its exhibits construct a bible that is consistent with the interests of its white evangelical patrons. Many museums see their missions as educational, presenting unfamiliar and sometimes challenging perspectives to help their visitors learn how to think about the complexities of human knowledge and history. They deploy immersive experiences to help their audiences discover something new, perhaps even surprising. The MOTB has a different model of pedagogy that offers white evangelicals an experience of discovering what they already know. Jesus, Israel, and a Christian America. Their Bible tells them so.

CHAPTER 5

Biblical Capital

Because of people's passion for this book, many folks are willing to believe anything, desperately wanting to prove what they believe to be true.

Steve and Jackie Green, *This Dangerous Book*, 25

Featured on the web page for new Christian heritage tour company Inspire Experiences, cofounded by Steve Green's son-in-law Michael McAfee, is a video montage filmed in part inside the Museum of the Bible.[1] A group of mostly white Christian tourists overlook the US Capitol from the museum's fifth floor and make their way through the MOTB's immersive exhibits. They are then pictured walking through the US Capitol rotunda and later smiling and chatting with one another as they saunter out of the White House. Perhaps the most intriguing image, though, is the group's filing into and filling out the recreated first-century synagogue in the museum's "The World of Jesus of Nazareth" exhibit. Usually this exhibit is visually sparse, with design elements intended to envelop visitors in an aura of antiquity. An actor-rabbi dons robes and rope sandals. Lights flicker, imitating candlelight. Walls are painted with uneven patterns, a faux patina of wear and tear, age and use. The imagery in the Inspire Experiences informational video makes for a jarring contrast. The rabbi, with his scrolls, is gone. In his place, against the background of this "ancient" synagogue, stands Steve Green in modern apparel with a white board, dry erase markers, and an earnest grin.

A mustached music leader, eyes squinted in devotion, plays guitar. Worshippers are seated in rows, two by two, in contemporary chairs, observing Green's timeline scribbled on the white board, highlights of which include Abraham with a historical date of 2000 BC and Jesus at year zero. Another promotional photo on social media depicts McAfee in the same setting with guitar in hand, apparently leading the small congregation in praise songs. The juxtaposition of old with new, Christian worship in a Jewish space, has supersessionist overtones. The spliced together images of visitors at the MOTB, at the Capitol, at the White House, and back at the MOTB constitute further evidence of the ideological connections of this museum with Christian nationalist heritage tours in DC. The focus of this chapter, however, takes as its starting point the positioning of members of the Green family as authoritative figures and evangelical influencers on account of their association with MOTB.

Since the opening of the museum in 2017, the Green family has been conspicuous in the public eye, fashioning themselves into the MOTB's "founding family" as they write books and Bible studies, deliver speeches and sermons, and otherwise produce and publicize a white evangelical bible both inside and outside of the museum.[2] As individuals and in varying team combinations, MOTB board chair Steve Green, his spouse Jackie Green, their daughter Lauren Green McAfee, and her spouse Michael McAfee have published four books with Zondervan, an evangelical Christian publishing house, and made public appearances on dozens of conservative and Christian radio and television shows and other media. Sleek marketing makes the family's products shine. One promotional photo shows Jackie behind a confident Steve with her arms lovingly draped on his shoulders as they sit among green trees. Lauren and Michael are branded as hip, with a full docket of leather jackets, coffee, and just the right amount of self-deprecating humor. In this chapter, we interrogate the stories that the MOTB's founding family tell about themselves, the museum, and their Bible – and to what effect. We demonstrate in part that the Green family, in partnership with conservative networks and the evangelical publishing industry, has produced for its members a newfound stage on which to feature and promote their views on the Bible and particularly to lobby for their white evangelical bible to have a central place in American life and lives. Our fundamental thesis relates to money, a topic about which the Greens say very little but that is, in our view, indispensable for contextualizing the MOTB.

The popular adage "money talks" is actually not true. If the Bible does not speak for itself, neither does wealth. But the latter can be exchanged to create opportunities for speech. French sociologist Pierre Bourdieu called attention to the fact that "capital" is not always economic in nature.[3] Economic capital can, and often is, exchanged through complex networks that transform money into symbolic capital. Symbolic capital takes many forms. It can, for example, authorize its possessor, as with the credentialing power of a college degree, or it can distinguish its possessor from others, as an expensive suit marks one out as higher class. Elites, in particular, concern themselves with acquiring symbolic capital because they have excess economic capital that does not, by itself, confer on them distinction.[4] Crucially for our purposes, while economic capital can be acquired merely by the amassing of wealth, symbolic capital can only be created through what Bourdieu calls "misrecognition," a kind of collective magic that allows for economic exchange to be transformed into something other than itself before the eyes of all involved.[5] For Bourdieu, the exchange of economic capital for symbolic capital must be masked. Thus the value of a work of art might be said to reside in the "genius" of its author, or the philanthropist may couch her giving in altruism, concern for the poor, or devotion to the arts.[6] We argue that the Greens' building of the MOTB is the mechanism through which they have exchanged their excess wealth for social capital. The origin stories they tell about their becoming collectors engage in a process like misrecognition. The money part is virtually erased. Instead, their rhetoric reveals that what principally qualifies them is love for their Bible. Devotion masks massive wealth. Because the central pivot of the Greens' exchange revolves around claims of Bible fidelity, we suggest that "biblical capital" is a useful way to capture in language what is produced through the Greens' exchange. We argue that the MOTB functions for the Green family as a means both of generating and of expending biblical capital – by which we mean credential themselves, build their brands, and promote their conceptions of Bible as natural and self-evident.

GENERATING BIBLICAL CAPITAL: DEVOTION AND DISCOVERY

As patrons of evangelistic causes, the Greens have a long history of transforming their wealth into biblical capital among white evangelical groups and institutions, particularly those connected to Christian evangelism.[7] They have been lauded as a family that has helped to spread the Bible and the Christian message throughout the world. As we have already noted, the MOTB's first tax filing as a nonprofit entity indicates that such was the original rationale for the museum itself: "To bring to life the living word of God, to tell its compelling story of preservation, and to inspire confidence in the absolute authority and reliability of the Bible."[8] This mission statement casts the museum (then in-progress) as an act of devotion to the Bible and its god and a defense of the Bible's stability and authority. As the chief funders of the MOTB, the Greens become conspicuous devotees. The original mission statement provides a good example of Bourdieu's concept of misrecognition: the gift that the Greens have made to their god and their community is couched in altruistic insider language, without attention to how the gift might redound to Hobby Lobby's bottom line through tax breaks for charitable giving and/or increased brand loyalty to Hobby Lobby and other Green-owned business ventures.[9] As Bourdieu notes, to name anything other than altruistic motivations would give the game away, would disrupt the process by which money is transformed into social capital.

One succinct version of the Greens' account of how their family came to collect artifacts and build a museum appears in a book by Jackie Green and daughter Lauren aimed at Christian women. In *Only One Life: How a Woman's Every Day Shapes an Eternal Legacy*, they write:

> Each manuscript or volume we encountered was a thread in the ancient, colorful tapestry that is the story of our miraculous Bible. As we followed the path we found ourselves on, we began sensing a heart and a calling to share that story. In the process, a vision for something much larger and more ambitious began to come into focus: a national museum of the Bible. ... Within two short years, we found ourselves in possession of what one magazine article described as "one of the world's largest private collections of rare biblical texts and artifacts." ... It seemed pretty clear that God was drawing us into the world of ancient artifacts,

manuscripts, and a Bible museum. . . . The only thing that really qualified
us, as a family, to oversee the creation of a world-class collection of ancient
Bible manuscripts and a center for Bible research was our common
reverence for the Book.[10]

Notice the deferral of agency here: this was a path they *found themselves* on
and a collection *they found themselves* possessing. It is not stated directly to
whom the heart, calling, vision, or ambition for the MOTB should be
attributed. The language depicts the Greens as passively drawn into this
project, attributing the doing to the divine, which is a rhetorical move
(even if also a belief sincerely held) that pushes responsibility away from
themselves and on to an agent that they ostensibly don't control: God.

This altruistic account of their philanthropy depicts the Greens as
possessors of white evangelical values: an authentic faithfulness born of
free choice, a willingness to follow God's individually directed calling,
and a zeal for the Bible and its story. Absent from view are messy details
better left to accountants and attorneys. For their community, this story
sets them up as models and masks the processes by which their wealth is
translated into a divinely inspired mission. As scholar of American religion Daniel Vaca points out, evangelicals have focused more than other
Christian groups on marketing their message and branding their theological products and at the same time "have sought to interpret and
portray their commercial objectives and activities as forms of divine
service."[11] Christians, he goes on to note, "have expressed persistent
anxiety about the money and wealth that sales can generate." Even so,
those most heavily invested in the production of evangelical consumer
products, whether that be publishers like Zondervan or retailers like the
Greens, tend to see their corporate successes as part of God's plan.[12]
Vaca's insights further help us contextualize the Greens' rapid publishing, specifically of books, in the wake of the opening of the MOTB. Books
are particularly useful in masking the circuits of capitalistic enterprise
that produced them and that incite their consumption. As Vaca writes:

Although they come into being through complex networks of individuals and
ideas, books do not especially invite reflection about what causes people to
create or consume them. Even more than other commodities, books appeal
to the ideal that consumption derives not from corporate manipulation of

consumers and markets but instead from the object's quality and its alignment with consumers' authentic interests, convictions, or needs.[13]

The Greens present themselves as devoted Bible lovers motivated by altruism in their books, the sale of which both brings revenue to an array of corporate actors and further enhances the brand upon which the Greens' empire is built. Capitalist circuits are less visible through the pages of a book. Furthermore, part of the misrecognition at the heart of evangelical publishing is that the act of reading is connected with piety itself: "marketing materials for evangelical books often have presented reading as a matter of personal piety, spiritual duty, or divine intervention in readers' lives."[14]

The most extended narration of the Greens' entrée into the world of biblical antiquities and institution building comes in a book entitled *This Dangerous Book* by Steve and Jackie Green. Published by Zondervan in 2017, coinciding with the opening of the MOTB, it offers the reader a winding series of inspirational, nonsequential snapshots and reflections. The book shifts from autobiography to apology to affective appeal, as the Greens describe and sometimes defend their motivations for pursuing the project. One would not suspect from their self-presentation in *This Dangerous Book* that the Greens are billionaires with generational wealth. Using a folksy style, they present themselves as an ordinary American family whose love for the Bible propelled them on a great adventure they could not have anticipated. They are, in their words, "just like normal people."[15] The Greens evoke a democratizing impulse that puts them on the same level as their readers. "Our story," they write, "is your story." We go on to read a tale much like an American dream story centered on a nuclear family (with mom, dad, and kids) celebrating hard work and being careful with money. They write that they "fell in love just like normal people. Got married, bought a house, and started a family just like so many people do in this country. We both worked for the family business . . . Like so many young families, we had to wrestle with raising children, making ends meet financially, dealing with debt, and budgeting."[16] The frequent repetition of their normalness can be read as an anxiety that their wealth might make them seem unable to connect with regular folks.

A similar strategy likewise animates the next generation's book: Michael McAfee and Lauren Green McAfee's *Not What You Think*, a plea to their fellow millennials not to dismiss the Bible as outdated. Michael and Lauren refer to themselves as normal as they write that "the Bible is mostly about normal people like us and their search for meaning in life."[17] The McAfees frequently emphasize their perceived normalcy without considering any privileges that might have attended their being members of the Green family. "As millennials," they write, "we are all about clarity and transparency. We (Michael and Lauren) are not gurus, elite academics, or pundits. We are simply trying to ask questions, seek answers, and spur conversation."[18] A key component of the book's rhetorical appeal is empathy, as Lauren and Michael over and over again identify themselves with their intended readers. "In many ways, we (Michael and Lauren) are typical millennials." Yet, they go on to share, "in other ways we are complete outliers." They distinguish themselves from "typical" millennials in a few important ways, but their self-situating begins with a list of tongue-in-cheek likes and dislikes. "We live for brunch," they confess, "but we never went through a Chaco phase." The more sober differences start with our authors' marital status: while more millennials than not are unmarried, the McAfees share that they are not only married but also entered marriage earlier than most, at twenty-one years old. The list closes by distinguishing their devotion to the Bible, as they describe themselves as "among the 9 percent of millennials who read the Bible daily and among the 30 percent who believe that the Bible is the inspired and inerrant Word of God."[19] It's the middle two statements, likely to be glossed over by their intended readers, that are more striking given the McAfees' institutional connections to Hobby Lobby and the Museum of the Bible's founding family. The McAfees write that they are distinct from their generational peers because they "live on [their] own, apart from any parental support" and also "have had stable, engaging employment throughout [their] marriage." Other statements appear to indicate that this stable employment that provides income for living is a result of family connections. Lauren writes, for example:

Since 2013, we have traveled the country, speaking on behalf of the Museum of the Bible. I (Lauren) was one of the first employees of the museum. My dad, Steve Green, is founder and board chairman of the museum. When the idea for the museum was being formulated, I was completing my undergraduate degree and looking for a job. I was lucky enough to have my dad hire me for my first full-time gig, and I helped out as a curator for the newly formed museum collection.[20]

Some might wonder at the decision to hire someone with such little experience and professional training to work with antiquities, but inexperience is actually an asset in the Greens' telling of the MOTB origin story. To return to *This Dangerous Book*: Steve and Jackie frequently highlight their initial inexperience around biblical artifacts. They write, for example, "as we began this journey of acquiring biblical artifacts, we were like children learning to walk. The steps were elementary. We were like first-graders learning to read."[21]

These claims to inexperience on the part of the Greens also appear in a MOTB press release from March 2020 and have since been repeated in numerous news stories about the Greens' legal missteps in acquisitions.[22] Their inexperience is presented in these stories as a defense of the MOTB, and as part of a narrative arc of redemption for the institution. Yet the claims to inexperience also serve to highlight what is perhaps the most pervasive rhetorical framing of the Green family's project: "We had no idea that there was an entire library of books waiting to be read and discovered." The Greens present themselves not as collectors but as adventurers. Not as consumers but as explorers. And most importantly: not as buyers but as discoverers. The Greens narrate their experience as an expedition full of "wonder" and "mystery" not unlike those of Indiana Jones, a character anchoring a franchise now infamous for its white imperial fantasies. In a chapter entitled "On a Plane to the Holy Grail," the Greens characterize their first attempt to buy a manuscript with a sense of amazement that deemphasizes ambition: "The trip to Turkey and Israel was eye-opening. To see firsthand so many biblical artifacts! This was a whole new world we knew nothing about but were excited to explore. Little did we know we'd embarked upon an adventure that would prove to have meaning for us as a family, for our nation, and for the world."[23] They are here explorers and adventurers, only gradually apprehending the possibilities for a grand project of national and even global scope.

The Greens further analogize themselves to two key examples of elite, educated European treasure seekers who traveled to locations considered "exotic" to seek and save (read: take) biblical manuscripts: Agnes and Margaret Smith and Constantin von Tischendorf, the latter of whom "discovered" the important biblical manuscript known as Codex Sinaiticus.[24] Modern tales of the "discovery" of ancient manuscripts have become a veritable genre worthy of its own scholarly analysis.[25] As historian Eva Mroczek argues, discovery stories do more than entertain; they can reveal the storytellers' anxieties about access to a threatened past as they simultaneously authorize the taking, or "rescuing," of ancient artifacts by Western actors. Discovery tales often follow a colonialist plotline that results, in Mroczek's words, in "'recovering' a past that rightfully belongs only to some." In the case of the Greens, *This Dangerous Book* is functionally a discovery metatale that uses devotion to the Bible as the authorizing mechanism by which they make ancient artifacts theirs for the taking, and thereby the past theirs for the interpreting. Finders, keepers; keepers, knowers.

The adventure motif that permeates *This Dangerous Book* reaches its colonialist peak when the Greens compare themselves to Christopher Columbus in a section titled "To Explore is to See." The passage is worth quoting at length:

> Historians call the time between the fifteenth century and the eighteenth century the Age of Exploration. As a country, we[26] are most familiar with a certain character from that age: Christopher Columbus. Columbus worked at the pleasure of the Spanish monarchs and took on one of the world's most popular exploration adventures. He sought the New World.
>
> The world boomed with new commerce during this time. Capitalism spread its wings as the race to build empires took hold of world powers like Spain, England, and France. This economic activity spurred growth and exploration.
>
> But what about the human spirit? We possess a natural inclination to *know*. And to know, we must go. We must experience the thrill of discovering something new.

Today, if we want to know something, we ask our digital devices a question. Christopher Columbus had to board a ship and take on the ravages of sailing the Atlantic Ocean – disease, violence, the elements. He had to make a commitment to go, and to go on, and to keep going though the end of the journey was unknown.

And what did Christopher Columbus and his crew see in their journey? Some days, no doubt they saw little. The only thing that carried them was their determination, and the anticipation of what lay ahead.

Anticipation can wield great power. It's a natural ally to exploration and adventure. It fuels our curiosity. Even when we can't see the journey's end, we carry on with hope and anticipate the reward of the adventure. That's the beauty of exploration. And that was our experience. Anticipation led us along the journey.[27]

This passage shows the ease with which the Greens slip between sanitized versions of European colonialism, libertarian paeans to capitalism, and their own quest for biblical manuscripts.[28] Their presentation of such juxtapositions with approbation suggests to us one way that the Greens have turned capital into authority. Typically interpretive authority is not granted to buyers of an object or good merely for the fact of having purchased it. "Discoverers," on the other hand, are much more likely to have ownership over interpretation of what is discovered. Further, collectors are curators if not by intention then at least by default. But they are not thereby automatically authoritative commentators. The Greens' discovery rhetoric enables them to authorize themselves as interpreters of their collection.

"Discovery" language does not merely privilege the perspective of the purported discoverer; it simultaneously eclipses any moral questions associated either with the means or consequences of "discovery" or with that very privileging itself. The "discovery" motif in *This Dangerous Book* enables the Greens to frame the conversation with their own experience as primary, which in turn allows them to focus on their motivations, which they report as good and sincere because they see devotion to the Bible as fundamentally moral and right. Their own experience has apparently told them so, as Jackie comments that "using the Bible as a guidebook for all things that come our way works every time."[29] They claim, further, that their family, their business, and their country have been "blessed by [their] efforts to follow the Bible's direction."[30] The Greens here do not consider the possibility that something good for them is not automatically good for someone else, though history suggests that benefits to wealthy white American Christians often come at the expense of others with different socioeconomic, racial, religious, or national citizenship statuses. The Greens' discovery motif, then, in combination with their self-presentation as normal people, rhetorically inoculates them from thorny questions around identity and epistemology as they universalize their own subjectivity. These intellectual commitments and rhetorical moves help them resist any criticism, for example, that their collecting is actually conquest or their discovery, truth monopoly.[31]

Significantly, whereas Christopher Columbus did not find what he set out to find but rather "discovered" something completely unexpected (and yet with dire consequences for others), the Green family report that they did not actually discover anything that did not confirm what they already knew. Indeed, the joy of discovery came from confirming their preexisting beliefs: "For us, to see these artifacts that represent the foundation of what we've always believed is inspiring."[32] And elsewhere: "The depth and breadth of the material surrounding the Bible has allowed our confidence to go deeper. There's a richness to our faith we could not have imagined as we see all the surrounding evidence."[33] What they found confirmed and enriched, rather than complicated, what they believed. We would liken the knowledge that is produced by the Greens' quest to a puzzle-box epistemology. The box shows the picture that will be formed, and the pieces just need to be located and put together properly to reveal the image already envisioned. The end result, then, is predetermined, and the evidence for that conclusion is believed to exist somewhere out there waiting to be found and assembled into that end result. In the Greens' model, knowledge is not *produced* by weighing alternative interpretations of evidence, but rather *gained* by accumulation of evidence that self-evidently leads to a conclusion already held. The decor of the MOTB's "Bible Research Lab" on the History floor leans in to such an epistemological model, with its string of words adorning the large glass doors: Analyze. Discover. Reflect. Share. Preserve. Explore.

Reveal. Uncover. Engage. Learn. These words are consistent with a view of research that sees the process of investigating biblical artifacts as uncovering something that is there to be found, something revealed, something we need merely to discover and then preserve and learn from.[34] To explore is to find corroborating evidence; to know is to apprehend one's own reality as universal.

A key example of how this epistemological model works comes in the Greens' discussion of the Dead Sea Scrolls in *This Dangerous Book*. As they characterize them, the Scrolls "remain one of the most significant discoveries in biblical archaeology and continue to add to the discussion surrounding the accuracy of what we have for the Old Testament."[35] For the Greens, the Scrolls represent a key piece of the puzzle that proves their Bible's textual stability through time. We observe that the authors here incorporate a direct quotation into one of their sentences, though it is conspicuously unanchored by a footnote or any other kind of attribution or indication of whose words are being quoted. The text reads: "most would agree that this 'select group of Essenes lived at the Qumran site from about 100–50 BC until AD 68 … and when moving to the desert, they took with them scrolls deriving from various places in Israel'." While no citation for this quoted material is offered in *This Dangerous Book*, an Internet search on our part revealed that the text is near verbatim a sentence authored by leading Scrolls scholar Emanuel Tov and published in a volume entitled *The Book of Books*.[36] This volume was apparently published to accompany a 2013 special exhibition by the same name, sponsored by the MOTB and the Green Scholars Initiative and held at the Bible Lands Museum in Jerusalem.[37] Tov's name does not appear anywhere in *This Dangerous Book*. This apparent appropriation of preexisting written material could accurately be described as plagiarism, even if it is a result of well-intentioned but sloppy editing or ghostwriting. Such is not our main point, however, as what is most important for our purposes here is to suggest that if indeed this sentence comes from Tov's work, the Greens stop short of letting Tov finish his thought. The suspected original source here goes on to say that the Qumranites also wrote new compositions and copied scrolls at Qumran (rather than merely preserving preexisting scrolls from elsewhere). If we are right about the origins of this quoted material, the Greens, who have sponsored the

project in which Tov's words appear, here behave as though Tov's intellectual property is now theirs for the taking to reappropriate to fit their
own ends. Tov's essay ends by summarizing scholarly conclusions, which
he helped pioneer and develop, around what the discovery of the DSS
did for our understanding of the textual transmission of biblical texts. He
concludes with a focus on the variety of textual readings preserved in the
scrolls, with data that more naturally leads to unseating, rather than
confirming, the received Masoretic text as exclusively authentic:

> These scrolls show that 2000 years ago the biblical scrolls, all considered
> authentic for different communities, differed much from one another.
> The texts from Qumran and other sites in the Judean Desert include the
> Masoretic Text as contained in modern Bibles in Hebrew and translation,
> Hebrew scrolls resembling the Samaritan Pentateuch and the Greek
> Septuagint translation, as well as scrolls different from all texts known
> before the discoveries near the Dead Sea. All the scrolls differed among
> each other in small and large details, and they contribute much to our
> understanding of the early Bible text.[38]

Rather than follow Tov, however, the Greens, in our judgment, have
discarded what does not fit with their preferred solution and recast the
Dead Sea Scrolls as proofs for what they already know. They move
immediately from what appear to be co-opted words of a leading Scrolls
expert into the lines of a prominent Christian apologist, Josh McDowell,
to argue that the Scrolls confirm the veracity of their Bible. "Discovery
doesn't always prove something right away," they write:

> Discoveries build upon each other. With the discovery of the Dead Sea
> Scrolls, each fragment, each scroll, provides further insight. It joins pieces
> of the biblical puzzle together. And these pieces tend to confirm what we
> believe, the integrity of the Old Testament Scriptures. As the pieces join,
> we're able to read the Bible with increasing confidence in its veracity.[39]

Seek and ye shall find what you expect to find – especially if you are able
to take and reshape a leading scholar's words to square them with those
of a Christian apologist.

This puzzle-box epistemology shows the limits that were placed upon
the Greens' adventures from the start: "Now, when we suggest that we

should all do our best to explore God and the Bible for ourselves, that doesn't mean we will come up with different answers. Arriving at right belief is like a complex math problem. You can solve it in different ways, but in the end you get the same answer."[40] The fixity of the Bible's textual stability is mirrored in the fixity of meaning that can be drawn from it. There is always just one answer, regardless of how you get there. In this sense, discovering the Bible is like solving a Rubik's Cube: you can twist and swivel those squares in thousands of different ways, but the puzzle's solution always looks the same. The Greens' generating of biblical capital enables them to define the solution.

Yet biblical capital is not worth anything without an audience. The Greens' books can be read in a complex system of evangelical exchange. The Greens present themselves as those who speak for and in defense of white evangelicals and their bible, which has the result of potentially inciting new audiences to see them as sites for further evangelical consumption. As Vaca has shown, entire evangelical industries have sprouted in the United States not just in response to demand from evangelical consumers, but as forces that "generate evangelical demand, evangelical identities, and the very idea of a coherent evangelical population."[41] Evangelical identity, for Vaca, is created and sustained through consumption. Evangelical beliefs and traditions "have been drawn together through commercial technologies and initiatives, which have enabled consumers to cultivate shared ideas, practices, and sensibilities across denominational, ecclesiastical, and geographic contexts."[42] Vaca focuses on the evangelical publishing industry, but the same could also be said for the Greens' various business ventures, from their crafting empire to the Mardel chain of Christian bookstores, started by Steve Green's elder brother Mart. While Hobby Lobby is known for its fight against Obamacare's contraception mandate and its regular publication of Christian nationalist advertisements, its stores also carry a wide assortment of products designed to allow Christian consumers to showcase their "faith" through what they buy and display in their homes. As scholar of American Christianity Kristin Kobes Du Mez has recently written of Hobby Lobby's "cultural evangelicalism," such marketing and consumption are highly gendered, mirroring the traditional gender stereotypes that, as we demonstrate further below, also animate the Greens' oeuvre.[43]

Du Mez helpfully points out that "for evangelical women, shopping at Hobby Lobby can be akin to an act of religious devotion."[44] When studying the Greens' philanthropic and cultural products, we have to keep in mind that their wealth is supported by selling evangelical products to evangelical consumers. We believe this is true also of the MOTB.

Further, as economists often are quick to note, capital *flows*. Capital has to be spent to be useful, and this is all the more so with the more ephemeral accounting of social capital. The Greens have begun to spend their biblical capital to become influencers within what Skye Jethani has called the "evangelical industrial complex."[45] Jethani's phrase plays off of Dwight Eisenhower's famous warning about the "military industrial complex," a network of defense industries, lobbyists, and politicians that collectively urged more defense spending and more hawkish policies to increase war (or its threat) and, simultaneously, profits. Jethani sees a similar collection of networked interests at play in contemporary evangelicalism's creation of a class of celebrity pastors. He points, in particular, to evangelical book publishers and conference organizers, who see profit in publishing and promoting pastors who already have large congregations, and therefore large in-house markets, for their products. It is thus not the best writers or theologians that make it to the top of the bestseller lists or conference programs, but those who already have an audience.[46]

Though the Greens are not pastors of megachurches, like the authors described by Jethani, they do have a similar position in the economy of evangelical book culture: a massive audience through their retail stores. Following the path of celebrity pastors aligned with Christian publishers, we observe that the Greens have begun to build a brand – through books, high-profile political speeches, social media presences, and heritage tours – that sells their brand of Christianity within the white evangelical marketplace. It is no accident, we suggest, that *This Dangerous Book* and the others published by Green family members are sold in Hobby Lobby stores, Mardel bookstores, and the MOTB gift shop. While all bookstores, Christian and otherwise, have lost market share in the book industry to Amazon, the Greens have the potential to offer publishers a venue for selling their products to curated audiences that are drawn to the Greens' evangelical identity as much as to their craft supplies.

EXPENDING BIBLICAL CAPITAL

We endeavor now to show that the MOTB's founding family is expending biblical capital as quickly as they generate it. Their aim, it appears, is to conscript others into their discovery: "Wouldn't it be great," they report having mused, "if a place existed that encouraged exploration and discovery? A museum, perhaps?"[47] Just as the Greens explored and found what they already knew, now others too can discover what the Greens know. "We believe there are multiple applications for Scripture," they write, "but only one interpretation."[48] We argue that the Greens' public-facing interventions envision a country, and indeed a world, in which everyone lives in a hierarchical, patriarchal order in which God reigns supreme over humans and men lead women. The evidence suggests that they envision as "biblical" a world in which white American evangelicals are privileged to tell everyone else how to live and in which capitalism, colonialism, and Christianity merge as unalloyed goods. Significantly, the Greens' claim to the MOTB, presented as an objective, neutral institution, allows the Green family to present their totalizing biblical interpretations as if they are natural, self-evident, and universally beneficial rather than constructed, perspectival, and dominionist.

One major theme of *This Dangerous Book* centers on the Greens' claim that the Bible "is a book for all, with a message for all, describing a set of principles of living for all." Steve and Jackie promote the Bible as fundamentally benevolent and universally applicable in the ways that they interpret it. Evidence suggests that their interpretations are guided, in part, by assumptions about the marriage between American capitalism and Christianity. For example, after citing a quotation attributed to Abraham Lincoln expressing appreciation for "the good old maxims of the Bible,"[49] the Greens acknowledge that not all of America's famous past leaders were equally devout Christians. Yet, they say, everyone – even non-Christians – can and should live by a "worldview" derived from the Bible. For the Greens, the Bible's perceived universal goodness transcends particularity to such a degree that they can envision a pluralistic society in which everyone, regardless of official religious affiliation, benefits from "biblical principles." As anecdotal evidence, Steve Green offers a reflection from his twenty years of business trips to China starting in the late 1980s. He describes having observed a Chinese rice farmer originally destined to a life of "planting, harvesting, planting, harvesting" whose world eventually expanded with positive economic development and personal opportunity. Green attributes this change to two factors: the United States opening up to trade with China (in 1972)[50] and the fact that China, in his words, "violated its own communistic principle and embraced a biblical principle: transferring property rights from the state to the individual."[51] The takeaway from Green's travels: "My observation? When a society employs biblical principles in establishing its rules, this is good for the society."[52] What it means to live in such a society is only hinted at with broad buzzwords, though it appears that libertarian forms of capitalism are required.

While the Greens usually use the language of "biblical worldview" to name this plan for everyone else's lives, they at times employ the troubled term "Judeo-Christian ethic," which they explain as follows: a "Judeo-Christian ethic simply means a set of life-governing principles based on principles found in Judaism and Christianity. And we find those principles in the Bible. They are principles that have proven beneficial in governance and in family life. You don't have to adhere to a certain faith to enjoy the benefits of a Judeo-Christian ethic."[53] Scholars of Judaism and the Bible are quick to point out that while "Judeo-Christian" might appear to sound inclusive, it is actually an exclusionary term that functions rhetorically to protect and prioritize Christians.[54] Further, as American religious historian K. Healan Gaston has shown, the term has not had any stable meaning since its invention in the American political imagination in the 1930s.[55] The Greens equate their "biblical worldview" with a "Judeo-Christian ethic" derived from the Bible as they commend both to all. "You can be a Hindu, a Muslim, an atheist, or," they write, "*even* a communist" (italics added) and still benefit from "the Bible's way to live."[56] Though the Greens couch their vision for society in pluralistic terms, what they are describing sounds like white Christian nationalism and supremacy: a society in which the white evangelical bible is at the center and in which various others are permitted to exist, though only on terms set by white evangelicals.

In what follows, we examine in depth two case studies of various Green family members' expending biblical capital through connections to

MOTB, the first a speech about divinely ordained government from Michael McAfee and the second the Green women's writing on the divinely ordained organization of women's lives.[57] In both examples, members of MOTB's founding family use their connection to the museum to offer their biblically ordered lives as natural examples of what it means to live biblically. As they credential themselves, they simultaneously offer normative claims based on their readings of what is biblical.

CASE STUDY #1: THE BIBLE AND GOOD GOVERNMENT

Michael McAfee is probably not the first "Michael" that most people would associate with the Bible. That honor might be reserved for, say, the archangel Michael. Yet McAfee has acquired an auspicious platform on which to market his brand: www.michael.bible. The domain name .bible, owned and operated by the American Bible Society, includes the stated mission: "The positive promotion of the Bible by allowing business, not-for-profits and individuals to positively associate their products, services, information and selves with the Bible."[58] McAfee's own mission on michael.bible is articulated with less precision:

> Michael has been a respected voice in Bible Exploration, tackled many initiatives, and is passionate about personal connections. His position at the esteemed Museum of the Bible grants him that opportunity daily. Michael has forged a relationship of modern Christianity through artifacts and urges the country to renew their spiritual quest for genuine Truth through applicability.

In his double capacity as member of the Green family and representative of the MOTB, Michael McAfee delivered a speech on chapter 13 of the apostle Paul's letter to the Romans in July 2018.[59] He spoke at the Western Conservative Summit (WCS), an annual conference hosted by the Centennial Institute at Colorado Christian University. The WCS bills itself as "the largest gathering of conservatives outside of Washington, DC ... All to advance faith, family, and freedom for our future."[60] The institute says that their mission is to foster the alliance between capitalism and evangelical Christianity and aims "[t]o impact our culture in support of traditional family values, sanctity of life, compassion for the poor, Biblical view of human nature, limited government, personal freedom, free markets, natural law, original intent of the Constitution and Western civilization."[61] McAfee spoke alongside scandal-plagued members of the Trump administration Jeff Sessions and Scott Pruitt, Senator Corey Gardner, the NRA's Dana Loesch, and white evangelical actor Kirk Cameron. McAfee was formally introduced as the MOTB's director of community initiatives. Among his opening words were "I bring you greetings from Museum of the Bible." He went on to identify himself as part of the Green family, whom he named as the museum's founding family. Neither the person who introduced McAfee on stage nor McAfee himself named any qualification for his presence and performance other than his affiliation with the MOTB.[62] He fashioned himself as an authoritative interpreter of the Bible's relevance for contemporary politics because of his affiliation with MOTB. McAfee's speech shows how the Green family's philanthropy has widened their platform within the evangelical industrial complex. Building on the biblical capital of their Supreme Court fight, the creation of the MOTB offers family members like McAfee a platform from which to speak for and about the Bible.

Before diving into interpretive specifics or imperatives, McAfee articulated an ideological commitment underpinning his participation, as representative of MOTB, in this politically engaged arena:

> Museum of the Bible is founded on this conviction: that the world is a better place when people read the Bible. That regardless of your background, regardless of your political preference, regardless of your religious affiliation, that we see time and time again that when people engage with this book it causes the flourishing of society for all people, for religious and irreligious.

We suggest that this is a similar form of the white evangelical supremacy offered in *This Dangerous Book*, though here it is presented as part of a choice within a variegated landscape of religious products: non-Christians are always able to choose to "engage" with the Bible, and (though McAfee does not offer evidence) are guaranteed a better world as a result. The slippage between individual choice and world transformation is interesting. If individuals choose to read the Bible, the world will be better and society will flourish. But what would it take, short of conversion, for a non-Christian to engage the Bible in such a way that it caused the world to be better?

McAfee does not provide an answer, though his speech suggests that one way this might manifest itself is through a government that operates according to "biblical" principles, a move that is similar to Steve Green's reflections on Chinese property rights. McAfee asks, "What does the Bible have to say about the government's role? And again I think this is gonna be a benefit to you even if you wouldn't define yourself as a Christian or a Jew or a religious person whatsoever." This is McAfee's segue into a discussion of Romans 13. His rhetoric here, which invokes a deceptively pluralistic orientation and a neutral "engagement" with the Bible, allows him to continue as though the subsequent reading of the chapter is merely "what the Bible says." And it further allows him to commend "what the Bible says" not only as universally self-evident but also as universally applicable and beneficial.

McAfee's disquisition on Romans 13 also includes an attempt to distance his reading from "politics" as such, a move that mirrors the use of the MOTB as a neutral arbiter of biblical interpretation.[63] The first principle that he takes from Romans 13 is that "God has absolute authority over all governments." Thus, "we don't place our hope in any one nation ... Because God has absolute authority we don't even place our hope in politics." Attention to the "we" in this statement is instructive. McAfee continually slips in and out of speaking to a community that already takes the Bible as its authoritative scripture. This rhetorical move blurs the lines between insider and outsider, between participant and observer. McAfee then switches to a different "we":

And the world we live in today is hyper political. We politicize everything that we do. We live in a pluralistic society, under a secular government, many of whom has [sic] a rich tradition of religious leaders that were involved in politics and much of our government was founded on principles found in the Bible. As we become more and more diverse, the question for us as a society is how are we going to navigate these waters, how are we going to sort the divides that exist between us. And I want to come to you today to suggest that those are not going to be sorted out

> through politics. That while politics is important and that politics is power, that ultimately it is like fire.

Here McAfee is addressing a broader audience of Americans who are democratic participants in American politics, regardless of their religious affiliation, and who are worn out on "partisanship." McAfee reasserts his claim that the institutions of American government, and many of its officeholders, are founded on biblical principles while also positioning himself as outside of politics proper. The logic appears to be that if our institutions and our best politicians were shaped by the Bible, it is apolitical to claim that we should go back to our roots.

Turning to the gospels, McAfee claims that Jesus rose above politics, a notion that invites particular interrogation given that Jesus lived in a society ruled by an imperial dynasty and in which the few existing democratic institutions would not have been available to a noncitizen like Jesus. McAfee can only reach for different Jewish groups as analogues to modern American political parties. Republicans, for example, are Pharisees and Democrats are Sadducees. While the rationale for these identifications is not offered, we believe the point of casting the two main American political parties as "the bad guys" from the gospels is to support McAfee's statement that "we should be primarily identified, not by our political persuasion, but by the principles we hold that work themselves out in politics." McAfee does not explain how he reconciles this recommendation with the fact that the Greens, through Hobby Lobby, have helped fund a vast network of entities working to advance conservative causes in alliance with the Republican Party.[64] Putting that aside, we can see that McAfee's "we" has shifted yet again, this time suggesting that the "conservatives" that he is addressing need to see themselves, like Jesus, as above politics, concerned with principle rather than party.

Having positioned himself and his ideal audience as outside of politics, McAfee returns to what he thinks Romans 13 says about governments. McAfee uses Romans 13 to make two interlocking assertions. The first is that "God delegates authority to all governments." Thus any government that exists is given its authority by God. To clarify his point, McAfee uses his relationship to the Green family as an analogy. During the family's legal challenge to the mandate to provide birth control to Hobby Lobby's employees by the Affordable Care Act, McAfee says, he was commissioned to speak for the family and the Hobby Lobby company. This mirrors how, he explains, God delegates authority to governments. McAfee's reading of Romans 13 draws its content from unmentioned parallels that flow from other New Testament texts like Colossians, Ephesians, and the Pastoral Epistles, allowing him to structure divine authority as a model for other social and familial relationships: parents over children, employers over employees, pastors over their church members. Noticeably absent from McAfee's examples, though not absent from the biblical texts that he relies on, are references to the authority of husbands over wives and enslavers ("masters") over enslaved persons ("slaves").

The inverse side of God's delegation of authority to governments is the response that such delegation requires of citizens of those governments: "Obeying government is obeying God. When we serve the government we serve God." McAfee recognizes that there is some relativism built into this framework, given that different countries at different times have had different kinds of governments. For McAfee, the conditions of American democracy are such that the American people have been delegated authority by God to govern themselves wisely. While democratic citizens are obligated to participate in their own governance, the point of doing so is to render Christian worship to God: "We honor the government as an act of worship to God." Here again is more slippage of McAfee's "we" between citizens, conservatives, and Christians, which rhetorically enables McAfee to position his reading of Romans 13 as a nonsectarian primer on civics.

Further, we would note the naïve white privilege with which McAfee appears to confront questions of obedience to governing authorities. In a joking tone, he suggests to the audience: "When a police officer pulls you over when you're speeding to get here on time, you can thank him as a minister, as a servant of God it says in [Romans] 13, for carrying out his God-given duty." McAfee's words and affect give no sense that he might ever worry that such a traffic stop might escalate to a violent confrontation.

McAfee concludes his reading of Romans 13 by wrestling with a tension that this chapter has created for interpreters for two millennia, namely that Romans 13 does not grapple with the possibility that ruling powers might do something wrong. McAfee recognizes that his various and sundry "wes" would not be comfortable with political advice that sanctioned blind allegiance to government as a divine fiat: "When the government asks us to violate God's commands, we must honor God as primary. We must make our own appeal to heaven." This final phrase is a reference to a revolutionary war flag from Washington's army that was, in turn, lifting this phrase from John Locke. As so often happens in such cases, McAfee turns to the problem presented by the Nazis: certainly God would not want citizens to support genocide and fascism because God had granted authority to the National Socialists. There must be some space for resistance, though because Romans 13 does not lend itself to support such a position, McAfee must turn to biblical texts outside of Romans 13, as we will see.

McAfee's civics lesson so far has played carefully with a variety of publics. A society governed by the Bible is one in which governmental authority is seen as deriving from God and in which the default option is to obey the government. Christians, those concerned with following God's commands and, thus, honoring God, are given the ability to exempt themselves from the normal expectations. McAfee appears to envision a society in which white evangelical Christians determine the state of exception, to use a phrase from Giorgio Agamben, while non-Christians are expected to obey. The model of resistance that McAfee articulates is Hobby Lobby's Supreme Court case. The Greens' resistance to the Affordable Care Act's birth control provision is offered as the ideal model for the Christian exception to democratic governments that attempt to trample on religious principles.[65] McAfee claims that the family's fight was really for the rights of all religious people: "We must contend for the religious faith of all peoples. One of the things that makes America unique is that our government does not give us our rights. It recognizes that we already have God-given rights." This invocation of pluralism is likely meant to placate those who might be wary of Christian nationalism here, but it is worth asking for whom it matters that a Hindu's or an atheist's rights are "God-given." In McAfee's schema, the best-case scenario is a government that implements biblical principles (presumably as he conceives them). A stand in resistance to unbiblical laws is only necessary when the government has not, in his logic, done its God-ordained job of governing like (the Christian) God desires.

McAfee closes his talk with an explicit turn to Christian theology and a collage of biblical allusions. Starting with Jesus's response to a question about paying taxes (Matthew 22:15–22, Mark 12:13–17, Luke 20:20–26), he dodges the issue of paying taxes and asserts that the real takeaway from the discussion is that God has granted his authority to Caesar. McAfee then references a scene from the Gospel of John where Jesus talks with Pontius Pilate before his crucifixion. McAfee does not follow the literal text of John but improvises his own exchange using language from Romans 13: "Jesus's response to him is 'You have no authority, except what has been given to you, what has been delegated to you by my Father.'"

This rescripting sets up McAfee's final christological turn, wherein he reads Christ's death on the cross as an example for thinking about the relationship between the individual, God, and government. Given that McAfee's God is always delegating authority to his subordinates, it must be God who sent Christ to the cross:

> He [Jesus] went to the cross, not because Pontius Pilate went to the cross, but because God ultimately sent him to the cross. That Christ's appeal to heaven in the Garden of Gethsemane asking for the cup to pass from him and on the cross crying out "My God, my God …," by not calling down angels to take him off the cross, Jesus subjected himself to governing authorities, demonstrating to us that even in suffering, how we are to live. And as he did that the wrath of God was poured out on Jesus so that the love of God and the grace of God could be poured out on us. And now Jesus is our perfect appeal that we can make to heaven.

The logic here is tortured, given that it appears to imply the opposite of the principle McAfee has read into Romans 13: while the Greens believed that God would want them to resist governments that pass unjust laws, Jesus submits to governmental authority such that he dies as a result. What McAfee seems to be saying in this final example is that Christians have their crosses to bear sometimes, which means suffering for a righteous cause. But at the core of his argument is the presumption that government is there to be obeyed until Christians like himself determine that exceptions must be made.

McAfee's speech at WCS is not a unique reading of Romans 13.[66] It dovetails with the dominant mode of reading the chapter in modern evangelical theology. And it commends the Bible to McAfee's audience as a resource for what is ultimately the conservative politics of white Christian hegemony, in which citizen-believers are to serve their government and obey it out of fidelity to God, to read and follow the Bible so that that same God will bless America, and to resist liberal governmental policies when they conflict with evangelical privilege. Speaking as a representative of the nation's Bible museum, McAfee rhetorically casts his biblical expositions on government as objective ("what the Bible says"), apolitical, and civically minded. If everyone just let the Bible and its God (accessed via the Bible) be in charge, all would benefit.

CASE STUDY #2: THE BIBLE AND GOOD GIRLS

Earlier in the chapter, we featured a vignette from *Only One Life*, written by Jackie Green and her daughter Lauren Green McAfee and pitched at helping women find biblical and historical models for living impactful lives. Aside from its celebration of the Greens' calling to build a Bible museum, the book also marks its female authors at the intersections of philanthropy, biblical devotion, and traditional patriarchal values. For example, Jackie Green is described on the back cover in this way: "Jackie Green, cofounder of Museum of the Bible with her husband and Hobby Lobby president, Steve Green, is an author, full-time homemaker, mother of six, and grandmother of four."[67] As American religious historian Kate Bowler has shown in her study of evangelical women celebrities, the title "cofounder" has in recent years become a popular mantle for women in American megaministry, particularly among white evangelicals and especially for (male) pastor's wives in this movement where "copastor" would violate hierarchical gender norms.[68] The "co-" further communicates to insiders that the wife has not wielded influence outside her home without the approval of her husband.[69]

Each of the twelve chapters of *Only One Life* is organized around a virtue, such as compassion or tenacity, and unfolds in parallel structure, with illustrations of how three women are believed to exemplify the virtue: a woman depicted in the Bible, a woman from sanitized annals of Western history, and a well-known Christian woman alive at the time of writing. The segments are also peppered with autobiographical reflections on the lives of the two authors. They are careful to attribute everyone's successes, though, to God. Throughout the book, Green and McAfee go to great lengths to portray women with extraordinary accomplishments as ordinary women whose extraordinary feats are due to providential power and who can be imitated in small, ordinary ways by their readers, who are themselves presumed to be ordinary. "Whatever you do," they assert, "your every day matters! Whether it's changing diapers and cooking meals or preparing reports and sending emails, it matters."[70]

In the chapter entitled "Courage," Green and McAfee treat the biblical character of Esther, who risked her life to save the Jewish people from annihilation in ancient Persia. In the biblical story, Esther, a Jewish woman who is married to the Persian king, takes upon herself great personal risk by confronting the king and revealing a genocidal plot against the Jewish people. Her risk leads to their salvation from the murderous scheme. Green and McAfee's imaginative shaping of Esther's story is revealing. Our authors impose onto the biblical character, for example, a temerity and developed sense of self-doubt that lack warrant in the text in their Bibles. In *Only One Life*, Esther is given an internal monologue: "Everyday her heart cries out in wonder, *What am I doing here?* And in the same breath, *I don't belong* . . . Her heart has a thousand objections. You can hear them: *I'm not a speaker. I'm just a young girl. No one can approach the king without permission.* And perhaps the darkest thought: *I'll have to reveal my true identity*" (33).

The biblical story of Esther in the Protestant Bible does not offer clues to the heroine's internal musings. While the narrator states that Esther was distressed when she heard about the king's decree to kill her people (4:4), the plan to undo this death edict is executed in the narrative with precision devoid of agonizing. In fact, both Esther and the story move very quickly. Esther's only expression of hesitation to risk her life to approach the king is brief and couched in logical, pragmatic terms as she communicates to her uncle Mordecai about the plan:

> All the king's servants and the people of the king's provinces know that if any man or woman goes to the king inside the inner court without being called, there is but one law – all alike are to be put to death. Only if the king holds out the golden scepter to someone, may that person live. I myself have not been called to come in to the king for thirty days. (4:11 NRSV)

She could be read here as taking initiative to assess risk, as negotiating with Mordecai about the best plan forward. Once she is convinced by his message back to her, she acts decisively. "If I perish, I perish," she concludes (4:16 NRSV).

One of the challenges facing biblical expositors of all stripes is how to make biblical stories, laws, and teachings legible across historical difference. How do stories of nomadic pastoralists, itinerant peasant wonder-workers, or palace courtiers apply to modern readers? Green and McAfee's psychologizing of Esther is a way to negotiate this historical and cultural gap since the circumstances that required courage in Esther's story are not likely to be repeated in the lives of evangelical Christian women in today's United States . Green and McAfee's additions to the story turn Esther into an imitable heroine for themselves and their readers. "We are all like Esther," they write. And further: "In so many ways, the world tells us that we don't belong and that we don't fit. Truly, we are exiles and outcasts. This world is not our home, and we all have our fears" (34).

Green and McAfee analogize Esther's Jewishness to outsiderness and then adopt that outsider mantle for themselves on the basis of their belief in an otherworld. They do this via a clever intertextual alignment of Esther's story with 1 Peter 2:11, where followers of Jesus are described as "aliens and exiles."[71] Our authors emphasize Esther's distinctiveness in order to make her distinctiveness generic enough that any woman can identify with her: "Esther doesn't belong. She is not of royal descent. She is no princess, let alone a queen – at least that's what the voices inside her head are telling her. Worse still, she's Jewish" (33). This rhetorical move paradoxically uses what is unique about Esther to strip her of her particularity and make her available enough as universal paradigm that modern evangelical women can follow her courageous example.

Green and McAfee's focus on Esther as a woman to emulate fits well with tendencies within white evangelical biblical interpretation to read biblical characters as heroes (or heroines) and to prioritize individual action within political systems while overlooking possibilities of critiquing or resisting power structures. Rather than a story of a girl finding her voice, for example, the book of Esther could be read as a horror story that reveals the disastrous results of patriarchy and is ripe for exposing and critiquing sexual exploitation of women.[72]

Following their own logic that "we are all like Esther," Green and McAfee individually reflect on the ways they are each like Esther. For McAfee, it is pursuing a PhD. Though she does not name the institution, it provides helpful context here to observe that social media posts indicate she attends Southern Baptist Theological Seminary, the flagship educational institution of the Southern Baptist Convention. Her apparent area of concentration is run by Russell Moore, who, as president of the SBC's Ethics & Religious Liberty Commission and former chairman of the Board for the Council on Biblical Manhood and Womanhood, is a fierce advocate for a complementarian view of gender roles.[73]

Green's turn as Esther takes the form of public speaking about the MOTB. Jackie writes, "I helped organize women's events, decorate, design gifts, choose menus, and do whatever was needed in the development years leading up to the opening." Green sees the spotlight and the homemaker skills she brought to planning the MOTB as analogous to Esther's courage navigating a frightening political landscape and risking her life to prevent the genocide of the Jewish people. Because of the expectations on most evangelical Christian women, Green and McAfee must not only democratize Esther's courage but also domesticate it. Their readers can take Esther's public example and use it privately, showing courage they "raise a child with disabilities or emotional trauma" or "face an illness of your own or of a family member" or "persevere through a troubled marriage" (35). We get a clear look into how Green and McAfee imagine Esther's example playing out in the lives led by their intended readers when they write: "Courage often comes in the everyday, the common, the unrecognized. Sometimes it is simply courage to face the day, the crying baby, the distant husband, or the circumstances of your everyday life" (31).

Green and McAfee continue this pattern of finding in individual women's stories or lives a way that their intended audience, and indeed they themselves, can follow them by shaping these women's stories to make them fit within the bounds of the Biblical Womanhood movement. Our authors deftly contour each woman's story to fit the gender expectations that their apparent tradition, the Southern Baptist Convention, has made an issue bound up inextricably with an affirmation of the Bible's infallibility.[74] An interesting conundrum that Green and McAfee must navigate is the dual commitment to celebrate women with great influence and to ensure that the patterns and resources they provide to their intended readers do not violate standards of Biblical Womanhood. To accomplish their project, Green and McAfee must account for the influence of the women they treat without violating tenets of male headship and without sacrificing marriage and home as a woman's centerpiece.

One way our authors maintain this precarious balance is to emphasize that the women they write about did not seek out attention. Rather, it is conceived as thrust upon them. These women of faith were not, as their readers are not expected to be, inherently ambitious. The pattern is so pervasive in *Only One Life* that in a flat reading one might fairly conclude that reluctance is a prerequisite for acceptably entering the public eye or wielding influence. Take for example, their summary statement of the summit of Mary Beth Chapman, wife of popular Christian musician Steven Curtis Chapman: "Never ambitious for the spotlight, leadership responsibility, or a complicated life, Mary Beth nevertheless found herself serving as president of the innovative nonprofit organization [Show Hope, an adoption support ministry]."[75] Likewise, Catherine Booth, famed founder of the Salvation Army: "a general shyness and reticence about being in a public position characterized her approach to ministry."[76] Of Marilynn Hickey, to take another example, Green and McAfee write: "Her aspirations were not to be spotlighted on the stage. She was committed to being a pastor's wife."[77] Of Rosa Parks: "boldness was not her natural tendency. Parks considered herself a meek and timid person. She was a shy, quiet child."[78] The same is true, they write in a self-authorizing move, of themselves: "Legacy often starts in unlikely places. Neither of us would have anticipated sharing our own story on a public stage. If anyone had told either of us that we'd stand to speak to hundreds, even thousands, we'd have said they were crazy. We are assuming that is true for you too."[79] Green and McAfee reconceptualize female agency in such a way that it can be sanctioned biblically from within their hermeneutical frame.

Accomplished women are remembered – as we have seen with the character of Esther – as having running internal monologues that express self-doubt about their capability. Readers are invited into our authors' imagined inner thoughts of Florence Nightingale, for example: "It may be difficult to imagine pursuing a calling like Florence did. But I (Lauren) like to think that she felt it would be difficult to. No doubt, she felt plenty of fear, doubt, and uncertainty as she stepped onto a path that no one had ever walked before."[80] Normalizing this phenomenon encourages readers that they too can overcome negative "self-talk" even as it, significantly, encodes an expectation that women *should* feel fearful of their own incompetence. To Nightingale are added Sarah Bowling, founder of the mission organization Saving Moses, and Pharaoh's daughter (named "Ahmose" by our authors) from the book of Exodus, who rescues baby Moses: "Ahmose, Florence, and Sarah all experienced the same doubts and fears along the way. They are no different than us. They just took the next step God put in front of them, leaving the results up to Him."[81] Green and McAfee foreclose the possibility that these women could be naturally self-assured, confident, or even cunning. Ambition and moxie are traded for humility and availability. Our authors frame their own apparent success with the MOTB as part of this pattern, crediting divine activity while celebrating their own passivity: "it was God who made it happen. Only He could have pulled off something like this. We're just not that clever, but we do try to be available."[82]

Green and McAfee's storycraft further suggests an underlying anxiety about a woman's influence interfering with her primary calling as a devoted wife. The story of Ruth Bell Graham, wife of famous evangelist Billy Graham, is manicured to point the way for women to prioritize their men. Characterizing Bell as Graham's "future helpmeet," Green and

McAfee praise Ruth for relinquishing her own dream, her perceived calling from God to go into international missionary work, in favor of supporting her husband's aspirations. Ruth's decision is couched in terms of obedience to the Bible, which is assumed to demand hierarchy of husband over wife within the family: "As a young woman who placed the highest value on the Word of God, she came to recognize that she was not only called to follow her husband as he led their family; her primary mission was to support and help him succeed in *his* calling."[83]

The self-sacrifice of women for the benefit of others, and particularly for that of men, is a repeated thematic virtue in *Only One Life*. In a chapter celebrating women who teach, Green and McAfee appear unbothered by a model of giving of oneself that ultimately destroys the self: "There is an old saying that asserts, 'A good teacher is like a candle – it consumes itself to light the way for others.' There is truth in that statement. No matter what the context ... the woman who chooses to teach gives of herself sacrificially, but the light of the sacrifice illuminates the future."[84] Women are expected to give so much of themselves that there is nothing left. And yet in keeping with the trope of home and family as centerpieces of women's lives, the teaching scenarios that Green and McAfee imagine as possibilities for their readers are much more mundane than one might otherwise suspect based on their candle analogy:

> The gift of lighting the way for others is a powerful culture changer and an opportunity for us to make change happen wherever we are – in our homes, our churches, our neighborhoods, and beyond ... Maybe you don't think of yourself as a teacher, but we all have strengths to offer ... Maybe the new staffer in your office needs help with the printer. Or you could show a new bride how to cook a homemade meal. The kid next door might enjoy learning how to plant flowers. The teenage boy could use a hand finding books in the library.[85]

In a related move, Green and McAfee frequently celebrate, rather than critique, the apparent invisibility of women's labor. Of Elizabeth Everest (*circa* 1832–95), nanny to Winston Churchill, they write: "God used the faith of an obscure woman of humble origins to shape the character of one of history's key figures."[86] Women, we find in this book, should take pleasure in obscurity, satisfaction in self-abnegation. Rather than an injustice to be named and lamented, unrecognized female labor becomes in *Only One Life* a condition to emulate – even unto immolation.

Alongside this expectation that women will burn like candles, shining a way for others as they slowly melt away, Green and McAfee must reckon with stories in the Bible of "fiery" women whose assertiveness or authority on the face of it present counterexamples. Take Deborah, for example, ancient Israel's only female judge and warrior, who in Judges 4:4 is called by the narrator *eset lappidoth* – a phrase that can be rendered in transla-tion, to opposite effect, either as "woman of flames" or "wife of Lappidoth."[87] Deborah is a commanding prophetess who communicates that God will help the Israelites defeat the enemy general Sisera, whom God, she prophesies, "will sell into the hand of a woman" (Judges 4:9). Green and McAfee do not mention that woman, though. That woman, who is arguably the central heroine of this story, is Jael, who quenches the general's thirst and then speaks softly to him while he sleeps – right before driving a tent peg through his skull (Judges 4:21–22).[88] Her cunning kill is then celebrated in the song of Deborah and Barak in the following chapter (Judges 5:24–31): "Most blessed of women be Jael."

Ignoring Jael, Green and McAfee focus on Deborah as a purveyor of wisdom due to her saturation, they assert anachronistically, in God's Word. They further see in Deborah a model for women today who must balance a home life with an additional divine calling. She is, they write, both a prophetess and a wife. Joining centuries of commentary wrestling with how to square Deborah's apparent public role and authority with traditional gender norms,[89] our authors make much of the identifier "the wife of Lappidoth." Adopting the easier translation for their project, Green and McAfee interpret the formulaic identifier as evidence that women entering the public sphere should not do so at the expense of their marriage: "the Scriptures are intentional in recording [Deborah's husband's name]. Deborah's rise to prominence was not at the cost of her marriage; she didn't forget her ties to her husband. Instead both were wonderfully woven together – a celebration of her wisdom and her marriage." *Only One Life* thereby fashions a biblical woman into a resource for Biblical Womanhood.

Perhaps unsurprisingly, the rhetoric in *Only One Life* reveals a particular anxiety around unmarried women. Singleness, when it comes to women, is framed not as an opportunity or a legitimate choice but rather as a problem to solve, a condition to lament, or a second-best compromise. Our authors use the derogatory term "spinster" without irony and imply that single mothers – not unlike orphans – need rescuing.[90] As a ministry to single mothers, Green proudly explains, her (married) daughter-in-law helps their church provide "childcare, spa treatments, and car repairs."[91] Elizabeth Everest (*circa* 1832–95) is said to "as a single person" have "accepted her status in life."[92] Lottie Moon (1840–1912), a missionary whose efforts are now commemorated in Southern Baptist churches in an annual "Lottie Moon Christmas Offering" for international missions, is another example. "In 1873," we read "Lottie, thirty-three years of age and single, stepped *alone* onto a steamship bound for China." Her "having no accompanying partner" is an "apparent deficit" she would need to overcome.[93]

Sex is not directly addressed in *Only One Life*, but widespread evangelical notions of purity culture frequently bubble up to the surface. At first glance such apparently parenthetical lines as "What girl doesn't enjoy tales of queens and princesses?"[94] might strike a reader as the authors' folksy attempt to connect to readers, one that reproduces essentialist assumptions about traditional gender expectations of what girls are supposed to like. Reading such comments alongside Green and McAfee's teleology for women's lives, however, reveals their explanatory power for identifying an ideology that is unarticulated but assumed throughout *Only One Life*. As scholar of American religion Amy DeRogatis has traced, a fairy-tale narrative is pervasive in literature aimed at young evangelical women – a story that in its basics promises girls who remain "pure" a divinely ordained "Prince Charming" of a husband.[95]

In Green and McAfee's interpretive frame, to be unmarried is to be unmoored from a woman's primary calling – a limited set of duties demarcated by, in their view, divinely crafted aptitudes inherent to "feminine" bodies. "God's design of the human body," they assert, "testifies to this feminine capacity for legacy."[96] While such feminine facility is

envisioned as geographically and temporally expansive, it is not cap-
acious in range. They write:

> there are certain cultural and societal impacts that we women are uniquely
> gifted by God to make. In every place on earth and in every time in history,
> right down to ours, women have been keepers of the flame of family unity
> and the binders of the cords of connectedness. We are seemingly
> handcrafted by God Himself to be the conversation starters, the
> communication hubs, and the culture keepers.[97]

Only One Life ascribes to women traditionally "feminine" attributes of
"relational skills and emotional intelligence."[98] Frequently such an ascrip-
tion is accompanied by Green and McAfee's assigning emotions to women
characters that their stories do not necessitate. Perhaps no example is
clearer than their retelling of the women who found Jesus's empty tomb
in the gospel story. Mary Magdalene takes center stage in a section entitled
"The Unique Witness of Women."[99] Green and McAfee narrate the discovery of Jesus's empty tomb by Mary and several other women in Luke 24 and
then reflect on God's choice of women (versus men) as witnesses.
A woman's crying is described as "breathless" and "inconsolable." Rather
than speaking with confidence, she "manages to stammer out a response."
Rather than summon constitutional grit, she "feels a surge of desperate
boldness." The Bible intentionally highlights, our authors claim, an essential feature of gender difference: the women "feel," while the men think.
Women are "wired" with "emotion" and "compassion," whereas men are
logical. This reading lifts details from the plot of Luke 24 and interprets
them as clues implanted by God in the text that instruct the reader on what
characteristics are essential to men and women.

Having established their white evangelical bona fides through their
altruistic zeal for the Bible, their generosity in defense of the Bible, and
their devotion to family and home, Green and McAfee argue that their
values are rooted in both the Bible and famous women in Christian
history. *Only One Life* traces the circuitous transformation of biblical
capital: Green and McAfee present themselves as evangelical exem-
plars then read the Bible in support of their exemplarity which in
turn is read as the inspiration for other "biblical" women in history

who are then examples emulated by Green and McAfee. Each chapter spins this hermeneutical circle round and round, with the effect that Green and McAfee cycle and recycle their biblical capital until it attaches to them.

CONCLUSION

The Green family is using their patronage of the MOTB to authorize themselves as biblical interpreters in political and religious spheres, avoiding traditional forms of credentialing from church institutions or academic training. We have argued that the Greens, as the Museum of the Bible's "founding family," have produced biblical capital for themselves with two key moves. The first is by recoding their philanthropic efforts – from their purchase of ancient manuscripts and objects to the founding of the MOTB itself – in altruistic tropes valued by white evangelicals. Because these tropes hide the economic inequalities and gains afforded the Greens, they allow them to rhetorically cast their expenditures as fidelity and devotion to the Bible. Second, the Greens also generate biblical capital by laboring to "let the Bible speak for itself." Because white evangelicals have weak institutional constraints on their members, religious professionals have to tailor messages that will speak to what their audiences want to hear. If they hear a message they do not like, they can easily choose a different church or authority. Lacking institutional backing, religious elites have little room to speak "prophetically" to their audiences; rather, they gain biblical capital by coding what their audience wants to hear as "what the Bible says." The Greens are not pastors, but they produce biblical capital by claiming to have "discovered" what they and their audience already believe. As discoverers of these always already known truths, the Greens claim for themselves the privilege of coding their interests as what the Bible says. Successfully masking one's own beliefs as what the Bible says for itself generates biblical capital, in the same way that coding their giving in altruistic terms transforms economic expenditures into acts of pious devotion.

Conclusion

THE MUSEUM OF THE BIBLE IS A WHITE EVANGELICAL INSTI-
tution. We have argued that it produces a white evangelical
bible, one that can do no wrong, tell no lies, encounter no
obstacle that can't be overcome by tenacity, whether human or divine. It
is a bible that works to authorize, affirm, and protect white Christian
privilege and advance the interests of Christian nationalists and Christian
Zionists. By focusing on how the museum has produced a particular
bible, we have been able to pay attention to aspects of the museum that
have evaded critical attention. Reading the MOTB as a bible manufac-
turer of sorts allows the combined effect of the museum's exhibits,
publications, rides, experiences, and patronage to come into sharper
focus. These elements combine to construct and then publicize a bible
steeped in the traditions of white evangelicals.

WHAT SHOULD WE MAKE OF THE MOTB?

What comes of this institution is hard to know. Will it anchor increased
bible reading among otherwise skeptical American audiences? Will it
advance the Christian nationalist and Christian Zionist political projects
further than they advanced under the Trump administration by serving
as an amplifier for these constituencies? Will it make the Green family
into a new face among evangelical influencers, a future dynasty akin to
the Grahams, Falwells, and Robertsons? As we saw in Chapter 1, white

evangelical institution-building has a mixed history of influence. Many investments by donors like J. Howard Pew fell flat, such as his attempt to woo Protestant clergy through tone-deaf fusions of evangelical theology and libertarian economics. Pew spent a fortune in donations that gained little traction, at least at first. Though Pew's efforts proved futile at the start, they eventually reshaped white evangelicalism when they were allied with the right forces, as with the potent assemblage that brought together Billy Graham, *Christianity Today*, the National Association of Evangelicals, and libertarian-minded, anti-Communist business leaders in the form of neo-evangelicalism. A similar situation bore out with Lyman Stewart's massive investment in *The Fundamentals*, a project that frustrated his own interests in liberal muckraking and dispensationalist promotion, but ultimately served to forge the first truly national network of mutual interest among dispensationalist and conservative evangelicals through the careful attention to curation, distribution, and branding by Moody Bible Institute's Henry Crowell. In looking at the institutional history of white evangelicalism, we see that it is the most networked institutions, organizations, and projects that have the most impact. The MOTB has worked to forge connections with other evangelical institutions and political interests, efforts that overlap with and extend those already forged by the Greens' previous and continued philanthropy to evangelistic causes. If the MOTB can become a prominent node in this network, it stands a good chance of having its bible amplified across white evangelicalism and beyond.

Were this to happen, we wonder about what effect it might have. Christian nationalist and Christian Zionist positions would likely see further advances with MOTB and the Greens, but these are already widely held positions within white evangelical culture. So too is the particular form of MOTB's good, reliable, and divinely inspired bible. Few white evangelicals would question these attributes of "the Bible." It may be that the MOTB's contribution to white evangelical discourse would be what it leaves out: the apocalyptic end of the world and the cultural antagonism that precedes it. Ever since dispensationalist premillennialism fused with white evangelicalism in the late nineteenth century, speculation about and expectation of the imminent end of the world has followed white evangelicals, to the ends of the earth as it were.[1] In our examination of the MOTB, we saw little evidence that its bible is committed to an imminent, apocalyptic view of the world's end. The New Testament film on the Stories of the Bible floor ends with a benign hopefulness about humanity's redemption and the arrival of the millennial kingdom, without the violent fantasies of the canonical book of Revelation or the esoteric predictions of dispensationalists. The MOTB's scriptural story has its telos not in the end of the world but in its scripturalization. There is an optimism to the museum's bible that expects biblical literacy and biblical accessibility to proceed toward its final saturation. Soon and very soon the Bible will be everywhere. Soon and very soon the Bible will be king.

At the same time, there is not a sharp dividing line between bible believers and their secular, cultured despisers. The Impact of the Bible floor trades on the idea that the white evangelical bible always works toward the good and makes societies that adhere to it better, an argument steeped in white racism and Christian nationalism. And yet, the overriding ethos here is of persuasion, not confrontation. The MOTB wants to show us how great its bible is, and how impactful it has been and still could be, while hiding a darker history. Absent or downplayed as well are the culture war tropes that often animate white evangelical voters: evolutionary science, liberal dominance of institutions of learning, abortion, LGBTQ rights, or school prayer. The overall portrait offered in the MOTB is that the white evangelical bible is good for society, if only we'd let it do its work on us.

One might take this as a sign that the MOTB is offering a different kind of white evangelicalism, one less interested in fighting old culture war battles and more optimistic about the future. That may well be. But if we read the MOTB as part of the history of white evangelical institution building, we find other potential analogues. As Timothy Gloege has so thoroughly documented, the Moody Bible Institute, under the leadership of Henry Crowell in the first decades of the twentieth century, drew upon early corporate branding strategies, developed by Crowell himself at the Quaker Oats Company, to sell dispensational theology to a white middle class audience that might otherwise have been ill-disposed to it.[2] This was true as well for *The Fundamentals*. Crowell and the other editors worked assiduously against their benefactor Lyman Stewart's interests so that the essays published in the collection would appeal to white middle class audiences.[3] One could extend this line of analysis to other seemingly benign institutions and organizations created by white evangelical donors, all of which intentionally couched a particular set of doctrinal, political, or economic interests in an appealing garb for middle class consumption.

Looked at from this perspective, the MOTB is a class-based argument for white evangelical respectability. The media coverage of the museum has almost ritually invoked the museum's state-of-the-art exhibits, its LED screens, its stunning views, its impeccable design elements, its high-end cuisine.[4] While these aesthetic descriptions might seem anodyne when compared to the museum's scandals or underlying ideologies, their ubiquity suggests that the museum's design has successfully appealed to the middle- and upper-class dispositions of the news media. This is the pitch that the MOTB and its f(o)unders are making: *There is a white evangelicalism that is not backwards, anti-modern, and low-class.* Just as fundamentalists shed their name in the wake of the embarrassment of the Scopes Trial, eventually rebranding themselves as (neo-)evangelicals, the MOTB is a branding exercise for white evangelicalism, renarrating its history, its impact, and its bible to appeal to the same white middle class (and the cultural respectability imagined to reside there) that has always been the movement's target. Judging by the long-term successes of those earlier projects, we should not underestimate the MOTB's potential to "impact" the shape of white evangelicalism.

THE MOTB, AMERICAN RELIGIOUS HISTORY, AND BIBLICAL STUDIES

While we have attended to the museum as a kind of factory and advertising firm for its bible, ours is not the only heuristic frame with which to analyze the museum. Studying the MOTB is relevant for a number of important conversations animating American religious history and biblical studies.

In her pioneering work *Consuming Religion*, Kathryn Lofton, a scholar of religion in American history, has called for renewed attention to reading consumerism, capitalism, corporate structures, and religion together. Consumption has become an organizing principle of our social formations, which means that "what we consume, how we consume, and how we organize in order to facilitate ongoing consumption" are questions that need to focus our attention.[5] How, we might ask, is consumption organized and incited at the MOTB? As historians Kristin Kobes Du Mez and Daniel Vaca have persuasively argued, white evangelicals have long constructed their identities out of their consumption of religious products.[6] This does not make them unique. All religious traditions structure relationships between adherents and economic practice. However, this aspect of white evangelical history and practice has been understudied and undertheorized, given the evangelical rhetoric that belief, not ritual or sacred objects, is central to their identities. Recognizing this takes us back to the MOTB's bookstore, filled as it is with an array of books and study guides, but also the kind of evangelical consumer goods that might be purchased at a Lifeway Christian Bookstore or at Hobby Lobby. Tourism, souvenirs, experiences – the MOTB offers these to visitors all wrapped up in a carefully branded package that affectively bolsters and produces evangelical identity. The MOTB is enmeshed in evangelical consumer culture that produces evangelical identity through consumption.

Indeed, the MOTB is deeply entangled in evangelical consumption since it is both the result of excess capital produced by Hobby Lobby's sale of cheap craft goods and a recipient of donations from Hobby Lobby that accrue tax benefits back on the corporation. Through a careful reading of the Supreme Court's ruling in *Hobby Lobby* v. *Burwell*, Lofton notes that the court found in Hobby Lobby's favor by redescribing the corporation as a religious sect. It is only as a sect, a kind of religious minority, that Hobby Lobby could be granted legal protection of its religious freedom.[7] Lofton's point is not to accuse Hobby Lobby and the Greens of hypocrisy, but rather to push us to see corporations themselves as religious, and vice versa. "Corporations," she writes, "inscribe practices and promote worldviews beyond the applied scope of their product. Organizations denoted as religions possess marketing strategies and consumer interests. There have been legal and political reasons to distinguish between these two words. But there are substantive reasons to understand the ways that companies organize themselves as religious."[8] Hobby Lobby is a corporation that is entangled with and an extension of the family's religious commitments. MOTB representatives have always insisted that the MOTB is legally distinct from Hobby Lobby and, therefore, not committed to the corporation's religious mission. But their various entanglements suggest that it is better to read the two as part of the same corporation serving the same interests. This is especially important now that the MOTB's mission statement has evolved to frame the institution as religious in nature. Corporations and religions are two words, Lofton would have us understand, for the same thing.[9]

An alternative model for analyzing the MOTB would be to treat it as a parachurch organization, an interdenominational institution that serves as a node connecting Christian communities together.[10] Parachurch organizations can take many different forms, but the key element is that they are not churches but rather entities that connect churches together or perform functions outside of direct oversight and control by churches. As sociologist Christopher Scheitle has shown, parachurch organizations represent the public face of Christianity in the United States and constitute a major channel through which social capital flows.[11] Parachurch organizations range from campus ministries like InterVarsity Christian Fellowship to political activist groups such as Focus on the Family to social service providers and missionary societies and traveling revival ministries. They might also be nodes of connection, such as the National Association of Evangelicals or the Christian Business Men's Committee International.

The MOTB resembles a parachurch ministry in several ways. It links different Christian communities together. It has become a major stop on Christian heritage tours that promote Christian nationalist perspectives on American history.[12] It also is a meeting point for various Christian organizations. Many have put on events at the museum, in event spaces specifically designed for rental use. Other Christian organizations have filmed shows or recorded podcasts at the museum. The museum's exhibits explicitly name partnerships that the museum has developed with Christian organizations, such as the various bible societies that helped to sponsor (and solicit donations through) the illumiNations exhibit on the History of the Bible floor. Many of these organizations have previous and existing ties to the web of evangelical nonprofits supported by the Greens. Outside of the Greens, many evangelical institutions, groups, and prominent donors have contributed financially to the museum, as we saw by looking at the museum's donor wall in Chapter 1.

The MOTB could also be productively read as an evangelical think tank, another form of parachurch organization. The MOTB has shown itself to be a site for generating stories and events where knowledge about "the Bible" is produced, stored, and disseminated. It therein functions like a think tank, an advocacy organization that does interested research on a topic that can be pushed out in the form of policy and awareness campaigns. The MOTB has done this with its social media, events it puts on, the scholars it has onboarded and paid, and the research endeavors it sponsors. One could also consider here the public event the MOTB sponsored in which volunteers were recruited to unfold and stretch out the world's longest bible, the mile-long Wiedmann Bible, at the Lincoln Memorial Reflecting Pool.[13] Reading the MOTB this way points to its work as not unlike a laundering operation, pushing stories through its think tank and out into the mainstream media. The MOTB leadership became convenient contacts for reporters to call to get a quote in a story. And so the MOTB acts as both a junction in white evangelical networks and as an amplifier of that network's interests. It thus can play the role of linking, with the patina of objectivity and disinterestedness accorded to institutions named as museums, white evangelicals to other networks.[14]

One final site within which to analyze the MOTB is our own home discipline of biblical studies. In many ways, the MOTB resembles a biblical studies institute, not unlike the Moody Bible Institute in the Crowell era or Tyndale House in Cambridge, a partnering institution of the MOTB.[15] Like biblical studies institutes, the MOTB has a collection of materials, pays a staff of researchers and academics, engages in research and publication, and sponsors events and talks connected with the academic study of biblical texts. It has also developed links with academic biblical scholars working at American and British universities.

Much of the ire that has been directed at the MOTB by its critics has been the result of failures in its acquisitions practices, in line with standards set by other museums. But a fair number of these critics have been biblical scholars who are deeply invested in biblical manuscripts for their own intellectual and research interests, beyond what might bother a professional museum curator. Other critics, with whom we would place our previous work on the MOTB, argue that the MOTB gets the history of the Bible wrong, that they have insufficiently practiced biblical historical criticism according to the standards set by academic biblical scholars. Scholars associated with the museum push back, arguing that they too are professionals, with proper credentials for the field, and that their work for and at the museum is in keeping with what they deem to be appropriate standards for studying the Bible. This back and forth envisions a horizon in which, at some point, the museum and biblical studies will meet in agreement, once the museum has reformed fully and once biblical scholars have overcome their biases towards it.

But such criticism, we have come to conclude, is ultimately unproductive for a number of reasons, which is why we have approached the MOTB differently in this book. First, fighting over who interprets the Bible the right way replicates a fissure with which the professional guild of biblical studies, and the broader academic study of religion itself, has not fully grappled. Namely, scholars fight over whether secular critics, well-meaning caretakers, or pious practitioners can claim to be better interpreters of religious phenomena.[16] Within biblical studies there remain deep divisions over whether evangelicals are sufficiently critical to be classed among "real" biblical scholars. But this obfuscates a larger problem, which is how those who seek to define what is "real" biblical scholarship are often themselves enmeshed in white liberal Protestant forms of Christianity, or at least to the ecumenical politics that those entities espouse. In this sense, biblical studies remains caught in the same fundamentalist/modernist battles that pitted Lyman Stewart against John Rockefeller. As Lofton has rightly noted, "Fundamentalism emerged as a kind of lay religious studies: a way of naming proper tactics of religion in a world of wrong figurations, wrong on religious grounds and wrong on social scientific ones."[17] Fighting with the MOTB over biblical studies is merely an extension of a longer, inconclusive, and unspoken war between white liberals and white conservatives over who gets to interpret the Bible.

We can see this clearly in the ire directed at the MOTB, Hobby Lobby, and the Greens over their acquisition of illicit manuscripts and its publication of forged Dead Sea Scrolls fragments. While this criticism directed at these shoddy and illegal practices was justified, it also can be mapped onto a longer history of how Christian institutions controlled access to the biblical text. As biblical scholar Jennifer Wright Knust has written, in early modernity Christian scholars in Europe began the process of collecting, collating, and analyzing ancient biblical manuscripts with the goal of fixing the original or oldest text of the Bible, a process that has come to be called textual criticism.[18] This was made possible, in most cases, by the formation of academic institutions that were built from and housed the spoils of European colonial expansion.[19] Initially, the oldest biblical manuscripts were housed in Europe at prominent research universities and libraries. With the growth of American economic and geopolitical power, American universities and liberal seminaries acquired their own collections of biblical manuscripts and developed partnerships with European institutions to study them. In this they were financially supported by American industrialists like Rockefeller. In recent decades, liberal-minded corporate interests have ceased to funnel their donations into progressive Christian institutions while conservative evangelicals like the Greens have continued to do so, allowing white evangelical institutions to purchase their own manuscripts, fund text-critical research, and train their own text critics.[20] The power dynamics for those who have felt entitled to control the biblical text have shifted. Thus, the fight over the MOTB's manuscripts is both about best practices in the field of biblical studies *and* reflective of an anxiety about where the real power and capital lie.

Rather than engage in intra-Protestant intellectual warfare, we have taken a different approach in critically analyzing the MOTB as a white evangelical institution engaged in creating a white evangelical bible. We have done this because we are convinced that one of the paths forward for biblical studies is to move beyond fights over the meaning of the Bible as adjudicated by scholars who value only the original meaning that can be reconstructed through historical research.[21] The quest for authorial intent that is assumed in such a project is methodologically unsound, but also indicative of a failure to come to grips with the reality that biblical texts have had and continue to have long and varied lives among a vast array of religious communities. The bibles of these groups should have their stories told.

In this book we have tried to tell a richly contextualized story of the Museum of the Bible and its bible, to explore its dizzying array of parts and unspoken connections, to analyze the things it says and the things it leaves unsaid. We have also named its people and tried to tell their stories as well. In so doing, we have frequently called attention to the museum's whiteness, not because we want to slander it as a racist institution but because it is an accurate description of who made this museum and for whom. The history of white evangelicalism, as that of our own field of biblical studies, has been a history where whiteness has dominated the conversation while being left unspoken. Critical attention to the history of how bible readers and scholars have constructed, interpreted, and used their bibles requires attention to how race, class, and gender shape those endeavors. Such a project requires critically interrogating white supremacy and privilege just as much as recuperating and centering voices that have for so long been relegated to the margins. Any understanding of the Museum of the Bible must begin and end, then, with the study of the white evangelical bible.

Notes

INTRODUCTION

1. We are grateful to Michael Peppard for directing our attention to this exhibit in private correspondence. For a more detailed description of the installation, see Kathleen J. Martin, *Indigenous Symbols and Practices in the Catholic Church: Visual Culture, Missionization, and Appropriation* (Farnham: Ashgate, 2010), 128. For an excellent recent exploration of encounters between Christian colonists and Indigenous peoples, see Jennifer Graber, *The Gods of Indian Country: Religion and the Struggle for the American West* (Oxford: Oxford University Press, 2018). For a critique of the Bible's liberative potential from the perspective of Indigenous readers, see Robert Allen Warrior, "A Native American Perspective: Canaanites, Cowboys, and Indians," in *Voices from the Margin: Interpreting the Bible in the Third World*, ed. R. S. Sugirtharajah (New York: Orbis, 2006), 287–95.
2. Larry W. Hurtado, *The Freer Biblical Manuscripts: Fresh Studies of an American Treasure Trove* (Atlanta: Society of Biblical Literature, 2006), 4–9.
3. See National Museum of Asian Art, press release, October 21, 2006, https://asia .si.edu/press-release/the-arthur-m-sackler-gallery-presents-in-the-beginning-bibles-before-the-year-1000/
4. National Museum of Asian Art, press release, October 21, 2006, https://asia.si .edu/press-release/the-arthur-m-sackler-gallery-presents-in-the-beginning-bibles-before-the-year-1000/
5. For images and information see the National Museum of African American History and Culture website, https://nmaahc.si.edu/object/nmaahc_2011.28. On Bibles and religion more broadly in this museum, see Judith Weisenfeld, "Religion on Display at the National Museum of African American History and Culture," *Sacred Matters* (January 3, 2017), https://sacredmattersmagazine.com/religion-on-display-at-the-national-museum-of-african-american-history-and-culture/
6. Victoria Dawson, "Nat Turner's Bible Gave the Enslaved Rebel the Resolve to Rise Up," *Smithsonian Magazine* (September 13, 2016), www.smithsonianmag.com/s mithsonian-institution/nat-turners-bible-inspiration-enslaved-rebel-rise-up -180960416/
7. For images see the National Museum of American History website, https:// americanhistory.si.edu/jeffersonbible/. For the fascinating story of this bible, see Peter Manseau, *The Jefferson Bible: A Biography* (Princeton: Princeton University Press, 2020).

8. Manseau, *Jefferson Bible.*
9. On "Bible" as cultural icon, see Timothy Beal, *The Rise and Fall of the Bible: The Unexpected History of an Accidental Book* (New York: Houghton Mifflin Harcourt, 2011), 1–12.
10. Timothy Beal, "Reception History and Beyond: Toward the Cultural History of Scriptures," *Biblical Interpretation* 19 (2011), 357–72.
11. "David Green," *Forbes,* https://www.forbes.com/profile/david-green/
12. For a recent catalogs of these scandals, see Jane Arraf, "After 'Missteps' and Controversies, Museum of the Bible Works to Clean Up Its Act," *NPR* (June 23, 2020), www.npr.org/2020/06/23/877581382/after-missteps-and-controversies -museum-of-the-bible-works-to-clean-up-its-act; and Erin L. Thompson, "That Robby Hobby," *Slate* (October 4, 2021); https://slate.com/news-and-politics/ 2021/10/museum-of-the-bible-looted-art-track-record.html. See also Candida R. Moss and Joel S. Baden, *Bible Nation: The United States of Hobby Lobby* (Princeton: Princeton University Press, 2017), esp. 22–61; Roberta Mazza, "The Green Papyri and the Museum of the Bible," in *The Museum of the Bible: A Critical Introduction,* edited by Jill Hicks-Keeton and Cavan Concannon (Lanham: Lexington Books/Fortress Academic, 2019), 171–206; and Morag M. Kersel, "Redemption for the Museum of the Bible? Artifacts, Provenance, the Display of Dead Sea Scrolls, and Bias in the Contact Zone," *Museum Management and Curatorship* 36, no. 3 (2021), 209–26.
13. Coptic Christian Romany Erian Melek Hetta has filed a civil complaint against the MOTB for being detained at security during an attempted visit to the museum in January 2018. For more context and helpful critique, see Amy Fallas, "American Protestantism's Commodification of the Middle East's 'Holy Lands,'" *Sojourners* (September 21, 2020), https://sojo .net/articles/american-protestantisms-commodification-middle-east-s-hol y-lands.
14. Current admission prices may be found on the Museum of the Bible website, https://museumofthebible.org/plan-your-visit
15. A MOTB Facebook post from October 20, 2015 explained the significance of the Codex Vaticanus this way: "The Codex Vaticanus is the most famous manuscript of the Bible in the possession of the Vatican library, thought to be from as early as the 4th Century. It's important for its quality and exten- siveness, but it's also believed to be one of the most reliable early biblical texts – written entirely in Greek and containing most of the New Testament, the Old Testament and many other books" (www.facebook.com/museumof theBible/posts/codex-vaticanus-hardly-a-household-term-i-grant-you-a-code x-simply-put-is-an-anc/861666237281669/).
16. Curation itself is also a category worth interrogating and is a constraining endeavor. On the Greens as curators, see Moss and Baden, *Bible Nation.*
17. Other attractions include a David-and-Goliath skeeball, an Esther pinball game, and a multilevel playscape structure themed as Noah's Ark.
18. For how such concerns governed the creation of another Bible-themed museum, see James Bielo, *Ark Encounter: The Making of a Creationist Theme Park* (New York: New York University Press, 2018).

19. Museum of the Bible website, www.museumofthebible.org/newsroom/muse
    um-of-the-bible-announces-amazing-grace-the-musical-to-inaugurate-its-new-
    world-stage-theater
20. Museum of the Bible website, www.museumofthebible.org/world-stage
21. On the entanglements of the research arm with evangelicalism, see especially
    Moss and Baden, *Bible Nation*, 62–98; and Jill Hicks-Keeton, "What the
    Museum of the Bible Conveys about Biblical Scholarship Behind Church
    Doors," *Religion & Politics* (March 13, 2018), https://religionandpolitics.org/
    2018/03/13/what-the-museum-of-the-bible-conveys-about-biblical-scholarship-
    behind-church-doors/. On the sectarianism of the MOTB's school curriculum,
    see Mark Chancey, "Can This Class Be Saved? The 'Hobby Lobby' Public School
    Bible Curriculum," Report from the Texas Freedom Network Education Fund,
    May 2014; and Moss and Baden, *Bible Nation*, 99–136.
22. David A. R. White, "God's Not Dead: A Light in the Darkness," Facebook
    (March 16, 2018), www.facebook.com/watch/?v=1696057123795813
23. A Twitter search with the hashtag #EFL20 reveals numerous photos of this
    event, including one in which Lauren Green McAfee, daughter of Steve
    Green, appears on stage.
24. Jenna Browder, "Excruciating Pain Left Fox Anchor Shannon Bream in
    Total Despair, then She Heard the Voice of God," *CBN* (January 23, 2020),
    www1.cbn.com/cbnnews/us/2019/may/fox-news-anchor-opens-up-about-
    life-faith-i-just-try-to-be-open-to-what-the-lord-may-have-nbsp
25. *Colorado Times Recorder* (January 23, 2020), https://coloradotimesrecorder
    .com/2020/01/devos-weighs-in-on-abortion-funding-religious-schools
    /20864/
26. Nicole Guadiano, "DeVos Compares Abortion Rights Debate to Slavery,"
    Politico (January 23, 2020), www.politico.com/news/2020/01/23/devos-
    compares-abortion-rights-debate-to-slavery-102895
27. Moss and Baden, *Bible Nation*, 44–45.
28. John Fea, "Letting the Bible Do Its Work on Behalf of Christian America:
    The Founding Era at the Museum of the Bible," in Hicks-Keeton and
    Concannon (eds.), *Museum of the Bible: A Critical Introduction*, 229–32. Fea
    builds on his earlier work on the American Bible Society: John Fea, *The
    Bible Cause: A History of the American Bible Society* (Oxford: Oxford University
    Press, 2016).
29. *Washington Post* (December 23, 2020), www.washingtonpost.com/religion/
    2020/12/23/bible-museum-covid-restrictions-lawsuit/
30. *New York Times* (April 5, 2020), www.nytimes.com/2020/04/05/arts/bible-mu
    seum-artifacts.html; *Vox* (November 17, 2017), www.vox.com/identities/2017/
    11/17/16658504/bible-museum-hobby-lobby-green-controversy-antiquities;
    Politico, October (15, 2017), www.politico.com/magazine/story/2017/10/15/
    just-what-is-the-museum-of-the-bible-trying-to-do-215711/. For the official state-
    ments by the US Department of Justice, see www.justice.gov/opa/pr/rare-cunei
    form-tablet-bearing-portion-epic-gilgamesh-forfeited-united-states and www.just
    ice.gov/usao-edny/pr/united-states-files-civil-action-forfeit-thousands-
    ancient-iraqi-artifacts-imported
31. Moss and Baden, *Bible Nation*, 22–98.

32. This approach represents a development from our 2019 book *The Museum of the Bible: A Critical Edition* (Lanham: Lexington/Fortress Academic). We regard that volume to be an invaluable tool for studying and contextualizing the museum, even as our own orientation to the material has evolved.

33. Lauren R. Kerby, *Saving History: How White Evangelicals Tour the Nation's Capital and Redeem a Christian America* (Chapel Hill: University of North Carolina Press, 2020).

34. For a recent and particularly accessible treatment of white Christian privilege in the United States, see Khyati Y. Joshi, *White Christian Privilege: The Illusion of Religious Equality in America* (New York: New York University Press, 2020).

35. On Bible boosterism inside the museum itself, see especially Margaret M. Mitchell, "'It's Complicated.' 'No, It's Not.': The Museum of the Bible, Problems and Solutions," in Hicks-Keeton and Concannon (eds.), *Museum of the Bible: A Critical Introduction*, 13–14.

36. Vincent Wimbush, *White Men's Magic: Scripturalization as Slavery* (Oxford: Oxford University Press, 2012), 12.

37. This has been a foundational concern for feminist biblical criticism since its inception. Feminist biblical criticism has often been shunted to the margins of "malestream" biblical scholarship, but it has consistently pushed the guild to focus on the ethics of interpretation rather than on the establishment of a scientific process for fixing historical meaning. On this see the foundational work of Elisabeth Schüssler Fiorenza, *Rhetoric and Ethic: The Politics of Biblical Studies* (Minneapolis: Fortress Press, 1999). Here we also draw on the interventions of Timothy Beal, who pushes biblical scholarship to move beyond reception history to analysis of "the cultural history of the Bible, in all its material, literary, and ideal forms … pursued as a subfield within the cultural history of scriptures within academic religious studies" ("Reception History and Beyond," 371).

38. In this we are thinking with Wimbush's notion of "scripturalization" (*White Men's Magic*, 9), which has been helpfully applied to the study of American religious history by Seth Perry in *Bible Culture and Authority in the Early United States* (Princeton: Princeton University Press, 2018).

CHAPTER 1 PROVENANCE

1. For an introduction to some of these scandals, see Roberta Mazza, "The Green Papyri and the Museum of the Bible," in *The Museum of the Bible: A Critical Introduction*, edited by Jill Hicks-Keeton and Cavan Concannon (Lanham: Lexington Books/Fortress Academic, 2019), 171–206. See also Brent Nongbri, who has blogged extensively on the details involved in these controversies, https://brentnongbri.com. A good summary of the museum's scandals can be found in Erin L. Thompson, "That Robby Hobby," *Slate* (October 4, 2021); https://slate.com/news-and-politics/2021/10/museum-of-the-bible-looted-art-track-record.html. For the official statements by the US Department of Justice, see www.justice.gov/opa/pr/rare-cuneiform-tablet-bearing-portion-epic-gilgamesh-forfeited-united-states and www.justice.gov/usao-edny/pr/unit ed-states-files-civil-action-forfeit-thousands-ancient-iraqi-artifacts-imported

2. For important discussions of how provenance has emerged as a central concern in museum studies, see Gail Feigenbaum and Inge Reist (eds.), *Provenance: An Alternate History of Art* (Los Angeles: Getty Research Institute, 2012); Jane Milosch and Nick Pearce (eds.), *Collecting and Provenance: A Multidisciplinary Approach* (Lanham: Roman & Littlefield, 2019).

3. On provenance research, see Nancy Yeide, Konstantin Akinsha, and Amy Walsh, *The AAM Guide to Provenance Research* (Washington DC: American Association of Museums, 2001).

4. Milosch and Pearce, "Introduction," in *Collecting and Provenance*, xv.

5. Our characterization of white evangelicalism as an assemblage is indebted to William Connolly's notion of an "evangelical-capitalist resonance machine" (*Christianity and Capitalism, American Style* [Durham: Duke University Press, 2008]). We owe the idea that white evangelicals comprise a sect within evangelicalism to Tad Delay, *Against: What Does the White Evangelical Want?* (Eugene: Cascade, 2019).

6. See, for example, Sarah Posner, *Unholy: Why White Evangelicals Worship at the Altar of Donald Trump* (New York: Random House, 2020); and John Fea, *Believe Me: The Evangelical Road to Trump* (Grand Rapids: Eerdmans, 2018).

7. Robert P. Jones, *White Too Long: The Legacy of White Supremacy in American Christianity* (New York: Simon & Schuster, 2020); Khyati Y. Joshi, *White Christian Privilege: The Illusion of Religious Equality in America* (New York: New York University Press, 2020); Jemar Tisby, *The Color of Compromise: The Truth about the American Church's Complicity in Racism* (Grand Rapids: Zondervan, 2020).

8. Anthea Butler, *White Evangelical Racism: The Politics of Morality in America* (Chapel Hill: University of North Carolina Press, 2021), 3.

9. On the problems with using "belief" as a central element in a definition of religion, see Brent Nongbri, *Before Religion: A History of a Modern Concept* (New Haven: Yale University Press, 2013).

10. David Bebbington, *Evangelicalism in Modern Britain* (London: Routledge, 1989), 2–3. The same definition is used to describe the early phase of the evangelical movement by Matthew A. Sutton, *American Apocalypse: A History of Modern Evangelicalism* (Cambridge, MA: Belknap Press of Harvard University Press, 2014), x. Mark Noll makes use of Bebbington's definition, but notes that the four different elements "do not exist in the same proportions or exert the same effects in all times and places" (Mark Noll, *The Rise of Evangelicalism: The Age of Edwards, Whitefield, and the Wesleys* [Downers Grove, IL: IVP Academic, 2003], 17–18). For a discussion of the reception of Bebbington's quadrilateral, see Mark Noll, David Bebbington, and George Marsden (eds.), *Evangelicals: Who They Have Been, Are Now, and Could Be* (Grand Rapids: Eerdmans, 2019).

11. "What is an Evangelical?," National Association of Evangelicals, www.nae.net/what-is-an-evangelical/

12. Timothy Gloege, "#itsnotus: Being Evangelical Means Never Having to Say You're Sorry," *Religion Dispatches* (January 3, 2018), https://religiondispatches.org/itsnotus-being-evangelical-means-never-having-to-say-youre-sorry/

13. Gloege, "#itsnotus."

14. Thomas S. Kidd, *Who is an Evangelical?: The History of a Movement in Crisis* (New Haven: Yale University Press, 2019), 4.

15. Kidd, *Who is an Evangelical*, 4.

16. Kristin Kobes Du Mez, *Jesus and John Wayne: How White Evangelicals Corrupted a Faith and Fractured a Nation* (New York: Liveright Publishing, 2020), 6.

17. Eric C. Miller, "Who Is an Evangelical? An Interview with Thomas Kidd," *Religion and Politics* (January 14, 2020), https://religionandpolitics.org/202 0/01/14/who-is-an-evangelical-an-interview-with-thomas-kidd/

18. An alternative use of ideational concepts to mark modern American evangelicalism is offered by Molly Worthen, who argues that "evangelical" names communities marked by anxiety over the individual's relationship to god, faith and reason, and secularism in the American public square. See Molly Worthen, *Apostles of Reason: The Crisis of Authority in American Evangelicalism* (Oxford: Oxford University Press, 2004); and Molly Worthen, "Defining Evangelicalism: Questions that Complement the Quadrilateral," *Fides et Historia* 47, no. 1 (2015), 83–86. What is useful about Worthen's approach is that she eschews insider theological terms in her definition, which means that she can read evangelicals as enmeshed in debates that affect the wider society. She also sees her definition as temporary, local, and heuristic, meaning that new definitions are needed for different time periods and contexts.

19. One can see the visceral struggle over definition in Douglas Sweeney's survey of the various types of definitions offered by scholars (*The American Evangelical Story: A History of the Movement* [Grand Rapids, MI: Baker, 2005], 17–25). Sweeney writes as an evangelical and resists the various modes of classification that have been offered.

20. Mark Noll, *The Scandal of the Evangelical Mind* (Grand Rapids, MI: Eerdmans, 1994), 8.

21. As do Melani McAlister, *The Kingdom of God Has No Borders: A Global History of American Evangelicals* (Oxford: Oxford University Press, 2018); Mark Hutchinson and John Wolffe, *A Short History of Global Evangelicalism* (Cambridge: Cambridge University Press, 2012); Paul Freston, *Evangelicals and Politics in Africa, Asia and Latin America* (Cambridge: Cambridge University Press, 2001); and Orlando E. Costas, "Evangelical Theology in the Two-Thirds World," in *Earthen Vessels: American Evangelicals and Foreign Missions, 1880–1980*, edited by Joel A. Carpenter and Wilbert R. Shenk (Grand Rapids: Eerdmans, 1990), 235–50.

22. Du Mez, *Jesus and John Wayne*, 7–11; Daniel Vaca, *Evangelicals Incorporated: Books and the Business of Religion in America* (Cambridge: Harvard University Press, 2019).

23. Mike Altman, "'Religion, Religions, Religious' in America: Toward a Smithian Account of 'Evangelicalism,'" *Method and Theory in the Study of Religion* 31, no. 1 (2019), 71–82; Jon Butler, "Enthusiasm Described and Decried: The Great Awakening as Interpretative Fiction," *The Journal of American History* 69, no. 2 (1982): 305–25; Linford Fisher, "Evangelicals and Unevangelicals: The Contested History of a Word, 1500–1950," *Religion and American Culture* 26, no. 2 (2016), 184–226; D. G. Hart, *Deconstructing*

Evangelicalism: Conservative Protestantism in the Age of Billy Graham (Grand Rapids: Baker Academic, 2004).

24. This fourfold division of time largely follows that of Sutton, *American Apocalypse*, x.

25. Butler, "Enthusiasm Described and Decried"; Frank Lambert, *Inventing the "Great Awakening"* (Princeton: Princeton University Press, 1999); Thomas S. Kidd, *The Great Awakening: The Roots of Evangelical Christianity in Colonial America* (New Haven: Yale University Press, 2008).

26. Harry S. Stout, "What Made the Great Awakening Great?," in *Turning Points in the History of American Evangelicalism*, edited by Heath W. Carter and Laura Rominger Porter (Grand Rapids: Eerdmans, 2017), 1–18; Jerome Dean Mahaffey, *Preaching Politics: The Religious Rhetoric of George Whitefield and the Founding of a New Nation* (Waco: Baylor University Press, 2007); J. D. Dickey, *American Demagogue: The Great Awakening and the Rise and Fall of Populism* (New York: Pegasus Books, 2019).

27. Jon Butler, "Disestablishment as American Sisyphus," in Carter and Rominger (eds.), *Turning Points*, 44–64. Noll remarks on the effects of disestablishment: "The national government refused to support any particular denomination. The consequences for the churches were immense. They were now compelled to compete for adherents. ... The primary way the churches accomplished this task was through the techniques of revival – direct, fervent address aimed at convincing, convicting, and enlisting the individual" (Noll, *Scandal of the Evangelical Mind*, 66).

28. Noll, *Scandal of the Evangelical Mind*, 75. For further discussion of evangelicals and the Enlightenment in the early US, see Catherine A. Brekus, "The Evangelical Encounter with the Enlightenment," in Carter and Rominger (eds.), *Turning Points*, 19–43.

29. Nathan Hatch notes that this was a period in which elite expertise was challenged on a number of fronts in the name of democratic individualism and the common sense of direct experience and perception (Nathan Hatch, *The Democratization of American Christianity* [New Haven: Yale University Press, 1989], 17–46).

30. Albert J. Raboteau, *Slave Religion: The "Invisible Institution" in the Antebellum South* (Oxford: Oxford University Press, 2004), 128–50; Sylvia Frey and Betty Wood, *Come Shouting to Zion: African American Protestantism in the American South and British Caribbean to 1830* (Chapel Hill: University of North Carolina Press, 1998).

31. Sam Haselby, *The Origins of American Religious Nationalism* (Oxford: Oxford University Press, 2016); Tracy Fessenden, *Culture and Redemption: Religion, the Secular, and American Literature* (Princeton: Princeton University Press, 2013); Amanda Porterfield, *Conceived in Doubt: Religion and Politics in the New American Nation* (Chicago: University of Chicago Press, 2012); John Lardas Modern, *Secularism in Antebellum America* (Chicago: University of Chicago Press, 2015); David Sehat, *The Myth of American Religious Freedom* (Oxford: Oxford University Press, 2011).

32. Stephen Moore and Yvonne Sherwood, *The Invention of the Biblical Scholar: A Critical Manifesto* (Minneapolis: Fortress Press, 2011), 47.

33. Mark A. Noll, *The Civil War as a Theological Crisis* (Chapel Hill: University of North Carolina Press, 2006), 17–20. Noll locates the origins of these dispositions in the Scottish Enlightenment. On this see George Marsden, *Fundamentalism and American Culture: The Shaping of Twentieth-Century Evangelicalism 1870–1925* (Oxford: Oxford University Press, 1980), 55–61; and Mark Noll, "Common Sense Traditions and American Evangelical Thought," *American Quarterly* 37, no. 2 (1985), 216–38.

34. Noll, *Civil War*, 34.

35. As Noll argues, "By 1860 a substantial majority of articulate Americans had come to hold a number of corollary beliefs about the Bible – specifically, that besides its religious uses, it also promoted republican political theory, that it was accessible to every sentient person, that it defined the glories of liberty, that it opposed the tyranny of inherited religious authority, that it forecast the providential destiny of the United States, and that it was best interpreted by the common sense of ordinary people" (*Civil War*, 22).

36. John Fea, *The Bible Cause: A History of the American Bible Society* (Oxford: Oxford University Press, 2016); Peter J. Wosh, *Spreading the Word: The Bible Business in Nineteenth-Century America* (Ithaca: Cornell University Press, 1994).

37. Timothy Beal, *The Rise and Fall of the Bible: The Unexpected History of an Accidental Book* (New York: Houghton Mifflin Harcourt, 2011), 7.

38. "A wide range of Protestants were discovering that the Bible they had relied on for building up America's republican civilization was not nearly as univocal, not nearly as easy to interpret, not nearly as inherently unifying for an overwhelmingly Christian people, as they once had thought" (Noll, *Civil War*, 32–33).

39. J. Albert Harrill, *Slaves in the New Testament: Literary, Social, and Moral Dimensions* (Minneapolis: Fortress Press, 2006), 165–92.

40. Noll, *Civil War*, 34.

41. Noll, *Civil War*, 40.

42. Noll puts it nicely: "The supreme crisis over the Bible was that there existed no apparent biblical resolution to the crisis [of what the Bible said about slavery] ... [I]t was left to those consummate theologians, the Reverend Doctors Ulysses S. Grant and William Tecumseh Sherman, to decide what in fact the Bible actually meant" (*Civil War*, 50).

43. Luke E. Harlow, "The Civil War and the Making of Conservative American Evangelicalism," in Carter and Rominger (eds.), *Turning Points*, 107–32.

44. Walter Rauschenbusch, *Christianity and the Social Crisis* (New York: Macmillan, 1907).

45. Christopher H. Evans, *The Social Gospel in American Religion: A History* (New York: New York University Press, 2017).

46. Butler, *White Evangelical Racism*, 23–32.

47. Harlow, "Civil War," 130–31.

48. As Harlow notes, redemption became a popular biblical metaphor for southern whites during Reconstruction, who looked for redemption from a sinful North that had oppressed them and overturned the natural order of white supremacy ("Civil War," 126–30).

49. Timothy Gloege, *Guaranteed Pure: The Moody Bible Institute, Business, and the Making of Modern Evangelicalism* (Chapel Hill: University of North Carolina Press, 2015).
50. Marsden's description of how Scottish Common Sense traditions shaped dispensational readings of the Bible remains apt: "Common Sense philosophy affirmed their ability to know 'the facts' directly. With the Scriptures at hand as a compendium of facts, there was no need to go further. They needed only to classify the facts, and to follow wherever they might lead" (*Fundamentalism and American Culture,* 56).
51. B. M. Pietsch, *Dispensational Modernism* (Oxford: Oxford University Press, 2015).
52. Pietsch, *Dispensational Modernism,* 4.
53. Harlow, "Civil War," 131.
54. "'Inerrancy,' which was to become a code word for much of the fundamentalist movement, had a scientific quality that was related to the view of truth as directly apprehended facts. It was vital to the dispensationalists that their information be not only absolutely reliable but also precise. Statements found in Scripture would not deviate from the exact truth" (Marsden, *Fundamentalism and American Culture,* 56–57).
55. Darren Dochuk, *Anointed with Oil: How Christianity and Crude Made Modern America* (New York: Basic Books, 2019). Dochuk argues that western oil barons found common cause with forms of conservative and dispensational theology in what he calls "wildcat Christianity," arguing that there was a unique fit between theology and their business practices.
56. Sutton, *American Apocalypse,* 47–78.
57. John Compton, *The End of Empathy: Why White Protestants Stopped Loving Their Neighbors* (Oxford: Oxford University Press, 2020), 46–49. On the Klan, see also Kelly J. Baker, *Gospel According to the Klan: The KKK's Appeal to Protestant America, 1915–1930* (Lawrence: University Press of Kansas, 2011).
58. Sutton, *American Apocalypse,* 148–77. See also Adam Laats, *Fundamentalism and Education in the Scopes Era: God, Darwin, and the Roots of America's Culture Wars* (New York: Palgrave Macmillan, 2010).
59. Compton, *End of Empathy,* 82–86.
60. Compton, *End of Empathy,* 97–104, 111–15.
61. Bethany Moreton, *To Serve God and Wal-Mart: The Making of Christian Free Enterprise* (Cambridge, MA: Harvard University Press, 2009).
62. Darren E. Grem, *The Blessings of Business: How Corporations Shaped Conservative Christianity* (Oxford: Oxford University Press, 2016), 49–52.
63. Kevin M. Kruse, *One Nation Under God: How Corporate America Invented Christian America* (New York: Basic Books, 2015).
64. Butler, *White Evangelical Racism,* 39–52.
65. Compton, *End of Empathy,* 147–48; Grem, *Blessings of Business,* 49–81.
66. Darren Dochuk, *From the Bible Belt to the Sun Belt: Plain Folk Religion, Grassroots Politics, and the Rise of Evangelical Conservatism* (New York: W. W. Norton, 2011).
67. Compton, *End of Empathy,* 1–42.
68. Compton, *End of Empathy,* 199–228.
69. Dochuk, *From the Bible Belt,* xiv.

70. Dochuk, *From the Bible Belt*, 32–33.
71. On Christian use of popular media, see Paul Apostolidis, *Stations of the Cross: Adorno and Christian Right Radio* (Durham: Duke University Press, 2000); Shayne Lee and Phillip Luke Sinitiere, *Holy Mavericks: Evangelical Innovators and the Spiritual Marketplace* (New York: New York University Press, 2009).
72. Connolly, *Capitalism and Christianity*, 39–68; Delay, *Against*, 103–26.
73. Dochuk, *From the Bible Belt*, 259–396.
74. Compton, *End of Empathy*, 252–57; Butler, *White Evangelical Racism*, 60–62; David Swartz, *Moral Minority: The Evangelical Left in an Age of Conservatism* (Philadelphia: University of Pennsylvania Press, 2014).
75. Randall Balmer, *Thy Kingdom Come: How the Religious Right Distorts Faith and Threatens America* (New York: Basic Books, 2007), 1–34.
76. On this see Anne Nelson, *Shadow Network: Media, Money, and the Secret Hub of the Radical Right* (New York: Bloomsbury, 2019); Jeff Sharlet, *The Family: The Secret Fundamentalism at the Heart of American Power* (New York: Harper Perennial, 2008); Susan F. Harding, *The Book of Jerry Falwell: Fundamentalist Language and Politics* (Princeton: Princeton University Press, 2000); and Compton, *End of Empathy*, 257–78.
77. Bruno Latour, *The Pasteurization of France* (Cambridge, MA: Harvard University Press, 1988), 16.
78. See the useful summary of the family's causes in Candida Moss and Joel Baden, *Bible Nation: The United States of Hobby Lobby* (Princeton: Princeton University Press, 2017), 1–14.
79. This is documented by Steve Green in his book *Faith in America: The Powerful Impact of One Company Speaking Out Boldly* (Decatur: Looking Glass Books, 2011).
80. Wosh, *Spreading the Word*; Nord, *Faith in Reading*.
81. Bruce Barton, *The Man Nobody Knows* (Indianapolis: Bobbs-Merrill, 1925). According to Grem, "Barton collapsed the 'corporation' into 'the church,' with Jesus serving as a divine corporate executive and moral exemplar. No callous teacher of corporate strong-arming, Barton's Jesus was more than an executive. He was 'The Leader' and 'The Master' who taught that all must reject the bottom-line 'temptation of material success.' True leaders and masters of business sought out greatness by becoming the 'servant to all,' a progressive vision of the ideal corporate executive" (*Blessings of Business*, 18).
82. This was the impetus for the formation of the Pew Memorial Trust and Pew Freedom Trust out of capital earned by J. Howard Pew and Joseph N. Pew Jr. through the success of Sun Oil Company (Darren Dochuk, *Anointed with Oil*, 330).
83. Gloege, *Guaranteed Pure*, 21–22, 26, 59–60. Moody was also the beneficiary of money from the Rockefellers (Dochuk, *Anointed with Oil*, 159).
84. Robert F. Martin, *Hero of the Heartland: Billy Sunday and the Transformation of American Society, 1862–1935* (Bloomington: Indiana University Press, 2002), 58; Dochuk, *Anointed with Oil*, 169.
85. Dochuk, *From the Bible Belt*.
86. Dochuk, *Anointed with Oil*, 353. His production company produced two movies that told the story of oilmen who came to find Christ, making a connection between rags-to-riches entrepreneurialism and Christian

NOTES TO PAGES 34–36

faith that would benefit both evangelical ministries and corporate interests in selling the virtues of Christian capitalism (353–57). This stood in contrast to contemporary Hollywood portrayals of greedy oilmen, echoed more recently in the character of Daniel Plainview (played by Daniel Day-Lewis) in Paul Thomas Anderson's *There Will Be Blood* (2007).

87. Kruse, *One Nation Under God*, 36–39, 49–57.
88. Grem, *Blessings of Business*, 49–70.
89. These examples further help us to see the role and function of what B. M. Pietsch has called the "power of lay money" in American religion ("Lyman Stewart and Early Fundamentalism," *Church History* 82, no. 3 (2013), 645).
90. This is the important point made by Darren Dochuk, who traces the flow of oil money through both evangelical and progressive Christian groups (*Anointed with Oil*).
91. Gloege, *Guaranteed Pure*, 117.
92. Gloege, *Guaranteed Pure*, 122–61.
93. Grem, *Blessings of Business*, 21.
94. A key to this project of brand management was the reliance on select faculty members as the face of the institute's brand. MBI relied heavily on the charismatic and popular evangelist Reuben Torry and the respected academic James M. Gray (Gloege, *Guaranteed Pure*, 123–27).
95. The racist logic of the MBI began with its founder, who preached to segregated crowds, built alliances with supporters of the "lost cause," and used racialized language in his preaching (Gloege, *Guaranteed Pure*, 51–52).
96. Gloege, *Guaranteed Pure*, 217–19. Gloege also notes that MBI segregated its Black students (159–60).
97. We owe this insight to Steve Friesen, who pointed out the MOTB's class coding in a panel discussion with us at the Southwest Commission on Religious Studies in 2018.
98. On Stewart's career and role in funding fundamentalist causes, see Robert Martin Krivoshey, "'Going Through the Eye of the Needle': The Life of Oilman Fundamentalist Lyman Stewart, 1840–1923," unpublished PhD dissertation, University of Chicago, 1973; Pietsch, "Lyman Stewart," 617–46; Darren Dochuk, "Fighting for the Fundamentals: Lyman Stewart and the Protestant Politics of Oil," in *Faithful Republic: Religion and Politics in Modern America*, edited by Andrew Preston, Bruce Schulman, and Julian Zelizer (Philadelphia: University of Pennsylvania Press, 2015), 41–55; Dochuk, *Anointed with Oil*, 130–35, 171–76; and Gloege, *Guaranteed Pure*, 162–92.
99. Gloege, *Guaranteed Pure*, 165.
100. Pietsch notes that by 1884 Union Oil was a $125 million company with more than 800,000 acres of land in the western United States ("Lyman Stewart," 617).
101. Stewart had earlier run up against the problem of how to make sure that his bequests went to causes he supported. In 1906 he had given $3,000 to Occidental College's Bible department, but soon grew frustrated that this donation did not give him a say in hiring or curricula (Gloege, *Guaranteed Pure*, 166).

102. Museum of the Bible website, www.museumofthebible.org/leadership
103. Pietsch, "Lyman Stewart," 628–29; Dochuk, "Lyman Stewart," 50. While he gave vast sums to Christian institutions like BIOLA, he also heavily supported foreign missionaries (Dochuk, "Lyman Stewart," 50–53).
104. "*The Fundamentals* would not have existed without – as the first volume's title page stated – the 'Compliments of Two Christian Laymen.' The "laymen" were executives at Union Oil, Lyman and Milton Stewart" (Grem, *Blessings of Business*, 21).
105. Ernest Sandeen, "Towards a Historical Interpretation of the Origins of Fundamentalism," *Church History* 36 (1967), 77–81.
106. On Stewart's role, see Gloege, *Guaranteed Pure*, 162–92.
107. Gloege, *Guaranteed Pure*, 163.
108. Gloege, *Guaranteed Pure*, 178.
109. Gloege, *Guaranteed Pure*, 191; Benedict Anderson, *Imagined Communities: Reflections On the Origin and Spread of Nationalism* (New York: Verso, 2006).
110. Dochuk quotes Stewart as claiming, "Recognizing the fact that we are the Lord's stewards, and that soon we must give an account of our stewardship … it has been my purpose to have the means which the Lord has entrusted to me transmuted into living gospel truth, as far as possible, during my lifetime" (Dochuk, "Lyman Stewart," 50).
111. Pietsch, "Lyman Stewart," 628.
112. Pietsch, "Lyman Stewart," 631–33. He was a supporter of the California Progressive Party, worried about economic inequality, campaigned against immigration restrictions, and fought against the power of monopolies, embodied for Stewart by the colossus that was his major economic opponent, Rockefeller's Standard Oil.
113. Dochuk, *Anointed with Oil*, 90–92.
114. Dochuk, *Anointed with Oil*, 158–70.
115. Compton, *End of Empathy*, 22–27.
116. Dochuk, *Anointed with Oil*, 12.
117. Dochuk, *Anointed with Oil*, 12.
118. Dochuk, *Anointed with Oil*, 330–31.
119. Compton, *End of Empathy*, 130–31.
120. The fight against the New Deal preceded concerns over Communism in the 1950s. The first threat that conservatives attacked was collectivism at home, rather than Communism abroad (Kruse, *One Nation Under God*, 22).
121. Kruse, *One Nation Under God*, 4–6.
122. Clergymen became useful because "As men of God, they could give voice to the same conservative complaints as business leaders, but without any suspicion that they were motivated solely by self-interest. In doing so, they could push back against claims that business had somehow sinned and the welfare state was doing God's work." (Kruse, *One Nation Under God*, 6).
123. Compton shows how Pew pumped large amounts of money into Fifield's project, with little return on the investment (*End of Empathy*, 97–101). One of the problems that beset those who tried to integrate Christian theology with libertarian economics was that there wasn't much biblical or theological material to draw from. See also Kruse, *One Nation Under God*, 8–20.

124. Compton, *End of Empathy*, 101–02.
125. Dochuk, *Anointed with Oil*, 335–36.
126. Grem, *Blessings of Business*, 54–55.
127. Compton, *End of Empathy*, 85.
128. Dochuk, *Anointed with Oil*, 332, 335.
129. Compton, *End of Empathy*, 154–55.
130. Grem, *Blessings of Business*, 49–51; Compton, *End of Empathy*, 156.
131. Compton, *End of Empathy*, 157–63.
132. Dochuk, *From the Bible Belt*, 120.
133. Dochuk, *Anointed with Oil*, 336–38.
134. Dochuk, *Anointed with Oil*, 325–27. It would also serve as a launch pad for the neo-Pentecostal movement in the 1980s that currently serves as one of President Trump's most loyal bases. See the important work of Brad Christerson and Richard Flory, *The Rise of Network Christianity: How Independent Leaders are Changing the Religious Landscape* (Oxford: Oxford University Press, 2017).
135. Christerson and Flory, *Rise of Network Christianity*.
136. Compton, *End of Empathy*, 111–13.
137. This is the argument of Compton's *End of Empathy*, summarized most clearly at 17–42.
138. Grem, *Blessings of Business*, 27.
139. Grem, *Blessings of Business*, 32–33.
140. His four part test was "(1) Is it the TRUTH? (2) Is it FAIR to all concerned? (3) Will it build GOODWILL and better friendships? (4) Will it be BENEFICIAL to all concerned?" (cited in Grem, *Blessings of Business*, 33).
141. Sarah Ruth Hammond, *God's Businessmen: Entrepreneurial Evangelicals in Depression and War* (Chicago: University of Chicago Press, 2017), 113.
142. Moreton, *To Serve God and Wal-Mart*, 100–73.
143. "Taylor's Four-Way Test brought him cross-over appeal with nonevangelical groups in Chicago, especially with those he would have considered liberal or 'modernistic' Protestants. The Rotarian creed also aligned with Taylor's test and undoubtedly informed it. In part, the creed was the product of liberal Protestant approaches to managing corporate power, wedded to Taylor's concerns about state involvement in business. The test linked businessmen's authority to social service and welfare ... [T]he creed was a precursor to the mid-century managerial philosophy of 'servant leadership,' which would become a mantra in evangelical, service-oriented firms like ServiceMaster, Wal-Mart, and Chick-fil-A" (Grem, *Blessings of Business*, 33–34).
144. Hammond, *God's Businessmen*, 101–02.
145. Grem, *Blessings of Business*, 44; Hammond, *God's Businessmen*, 123. Taylor became a financial supporter of Fuller Seminary as a trustee in 1947.
146. Grem, *Blessings of Business*, 45.
147. Grem, *Blessings of Business*, 38.
148. Hammond, *God's Businessmen*, 104.
149. *The Week*, https://theweek.com/articles/446097/stop-calling-hobby-lobby-christian-business

150. This is a key point made by Moreton, *To Serve God and Wal-Mart*. The Greens have spelled out this vision in their books: David Green, with Dean Merrill, *More Than a Hobby: How a $600 Startup Became America's Home and Craft Superstore* (Nashville: Thomas Nelson, 2005); David Green, with Bill High, *Giving It All Away . . . and Getting It All Back Again: The Way of Living Generously* (Grand Rapids: Zondervan, 2017); Steve Green, *Faith in America: The Powerful Impact of One Company Speaking Out Boldly* (Decatur: Looking Glass Books, 2011).

151. Pietsch, "Lyman Stewart," 646.

152. Gregory L. Cuéllar, *Empire, the British Museum, and the Making of the Biblical Scholar in the Nineteenth Century: Archival Criticism* (London: Palgrave Macmillan, 2019).

153. Mark Chancey, "Museum of the Bible's Politicized Holy Land Trip for Students," in Hicks-Keeton and Concannon (eds.), *Museum of the Bible: A Critical Introduction*, 275–94.

154. These are the Richard and Helen DeVos Foundation, the Dick and Betsy DeVos Family Foundation, the Jerry and Marcy Tubergen Foundation, and the Douglas and Marla DeVos Foundation.

155. Fellowship of Companies for Christ International website, https://fcci.org /about-us/

156. DeSmog website, www.desmogblog.com/thirteen-foundation

157. Right-Wing Watch website, www.rightwingwatch.org/post/the-wilks-brothers-fracking-sugar-daddies-for-the-far-right/

158. https://www.philcooke.com/fundraising-and-donor-development-an-interview-with-museum-of-the-bibles-jon-sharpe/

CHAPTER 2 GOOD BOOK

1. To take one example, a museum press release from July 2020 indicates that MOTB "partnered with Trinity Broadcasting Network (TBN) to produce The Truth I'm Standing On, a concert featuring high-profile recording artists sharing songs about healing during this difficult time for our country and world" (www.museumofthebible.org/press/press-releases/museum-of-the-bible-and-tbn-gather-major-recording-artists-for-the-truth-im-standing-on -televised-concert). The two-part event was filmed at MOTB and was broadcast on TBN as part of the museum's response to the COVID-19 pandemic.

2. Including the famous "texts of terror" so-named by Phyllis Trible (*Texts of Terror: Literary-Feminist Readings of Biblical Narratives* [Minneapolis: Fortress Press, 1984]).

3. On interrogating the Bible's constructed and imagined "goodness" with respect to the apostle Paul, see Cavan Concannon, *Profaning Paul* (Chicago: University of Chicago Press, 2021).

4. Lauren R. Kerby, *Saving History: How White Evangelicals Tour the Nation's Capital and Redeem a Christian America* (Chapel Hill: University of North Carolina Press, 2020), 29. See also Paul Thomas, *Storytelling the Bible at the Creation Museum, Ark Encounter, and the Museum of the Bible* (London: T&T Clark, 2020). On heritage as a way of making meaning out the past (in contrast to "history"), see David Lowenthal, *The Heritage Crusade and the Spoils of History*

(Cambridge: Cambridge University Press, 1998). For a discussion of the boundaries of the category "white evangelical," see Introduction.

5. See, for example, Andrew Tobolowsky, "Did History Really Happen? Colin Kaepernick, MLK, and Historical Hindsight," *Eidolon* (April 13, 2018).

6. Mark A. Noll, *The Civil War as a Theological Crisis* (Chapel Hill: University of North Carolina Press, 2006), 31–51.

7. On the failure of the MOTB to represent Black Christianity, see Terrence Johnson, "Exploring Race, Religion, and Slavery at the Museum of the Bible," in *The Museum of the Bible: A Critical Introduction*, edited by Jill Hicks-Keeton and Cavan Concannon (Lanham: Lexington Books/ Fortress Academic, 2019), 37–46.

8. Steven K. Green has shown that the Mayflower Compact became an important part of myth of Christian nationalism only after the fact (*Inventing a Christian America: The Myth of the Religious Founding* [Oxford: Oxford University Press, 2015], 74–77).

9. According to the MOTB's signage, the "Native headdress" was presented to Billy Graham in 1974 during a rally in Phoenix, Arizona. The object is listed with a catalog number of IL 2017.002.002 and comes from the collection of the Billy Graham Library. The evangelist's name is spelled in beads on the headband.

10. Margaret M. Mitchell, "'It's Complicated.' 'No, It's Not.': The Museum of the Bible, Problems and Solutions," in Hicks-Keeton and Concannon (eds.), *Museum of the Bible: A Critical Introduction*, 13–14.

11. See the assessment of Stephen L. Young, "Religious Freedom for a Christian America: 'Don't You Agree?,'" in Hicks-Keeton and Concannon (eds.), *Museum of the Bible: A Critical Introduction*, 235–54. See also Thomas, *Storytelling the Bible*, 150–54.

12. Tisa Wenger, *Religious Freedom: The Contested History of an American Ideal* (Chapel Hill: University of North Carolina Press, 2017), 1.

13. Kerby, *Saving History*.

14. Kerby, *Saving History*, 6.

15. Mitchell, "'It's Complicated,'" 3–36.

16. The MOTB here repeats an interpretive move employed in "Passages," the DC museum's traveling precursor exhibition (Candida Moss and Joel Baden, *Bible Nation: The United States of Hobby Lobby* [Princeton: Princeton University Press, 2017], 161).

17. "Book Minute" does not mention slavery: https://www.museumofthebible.org /book/minutes/520

18. The reproduction can be seen in a MOTB-produced video on their website: https://www.museumofthebible.org/book/minutes/785

19. Stephen J. Stein, "George Whitefield on Slavery: Some New Evidence," *Church History* 42, no. 2 (1973), 243–56.

20. Allan Gallay, "The Origins of Slaveholders' Paternalism: George Whitefield, the Bryan Family, and the Great Awakening in the South," *Journal of Southern History* 53, no. 3 (1987), 369–94.

21. The MOTB is thus participating in a broader historical contestation over Whitefield's memory that has made him into a complex "religious icon." See

Jessica M. Parr, *Inventing George Whitefield: Race, Revivalism, and the Making of a Religious Icon* (Jackson: University Press of Mississippi, 2015).

22. See Michael G. Long, *Billy Graham and the Beloved Community: America's Evangelist and the Dream of Martin Luther King, Jr.* (London: Palgrave Macmillan, 2006); and Anthea Butler, *White Evangelical Racism: The Politics of Morality in America* (Chapel Hill: University of North Carolina Press, 2021), 42–55.

23. Michael McAfee and Lauren Green McAfee deploy this strategy in their book *Not What You Think*, as they attempt to persuade fellow millennials not to dismiss the Bible: "We readily admit that indefensible acts have occurred in the name of the Christian religion, not to mention the Bible itself. Men and women have often misused the text of Scripture for their own gain. This is inexcusably wrong. Instead we want to look at the Bible for what it says, and it never condones the violation of human dignity" (*Not What You Think: Why the Bible Might Be Nothing We Expected Yet Everything We Need* [Grand Rapids: Zondervan, 2019], 111).

24. Mitchell, "'It's Complicated,'" 14.

25. Moss and Baden, *Bible Nation*, 181–82.

26. Moss and Baden, *Bible Nation*, 182.

27. Mitchell, "'It's Complicated,'" 21.

28. Mitchell, "'It's Complicated,'"14–19. See also Thomas, *Storytelling the Bible*, 155.

29. "Many Christians on the antislavery side of the debate in the 19th century could tolerate (or explain) the existence of proslavery passages in their Old Testament by adhering to a dispensational view of God's revelation and/or by arguing that the New has superseded the Old. So the primary hermeneutical problem for such abolitionist interpreters was to explain how the New Testament cohered with their position" (J. Albert Harrill, *Slaves in the New Testament: Literary, Social, and Moral Dimensions* [Minneapolis: Fortress Press, 2006]).

30. Noll, *Civil War*, 33–36.

31. See the website Documenting the American South for a digitized version of this book: https://docsouth.unc.edu/church/stringfellow/stringfellow.html

32. E. N. Elliott, *Cotton is King and Pro-Slavery Arguments: Comprising the Writings of Hammond, Harper, Christy, Stringfellow, Hodge, Bledsoe, and Cartwright on This Important Subject* (Augusta: Pritchard, Abbott, & Loomis, 1860).

33. George Whitefield's arguments in favor of slavery often traded on the view that it was important for maintaining the colonial economy (Stein, "George Whitefield on Slavery," 245).

34. See the Internet Archive for a digitized version of this book: https://archive.org/details/ASPC0005022700/mode/2up

35. The slide also misrepresents Hodge's own complicated position on slavery (James H. Moorhead, "Slavery, Race, and Gender at Princeton Seminary: The Pre-Civil War Era," *Theology Today* 69, no. 3 [2012], 274–88). Hodge argued that the Bible did not consider slavery to be a sin and therefore the institution could not be attacked, as some abolitionists had done, as sinful.

Slavery was only sinful, wrote Hodge, when masters mistreated their slaves. That being said, Hodge also envisioned an end to slavery, though he vehemently resisted being classed with the abolitionists. He suggested that the gradual Christianization of enslaved Africans would increase their intelligence and virtue so that eventually they could become free men (Charles Hodge, "Slavery," *The Biblical Repertory and Princeton Review* 8 [1836], 15–17). It is true that Hodge later supported Lincoln and the Northern fight against slavery in the Civil War, but even at that point he resisted being called an abolitionist (Charles Hodge, "The General Assembly," *The Biblical Repertory and Princeton Review* 36, no. 3 [1864], 549–50).

36. This section is adapted and expanded from Jill Hicks-Keeton, "The 'Slave Bible' is Not What You Think," *The Revealer* (June 3, 2020).

37. Museum of the Bible website, www.museumofthebible.org/press/press-releases/slave-bible-exhibit-examines-use-of-religion-in-colonial-period

38. Dominic Holden, "A Bible Museum Backed By White Conservatives Is Suddenly Trying Hard to Attract Black Visitors," *BuzzFeed* (December 3, 2018), www.buzzfeednews.com/article/dominicholden/bible-museum-dc-black-visitors-hobby-lobby

39. Geoff Bennett, Twitter (April 21, 2019, 11:55 p.m.), https://twitter.com/GeoffRBennett/status/1120098700590817281. Garnering over 10,000 views, this video made it to the eyes and ears of thousands of people unlikely to have made it to the physical exhibit.

40. It is indeed the case that most of the book of Exodus was not selected for inclusion. The narrative in *Select Parts of the Holy Bible* cuts out at the end of the Joseph cycle in Genesis 45 and picks up again with the Israelites at Sinai in Exodus 19. MOTB representative Anthony Schmidt, associate curator of Bible and Religion in America, suggested in an interview with the Christian Broadcast Network that the editors thereby emphasized the positive outcome of Joseph's enslavement while skipping the Israelites' collective emancipation (Amber Strong, "The Shocking 'Slave Bible': Here Are the Parts That Were Deleted to Manipulate Slaves," *CBN News* [February 2, 2019], www1.cbn.com/cbnnews/us/2018/february/freedom-in-christ-how-this-bible-was-used-to-manipulate). But the main event of the Exodus narrative – God's redemption of Israelites from bondage in Egypt – is nowhere near absent from *Select Parts*.

41. Further examples include Exodus 19:4 and Deuteronomy 4:20, 34, 37.

42. All quotations are from the NRSV.

43. See the Internet Archive for a digitized version of this book: https://archive.org/details/alettertogovern01portgoog/page/n9/mode/2up

44. Here, Porteus is intervening in a larger debate among white colonists, who argued with each other about whether to provide education to the enslaved. Part of that conversation was wrapped up in claims that the Black intellect was inferior (can they even learn?) and also in arguments about whether property (akin to farm animals) was worth educating. The exhibit on the "Slave Bible" hides from view this larger – immensely ethically disturbing – conversation happening among British colonial Christians.

45. See the important work of Katherine Gerbner, *Christian Slaves: Conversion and Race in the Protestant Atlantic World* (Philadelphia: University of Pennsylvania Press, 2018). White Christians at this time were not actually arguing between "yes, slavery" and "no, slavery"; to return to the tug-of-war imagery: the rope only existed between "yes, convert enslaved Black people" or "no, don't convert enslaved Black people." Both of these latter options are today inconceivable moral positions, for to make a choice is to presume the existence of slavery and to enter the debate at all is to engage in a discussion built on questions about whether enslaved people are capable of being Christians and whether it is acceptable for Christians to own other Christians.

46. In the "Translating the Bible" exhibit on the History of the Bible floor, to take one illustration, we find on display a fourteenth-century book of hours and psalter (catalog no. MS.000761.), a pair of manuscripts bound together that belonged to Elizabeth de Bohun, Countess of Northampton (1313–56). It is described in a museum-produced video by one of its curators as "one of our most precious manuscripts, one of our most famous manuscripts" (https://museumofthebible.org/collections/artifacts/25231-hours-and-psalter-of-elizabeth-de-bohun-countess-of-northampton?&tab=description).

An extended written description of this artifact appears on the museum's social media: "Book of Hours were popular medieval Christian devotional works that included selections from the Bible, often from the Gospels and psalms, and included prayers to be read at various hours of the day" (Facebook [April 14, 2020]). Neither outrage nor judgment attends the museum's presentation of this artifact. It is not framed as an "incomplete Bible."

47. One prominent example, titled *The Children of the World Storybook Bible*, is a 256-page colorful book designed to appeal to children. The publisher's description reveals that this book is a compilation – parts of the Bible – chosen for and told for a specific audience of readers: "here are 100 best-loved Bible stories presented in a beautiful hardcover edition for children aged 5 to 8. The stories are written in a manner that is appropriate for either a read-to-me audience or early readers, and the collection includes both Old and New Testament stories … [B]y showcasing the unique perspectives that children bring to their understanding of these stories, this collection will allow young readers to see the Bible as something with which they can personally engage" (https://store.museumofthebible.org/Children-of-World-SB-Bbl/).

48. This quotation is taken from posts on Facebook when this book was twice featured as Artifact of the Day: July 7, 2018 and again on August 16, 2018.

49. As Timothy Beal points out, such consumer-oriented Bibles were produced within the competitive publishing environment that emerged in early modern England, particularly after the state awarded a monopoly on printing rights to the Authorized Version (also known as the King James Version) (*The Rise and Fall of the Bible: The Unexpected History of an Accidental Book* [New York: Houghton Mifflin Harcourt, 2011], 130–36.

50. The post was a repetition of the original placard text explaining the artifact when it appeared as part of the "Bible in America" exhibit on the Impact floor. It read in its entirety: "This volume is called 'Holy,' but it is deeply manipulative. Based on the King James Version, it omits all entries that

express themes of freedom. The story of Exodus, for example, describing the Israelites' escape from slavery in Egypt, is missing. The editors left out entire books and large portions of others; their selections stressed obedience, submission, and acceptance. The book was part of an inhumane process to make slaves docile and subservient, to break their spirits. #BlackHistoryMonth."

51. Indeed, the ABS was a major innovator of what Beal calls "value-added Bibles." These consumer-focused Bibles were produced in a dizzying array of formats as a means of appealing to as broad an audience as possible (*Rise and Fall of the Bible*, 136).

52. Allen Dwight Callahan, *The Talking Book: African Americans and the Bible* (New Haven: Yale University Press, 2008), especially 1–48.

53. Howard Thurman, *Jesus and the Disinherited* (Boston: Beacon Press: 1996), 30–31.

54. Consistent with other tracts published and distributed by the Society for the Propagation of the Gospel in Foreign Parts in the eighteenth century (see Raboteau, "African Americans," 1–2), Porteus himself argued that enslaved Christians are better, more docile workers because they have the Bible's instructions (e.g., 1 Peter 2:18; Titus 2:9–10; Colossians 3:22).

55. Noll, *Civil War*, 33–50.

56. Noll, *Civil War*, 34–51.

57. The complete list of Scripture references on this sign is as follows: Exodus 21:16; Exodus 6:6; Galatians 3:28; Deuteronomy 23:15; Exodus 1–18, 21–40; Revelation 18:11; Jeremiah 22:13; 1 Corinthians 4–12; Psalms 1–150; Galatians 2–4; Leviticus 25:39–41.

58. The complete list of Scripture references on this sign is as follows: 1 Samuel 17, 24; Ephesians 6:5; 1 Chronicles 17; 1 Peter 2:18; Job 1:17; Daniel 1–9; Exodus 20:10; Genesis 37:26–28; James 1, 3, 5; Luke 12:47–48; 1 John 3; Acts 1–28; Titus 2:9.

59. J. Albert Harrill, "The Use of the New Testament in the American Slave Controversy: A Case History in the Hermeneutical Tension between Biblical Criticism and Christian Moral Debate," *Religion and American Culture* 10 (2000), 149–86, at 170. The same is true of, for example, 1 Corinthians 7:21 and 1 Timothy 1:10.

60. Harrill, "Use of the New Testament," 149–86.

61. Harrill, "Use of the New Testament," 149.

62. Philippa Koch has argued persuasively that evangelical support for slavery and for the education of slaves was tied to notions of divine providence in evangelical theology ("Slavery, Mission, and the Perils of Providence in Eighteenth-Century Christianity: The Writings of Whitefield and the Halle Pietists," *Church History* 84, no. 2 [June 2015], 369–93).

63. Callahan, *Talking Book*, 26. Callahan's statement follows his quotation of a poem by Phyllis Wheatley, "On Being Brought from Africa to America," in which he finds "the beginnings of an apologia for the blight of African slavery on the Christian understanding of God's permissive will."

64. This move repeats an analogous problem from the MOTB's precursor traveling exhibit "Passages," which, as Moss and Baden showed, minimized Christian complicity in the Holocaust (*Bible Nation*, 161).

65. Of the four questions, the most innocuous asked visitors to articulate their own curiosities: "What questions does the Slave Bible raise about how the Bible is used today?" This prompt was formulated in such a way as to provoke normative ethical reflection since it was premised on the assumption that the artifact on display naturally elicits questions not merely about historical legacies but about the contemporary moment. Visitors were primed to use this artifact to make meaning in the here and now. As we've seen, though, the exhibit did not give visitors much material for any serious ethical reflection unless they first identified and then interrogated its narrative and also had access to more historical knowledge and context than the exhibit gave. Another question effectively cued, and thereby circumscribed, the reaction allowed to guests: "What surprised you most about the Slave Bible?" Visitors were not offered the option to be surprised or not – they were asked only to articulate what surprised them *most*. Why is surprise assumed as the primary reaction? The promotional email mentioned above offers some help: "Does this sound like the Bible you know?" it asks. The most natural interpretation is that surprise is anticipated on the part of visitors because the museum expects the "Slave Bible" to be very different from visitors' Bibles in terms of both content (full versus partial) and function (liberative versus oppressive).

66. The final question likewise conscripted visitors into a particular view of the Bible – that it is necessarily authoritative: "Does the Bible have the same authority if portions are removed?" Once again, no matter whether one answers yes or no, the premise of the question is baked into the answer. No answer that we observed among the visitor responses attempted to resist the premise. For example, on the negative side, one visitor wrote "Only half of the truth is still a lie. So my answer is NO, period." Another: "No. But it still has some authority." On the affirmative side: "Yes. All of God's words have authority. What doesn't have authority is man's manipulation of the message. No part of the Bible is to be changed or omitted. SO, reading only certain portions of Scripture still contains the authority of God but does not give the whole picture." See Thomas, *Storytelling the Bible*, 156–59, for another example of what can be learned from examining the visitor comment cards at this exhibit.

67. This group includes those known as "exvangelicals." See, for example, the collection of essays in Chrissy Stroop and Lauren O'Neal (eds.), *Empty the Pews: Stories of Leaving the Church* (Indianapolis: Epiphany Publishing, 2019).

68. Kerby, *Saving History*, 25.

69. Museum of the Bible website, www.museumofthebible.org/press/back ground/floor-2-impact-of-the-bible-bible-in-the-world

70. Byron R. Johnson, *More God, Less Crime: Why Faith Matters and How It Could Matter More* (West Conshohocken: Templeton Press, 2011).

71. The event was cosponsored by the Baylor Institute for Studies of Religion (which Johnson founded), the American Bible Society, and Prison Fellowship (a Christian nonprofit founded by Chuck Colson).

72. Interestingly, Johnson consistently defended the quality of his publications and attributed them to divine intervention. In one example, he said, "What I'd like you to understand is these are publications in journals that don't like

what we're finding. They don't like the fact that this prison is associated with these kinds of positive outcomes ... These are papers that are peer-reviewed by people who are looking to reject them, and yet God's helped us to be able to publish these in very good outlets."

CHAPTER 3 RELIABLE BIBLE

1. Erin Thompson, "That Robby Hobby," *Slate* (October 4, 2021), https://slate.com/news-and-politics/2021/10/museum-of-the-bible-looted-art-track-record.html

2. Another placard, a very small one explaining the color coding to visitors, effaces the identity of *who* is perceiving the need with the use of passive voice: "About 2,000 languages are considered to have no need of a Bible translation. Speakers of these languages tend to be fluent in another language or the community has not been supportive of translation for their language."

3. Jonathan Sprowl, "Mart Green: On a Quest to Eliminate Bible Poverty," *Outreach Magazine* (March 5, 2019), https://outreachmagazine.com/interviews/41163-mart-green-on-a-quest-to-eliminate-bible-poverty.html.
Outreach Magazine is described on its website as "a bimonthly publication helping local churches reach their community and change the world."

4. A floor-to-ceiling map offers visitors a visual representation of the Bible's "spread." The dates given for the "origins of the Bible" are rather vague: "ORIGINS OF THE BIBLE | ?? – 100 BCE."

5. Lawrence H. Shiffman and Jerry Pattengale (eds.), *The World's Greatest Book: The Story of How the Bible Came to Be* (Museum of the Bible Books, 2017).

6. While there are no dinosaur bones at the MOTB, there are skeletons in its closet. On the institutional connection between MOTB and Answers in Genesis, see James A. Linville, "The Creationist Museum of the Bible," in *The Museum of the Bible: A Critical Introduction*, edited by Jill Hicks-Keeton and Cavan Concannon (Lanham: Lexington Books/Fortress Academic, 2019), 257–73.

7. Originally posted in January 2016 and at time of writing on YouTube, https://www.youtube.com/watch?v=z3TKNR0kUAk

8. Jana Mathews, "The Museum of the Bible's 'Fake' History of the Bible," *Material Religion* 15, no. 1 (2019), 133.

9. The story, as is often the case, is not so simple. See on this Christian Hannick, "Le développement des langues regionals et l'introduction d'alphabets dans des communautés illettrées," in *East and West Modes of Communication*, edited by Evangelos Chrysos and Ian Wood (Boston: Brill, 1999), 205–22.

10. This bears concerning similarity to Jonathan Sheehan's description of the role of translation of the Bible in the production of modern national identity, particularly in Germany (*The Enlightenment Bible: Translation, Scholarship, Culture* [Princeton: Princeton University Press, 2005], 170–73).

11. See Megan Williams, *The Monk and the Book: Jerome and the Making of Christian Scholarship* (Chicago: University of Chicago Press, 2006), 63–95.

12. Candida Moss and Joel Baden, "The Museum of the Bible is Exploiting Jewish Tradition – and Saving Its Evangelical Christian Donors Millions," *The Daily*

Beast (September 1, 2018), www.thedailybeast.com/how-the-museum-of-the-bible-exploits-jewish-traditionand-saves-its-evangelical-christian-donors-millions. Moss and Baden's investigation into the Torah Scrolls at the MOTB, which includes allegations about how the Green family enjoy massive tax breaks for donating them, is essential reading on the MOTB's relationship to Judaism.

13. Museum of the Bible website, https://collections.museumofthebible.org/arti facts/1035-novum-instrumentum-omneerasmuss-new-testament?&tab=descripti on&fbclid=IwAR01t-qGW3Zca1B1iGhPT6ADKbX9RZqcvZmPcVCMaRG2Ay WBeQ60C2x4gpw

14. Museum of the Bible website, https://collections.museumofthebible.org/arti facts/25085-luthers-pentateuch?&tab=description&fbclid=IwAR0FjOvRl_7aI CmWTEk1b9Ep3OURYBBvSCTFdPgn7-OqZBMPKgG-MtlPmFc and https:// collections.museumofthebible.org/artifacts/320-erasmuss-paraphrases-o n-the-gospels-and-acts?&tab=description&fbclid=IwAR2J3d_j1gMl8eQofjz vFMogUfy44lxOLfjVHVmPNrOAHWWDiITg-yJy-u8

15. Museum of the Bible website, https://collections.museumofthebible.org/a rtifacts/27698-fragment-of-tyndales-english-new-testament?&tab=descriptio n&fbclid=IwAR2hSvNhaMy4557XlLOw8GoUvqMtWOMwiux2zbNOOCD9 UvxlAQGDTOE6U4w

16. Museum of the Bible website, https://collections.museumofthebible.org/a rtifacts/25997-tyndales-new-testament?&tab=description&fbclid=IwAR2eO L8G1xWVvWBvlihgxd0ebANhm3RovTbJoenoxvhXO1VuuODre0G86x4

17. Several videos produced by the Museum of the Bible and accessible online indicate that the Gutenberg Press was an essential development in service of the Protestant Reformation.

18. Margaret M. Mitchell, "'It's Complicated.' 'No, It's Not.': The Museum of the Bible, Problems and Solutions," in Hicks-Keeton and Concannon (eds.), *Museum of the Bible: A Critical Introduction*, 8.

19. Gutenberg Gates, @GutenbergGates, Twitter, https://twitter.com/Gutenb ergGates, accessed October 14, 2021.

20. For a digitized version of the "He" Bible, see the MOTB website, https://co llections.museumofthebible.org/artifacts/1270-king-james-bible?&tab=desc ription&fbclid=IwAR2WFDTiSws0P2v7lmTbUk2dJlX6_3RuqwTFTFt5CGO Fb9jJ-pzlzPcr8cw

21. For a digitized version of the "Wicked" Bible, see the MOTB website, https:// collections.museumofthebible.org/artifacts/95-the-wicked-bible–corrected ?&tab=description

22. We address the problematic term "Judeo-Christian" in Chapter 5.

23. Eva Mroczek, "Batshit Stories: New Tales of Discovering Ancient Texts," *Marginalia: Los Angeles Review of Books* (June 22, 2018), https://marginalia .lareviewofbooks.org/batshit-stories-new-tales-of-discovering-ancient-texts/

24. See Bryan Bibb, "Readers and Their E-Bibles: The Shape and Authority of the Hypertext Canon," in *The Bible in American Life*, edited by Philip Goff, Arthur E. Farnsley II, and Peter J. Thuesen (Oxford: Oxford University Press, 2017); and Jeffrey S. Siker, *Liquid Scripture: The Bible in a Digital World* (Minneapolis: Fortress Press, 2017).

25. Noble Warriors website, www.noblewarriors.org/the-noble-man-knows-some-facts-about-the-word-podcast-ep-12/

26. See Wayne Proudfoot, *Religious Experience* (Berkeley: University of California Press, 1985); and Russell McCutcheon, *Critics Not Caretakers: Redescribing the Public Study of Religion* (Albany: State University of New York Press, 2001). Proudfoot and McCutcheon pay particular attention to the ways "religious experience" operates as a protective strategy for claiming the *sui generis* nature of religion. For other uses of protective strategies, see Tyler Roberts, "Exposure and Explanation: On the New Protectionism in the Study of Religion," *Journal of the American Academy of Religion* 72, no. 1 (2004), 143–72; Stephen L. Young, "Protective Strategies and the Prestige of the 'Academic': A Religious Studies and Practice Theory Redescription of Evangelical Inerrantist Scholarship," *Biblical Interpretation* 23 (2015), 1–35; and Stephen L. Young, "Let's Take the Text Seriously," *Method & Theory in the Study of Religion*, Advance Articles (2019), 1–36.

27. We do not present these strategies as mistakes that the MOTB made, and which could be fixed if they only listened to biblical scholars like ourselves. Academic biblical studies has its own protective strategies, some of which are similar to those used by the MOTB. We note these strategies because they do work for the story told at the MOTB about their bible.

28. There is not one definition of inerrancy that is common to all white evangelicals, though the Chicago Statement on Biblical Inerrancy (1978) is perhaps the most influential definition.

29. Young, "Protective Strategies," 7.

30. Young, "Protective Strategies," 6–7.

31. Young, "Protective Strategies," 11.

32. Young, "Protective Strategies," 24.

33. The title of this subsection is borrowed from Lawrence Venuti, *The Translator's Invisibility: A History of Translation* (London and New York: Routledge, 2017).

34. Lawrence Venuti, "Genealogies of Translation Theory: Jerome," *boundary 2* 37, no. 3 (2010), 5–6.

35. Mitchell has discussed a similar approach in an interactive made for children near the "illumiNations" exhibit ("'It's Complicated,'" 23–24).

36. Venuti, "Genealogies of Translation," 22.

37. Willie James Jennings, *The Christian Imagination: Theology and the Origins of Race* (New Haven: Yale University Press, 2010), 119–68.

38. Jennings, *Christian Imagination*, 159.

39. Jennings writes as a Christian theologian and thus is not critiquing the use of biblical translation for having a theological rationale. Rather, he questions the ethics of instrumentalist, colonialist translation in favor of a theological ethics of "concurrency": "the possibilities of cultural inner logics being joined together, ... the possibility of freedom in the transgression of boundaries" (*Christian Imagination*, 154). For further exploration of the complexities of translation, see the surveys by Anthony Pym, *Exploring Translation Theories* (London: Taylor & Francis, 2014); Daniel Weissbort and Eysteinsson Astradur (eds), *Translation – Theory and Practice: A Historical Reader* (Oxford: Oxford University Press, 2006); and Susan Bassnett and

Trivedi Harish (eds), *Post-Colonial Translation: Theory and Practice* (London: Routledge, 1999).

40. Young, "Protective Strategies," 10.
41. What follows is a condensed and adapted version of analysis published earlier in Cavan Concannon, "Theo-Politics, Archaeology, and the Ideology of the Museum of the Bible," in Hicks-Keeton and Concannon (eds.), *Museum of the Bible: A Critical Edition*, 101–20.
42. See Drive Thru History website, https://drivethruhistory.com/
43. For a sustained argument about how the MOTB gives the Bible agency, see Mitchell, "'It's Complicated,'" 3–36.
44. The literature on the Dead Sea Scrolls is vast, but for a good overview, see, for example, Jodi Magness, *The Archaeology of Qumran and the Dead Sea Scrolls* (Grand Rapids: Eerdmans, 2002).
45. This narrative of the Bible's transmission is also one supported by Steve Green (Candida Moss and Joel Baden, *Bible Nation: The United States of Hobby Lobby* [Princeton: Princeton University Press, 2017], 84–85, 155–56). For more on the Greens, see Chapter 5.
46. These kinds of arguments also pervade the MOTB's public school Bible curriculum. On the curriculum, see Moss and Baden, *Bible Nation*, 99–136, wherein they discuss the important work of Mark Chancey on this topic.
47. The most oft-cited figure that evangelicals position themselves against is Bart Ehrman, a professor at the University of North Carolina at Chapel Hill. Ehrman has written many books that have emphasized the instability of the biblical text, including *The Orthodox Corruption of Scripture: The Effect of Early Christian Christological Controversies on the Text of the New Testament* (Oxford: Oxford University Press, 2011) and *Misquoting Jesus: The Story Behind Who Changed the Bible and Why* (New York: HarperOne, 2005).
48. Ludvik A. Kjeldsberg, "Christian Dead Sea Scrolls?: The Post-2002 Fragments as Modern Protestant Relics," in Hicks-Keeton and Concannon (eds.), *Museum of the Bible: A Critical Introduction*, 207–18.
49. The fragments were originally published in Emanuel Tov, Kipp Davis, and Robert Duke (eds.), *Dead Sea Scrolls Fragments in the Museum Collection*, Publications of Museum of the Bible 1, edited by Michael W. Holmes (Leiden: Brill, 2016).
50. Molly M. Zahn, *Genres of Rewriting in Second Temple Judaism: Scribal Composition and Transmission* (Cambridge: Cambridge University Press, 2020).
51. "Museum of the Bible Releases Research Findings on Fragments in Its Dead Sea Scrolls Collection," press release, Museum of the Bible (October 22, 2018), https://www.museumofthebible.org/press/press-releases/museum-of-the-bible-releases-research-findings-on-fragments-in-its-dead-sea-scrolls-collection.
52. The original exhibit has been remodeled since our most recent visit to the museum (https://www.museumofthebible.org/newsroom/museum-of-the-bible-opens-updated-dead-sea-scrolls).
53. The two real manuscripts were fragments of Romans 4:23–5:3 (Uncial 0220) and John 8:14–18 (P39).
54. See, for example, the press releases from the US Department of Justice outlining the forfeiture and repatriation of items purchased by Hobby

Lobby: www.justice.gov/usao-edny/pr/united-states-files-civil-action-forfeit-thousands-ancient-iraqi-artifacts-imported; https://www.justice.gov/opa/pr/rare-cuneiform-tablet-bearing-portion-epic-gilgamesh-forfeited-united-states.

55. Mathews, "'Fake' History," 133.

56. While there are many important works that describe the state of the field, our description of text criticism follows Eldon J. Epp and Gordon Fee, *Studies in the Theory and Method of New Testament Textual Criticism* (Grand Rapids: Eerdmans, 1993); Yii-Jan Lin, *The Erotic Life of Manuscripts: New Testament Textual Criticism and the Biological Sciences* (Oxford: Oxford University Press, 2016); Bruce Metzger and Bart D. Ehrman, *The Text of the New Testament: Its Transmission, Corruption, and Restoration* (Oxford: Oxford University Press, 2005); David C. Parker, *Textual Scholarship and the Making of the New Testament* (Oxford: Oxford University Press, 2012); David C. Parker, *An Introduction to the New Testament Manuscripts and Their Texts* (Cambridge: Cambridge University Press, 2008); David C. Parker, *The Living Text of the Gospels* (Cambridge: Cambridge University Press, 1997); and Emanuel Tov, *Textual Criticism of the Hebrew Bible* (Minneapolis: Fortress Press, 2012).

57. Lin, *Erotic Life of Manuscripts*; Gregory L. Cuéllar, *Empire, The British Museum, and the Making of the Biblical Scholar in the Nineteenth Century: Archival Criticism* (London: Palgrave Macmillan, 2019).

58. See Evangelical Textual Criticism blog, http://evangelicaltextualcriticism.blogspot.com

59. Brent Nongbri, *God's Library: The Archaeology of the Earliest Christian Manuscripts* (New Haven: Yale University Press, 2018); Parker, *Living Text*; Parker, *Textual Scholarship*; Eldon Epp, *Perspectives on New Testament Textual Criticism: Collected Essays, 1962–2004* (Leiden: Brill, 2005).

60. We would like to thank Brent Nongbri for helping us refine this point.

61. Jill Hicks-Keeton, "What the Museum of the Bible Conveys about Biblical Scholarship Behind Church Doors," *Religion & Politics* (March 13, 2018), https://religionandpolitics.org/2018/03/13/what-the-museum-of-the-bible-conveys-about-biblical-scholarship-behind-church-doors/

62. See in particular Jennifer Wright Knust, "Editing without Interpreting: The Museum of the Bible and New Testament Textual Criticism," in Hicks-Keeton and Concannon (eds.), Museum of the Bible: A Critical Introduction, 145–70; Moss and Baden, *Bible Nation*.

63. Peter J. Williams, *Can We Trust the Gospels?* (Wheaton: Crossway, 2018).

64. Williams concluded: "If you accept Jesus as the organizing principle for knowledge, you can explain a whole load of things more simply." No one is likely to contest the truthfulness of that claim: if you take something on faith as given, you don't have to do the hard work of assessing complicated and often contradictory evidence. Of course, not every person would want to claim Jesus as an epistemological starting point, and even among Christians the concept "Jesus" would likely lead to varying conclusions on account of the very fact that the gospels are not self-interpreting or self-evidently meaning-ful in one straightforward way.

CHAPTER 4   JESUS, ISRAEL, AND A CHRISTIAN AMERICA

1. On the Bible as transmedial, see James Bielo, "Performing the Bible," in *The Oxford Handbook of the Bible in America*, edited by Paul C. Gutjahr (Oxford: Oxford University Press, 2017), 484–501.
2. Biblical gardens are exceptionally popular devotional sites for Bible readers. Leading expert James Bielo estimates that 40 percent of the more than 400 sites around the world that boast Bible-themed attractions are biblical gardens (*Ark Encounter: The Making of a Creationist Theme Park* [New York: New York University Press, 2018], 40–42). These gardens feature plants of various kinds that are either mentioned in the Bible or are native to Israel. Functioning as sites for prayer or meditation, for connecting with God's presence on a quiet stroll, they teach via a bodily sensorium, inviting visitors "to learn the text of scripture better through a physical encounter with cultivated nature" (*ibid.*).
3. See Museum of the Bible website, www.museumofthebible.org/museum/ex plore/floor-6
4. *Dallas News* (November 28, 2017), www.dallasnews.com/arts-entertainment/tra vel/2017/11/28/new-museum-of-the-bible-in-washington-d-c-includes-stunning-garden/
5. *Dallas News* (November 28, 2017), www.dallasnews.com/arts-entertainment /travel/2017/11/28/new-museum-of-the-bible-in-washington-d-c-includes-stunning-garden/
6. Willows tend to grow in riparian contexts, along the banks of rivers, and are mentioned in Leviticus 23:40, Job 40:22, and Isaiah 15:7 and 44:4.
7. While biblical gardens are the most common form of Bible materialization, the Bible also becomes materialized through creation museums, biblical history museums, and recreations of biblical places (Bielo, *Ark Encounter*, 40). The MOTB at one point had an institutional connection to the creation museums run by Answers in Genesis (James R. Linville, "The Creationist Museum of the Bible," in *The Museum of the Bible: A Critical Introduction*, edited by Jill Hicks-Keeton and Cavan Concannon [Lanham: Lexington Books/ Fortress Academic, 2019], 257–74).
8. Museums in the US have long paid careful attention to the way in which their exhibits and physical spaces shape the experiences of visitors (Tina Roppola, *Designing for the Museum Visitor Experience* [New York: Routledge, 2012]). Bielo has interviewed the design firms involved in the creation of the Ark Encounter creationist theme park (Kentucky) and the MOTB, examining the ways in which they make choices that will shape the experience of visitors (*Ark Encounter*). While studies involving design choices add useful information about how the MOTB took the shape that it has, in this chapter we focus on how the museum's narrative exhibits retell biblical stories in immersive ways that mirror popular forms of entertainment as a different way to explore the ideological resonances of these exhibits and the narratives that they tell.
9. As Wilfred Cantwell Smith has noted, "The Bible, too, over much of its life, and not only for those many who were illiterate, has been heard, as well as – until recent centuries much more than – received through the eyes, off the page" (*What is Scripture?: A Comparative Approach* [Minneapolis: Fortress Press, 1993], 8).

10. On the Bible as performed, see Bielo, "Performing the Bible," 484–501.
11. *CBN* (November 15, 2017), www1.cbn.com/thebrodyfile/archive/2017/11/15/finding-jesus-at-the-museum-of-the-bible-isnt-so-easy.
12. Michel Foucault, *The History of Sexuality*, vol. I, *An Introduction* (New York: Vintage, 1990), 27.
13. See the Museum of the Bible website, www.museumofthebible.org/visit/current-attractions.
14. On the MOTB's collapsing of distinctions between the Tanakh and the Old Testament, see Jill Hicks-Keeton, "The Museum of Whose Bible? On the Dangers of Turning Theology into History," *Ancient Jew Review* (January 24, 2018).
15. Though it's a well-known trope, see specifically Stephen Prothero's helpful distinction in *God is Not One* between Judaism and Christianity. Prothero articulates that for Jews the main problem in the world is exile and the solution is return (a cyclical pattern mirroring the ways Jews read the Tanakh), whereas for Christians the problem is sin and the solution is salvation (a movement that necessarily treats the Old Testament as more teleological than cyclical). Stephen Prothero, *God Is Not One: The Eight Rival Religions That Run the World* (New York: HarperOne, 2010). On the diversity of ways Genesis 1-3 could be understood differently among Jews and Christians, see Amy-Jill Levine and Marc Zvi Brettler, *The Bible With and Without Jesus: How Jews and Christians Read the Same Stories Differently* (New York: HarperOne, 2020), 67–134.
16. That the MOTB frames God's actions here as "washing" the world stands in stark contrast to the stated motivations of God in Genesis 6:6–7: "And the Lord was sorry that he had made humankind on the earth, and it grieved him to his heart. So the Lord said, 'I will blot out from the earth the human beings I have created – people together with animals and creeping things and birds of the air, for I am sorry that I have made them'" (NRSV). In Genesis, God conceives of the flood as an act of de-creation, not as a cleansing of the world's wickedness.
17. Our thanks to Alan Levenson, who noted this to Jill Hicks-Keeton in private correspondence.
18. Mark Leuchter, "Smoke and Mirrors: The Hebrew Bible Exhibit at the Museum of the Bible," in Hicks-Keeton and Concannon (eds.), *Museum of the Bible: A Critical Introduction*, 5s.
19. Cynthia Baker, *Jew* (New Brunswick: Rutgers University Press, 2017), 29–32.
20. Leuchter writes: "The word 'Torah' never appears *even once* in either the book of Judges *or* the book of Ruth, and the characters in either book seem to have no awareness whatsoever of the Torah's existence" ("Smoke and Mirrors," 93).
21. On the MOTB's History floor, the Bible's history from antiquity to today is also framed as one of particularity being overcome in favor of universality. On this, see Hicks-Keeton, "Museum of Whose Bible?"
22. The earliest iteration of this use of Isaiah 11:1 comes in Justin Martyr's *Dialogue with Trypho* (86–87). The use of this prophecy then becomes widespread in Christian literature and theology. Consider, for example,

the long history of Christian artistic depictions of the Tree of Jesse, a genre that traces Jesus's genealogy back to Jesse on the basis of Isaiah 11:1. Similar connections between roots and branches can be found in Job 18:16, Jeremiah 17:8, Ezekiel 31:7, Sirach 1:20 and 40:15, and Romans 11:16–24.

23. For more reflection on the "Ezra Reveal," see Leuchter, "Smoke and Mirrors," 94–95.

24. Cary Summers, former museum president, writes about the intention behind its production: "In every way, the synagogue is real. Every detail is accurate and authentic, from the stones to the colors and from the columns to the seats. The fact that you can listen to and learn from the rabbi only makes the experience all the more impressive. You feel you are really there, transported back in time. And that, of course, is the goal." Citing these lines, Sarah Porter argues that Nazareth Village is part of a larger fetishization of the Land of Israel by both evangelicals, particularly those influenced by Christian Zionism, and the MOTB (Sarah F. Porter, "The Land of Israel and Bodily Pedagogy at the Museum of the Bible," in Hicks-Keeton and Concannon [eds.], *Museum of the Bible: A Critical Introduction*, 121–42). Jesus's hometown is thus made into a conduit that channels the past and the present, theology and history, into a potent contemporary body politics.

25. Further examples include "Cornerstone – The Wicked Tenant – Matthew 21:33–41"; "Pouch for seed – The Sower and Soils – Matthew 13:1–9"; "Ring – The Lost Son and His Brother – Luke 15:11–32"; and "Flasks of Oil – The Ten Bridesmaids – Matthew 25:1–12."

26. This exhibit in the MOTB in fact has a placard elsewhere that begins to do this but then culminates, perhaps not surprisingly given the Bible museum context, with Isaiah's use of "the life cycle of grain" as "an ideal metaphor for God's effective, life-giving words that yield 'seed for the sower and bread for the eater' (Isaiah 55:10–11)."

27. The selection of Proverbs 31 here is only explicable, we think, by noting the modern-day evangelical Christian trope of the "Proverbs 31 Woman" as shorthand for the ideal Christian woman who purports to embody the values laid out in this biblical chapter, usually connected to the labor of maintaining a household. See, for example, Proverbs 31 Ministries, which is described on its website as "a non-denominational, non-profit Christian ministry that seeks to lead women into a personal relationship with Christ, with Proverbs 31:10–31 as a guide" (https://proverbs31.org/). See also Rachel Held Evans, *A Year of Biblical Womanhood: How a Liberated Woman Found Herself Sitting on Her Roof, Covering Her Head, and Calling Her Husband 'Master'* (Nashville: Thomas Nelson, 2012); Amy DeRogatis, *Saving Sex: Sexuality and Salvation in American Evangelicalism* (Oxford: Oxford University Press, 2014); and Kate Bowler, *The Preacher's Wife: The Precarious Power of Evangelical Women Celebrities* (Princeton: Princeton University Press, 2019), 65–116.

28. Here one could point to the placards accompanying both the cistern (entitled "Preserving Water," citing Deuteronomy 11:11) and the olive press (entitled "Gift for Many Uses," citing Deuteronomy 7:13).

29. The emphasis we saw in the Hebrew Bible exhibit on the movement from particular to universal is mirrored here in Nazareth on the "Meals and Celebrations" placard: "these local [Jewish] celebrations fueled images of a global feast when 'the Lord Almighty will prepare a feast of rich food for all peoples' (Isaiah 25:6)." The stage is set for a universal solution.

30. What follows is a transcription of a recording made during a visit to the museum on August 1, 2018.

31. See Shawn Kelley, *Racializing Jesus: Race, Ideology, and the Formation of Modern Biblical Scholarship* (London and New York: Routledge, 2002); Amy-Jill Levine, *The Misunderstood Jew: The Church and the Scandal of the Jewish Jesus* (San Francisco: HarperOne, 2006); Susannah Heschel, *The Aryan Jesus: Christian Theologians and the Bible in Nazi Germany* (Princeton: Princeton University Press, 2008); Laura Nasrallah and Elisabeth Schüssler Fiorenza (eds.), *Prejudice and Christian Beginnings: Investigating Race, Gender, and Ethnicity in Early Christian Studies* (Minneapolis: Fortress Press, 2009); and Magnus Zetterholm, *Approaches to Paul: A Student's Guide to Recent Scholarship* (Minneapolis: Fortress Press, 2009).

32. Adele Reinhartz, *Jesus of Hollywood* (Oxford: Oxford University Press, 2007), 43–63.

33. In classic Coen Brothers' style, this scene plays with Cecil B. DeMille's famous religious advisory council for *The King of Kings* (1927), made up of Rev. George Reid Andrews, Bruce Barton, and Father Daniel A. Lord, SJ (W. Barnes Tatum, *Jesus at the Movies: A Guide to the First Hundred Years* [Santa Rosa: Polebridge Press, 2004], 47–8). Mannix, played by Josh Brolin, is not not-interested in the theology lesson but has more pressing concerns. This film is a big deal and it is costing the studio a lot of money. "It's a swell story – a story told before, yes, but we like to flatter ourselves that it's never been told with this kind of distinction and panache," he exclaims. This studio, therefore, cannot risk ruffling feathers: "Now *Hail, Caesar!* is a prestige picture, our biggest release of the year, and we are devoting huge resources to its production in order to make it first-class in every respect. Gentlemen, given its enormous expense, we don't want to send it to market except in the certainty that it will not offend any reasonable American, regardless of faith or creed."

34. MOTB website, www.museumofthebible.org/press/background/floor-3-stories-of-the-bible-the-new-testament

35. John as eyewitness plays a similar role to Mark, a recipient of Jesus's healing and the future author of the Gospel of Mark, in DeMille's *The King of Kings*.

36. Tatum, *Jesus at the Movies*, 2–6.

37. Martin Kähler, *The So-called Historical Jesus and the Historic Biblical Christ* (Minneapolis: Fortress Press, 1988), 80 n. 11.

38. Tatum sees the "harmonizing" approach as one of two ways to render Jesus in the medium of film, with the other way being a focus on single gospels or something more explicitly reimaginative (*Jesus at the Movies*, 12–14). Among the harmonizing films, Tatum lists *From the Manger to the Cross* (1912), (*The*) *King of Kings* (1927, 1961), *The Greatest Story Ever Told* (1965), *Jesus of Nazareth* (1977), and *The Passion of the Christ* (2004).

39. Reinhartz, Jesus of Hollywood, 21. "'We did not show any image of Jesus here and that was intentional,' [Steven] Bickley [vice president of marketing] says. 'We decided that its best not to because there is no actual photographic or actual image of him to not venture and bring our opinions here and so that's why you won't see a picture of Jesus in the museum'" (*CBN* [November 15, 2017], www1.cbn.com/thebrodyfile/archive/2017/11/15/finding-jesus-at-the-museum-of-the-bible-isnt-so-easy).

40. Seth Pollinger, former director of education at the MOTB, has said that the focus of the film was on the early spread of the Jesus movement: "So we decided that our main theme was going to be the spread of this small group, they start with a few Jewish believers, they expand into a larger pool of Jewish believers and then it expands into a church of Jew and Gentile" (*CBN* [November 15, 2017], www1.cbn.com/thebrodyfile/archive/2017/11/15/finding-jesus-at-the-museum-of-the-bible-isnt-so-easy).

41. For the biblically literate viewer, these are cues to read Jesus's disciple as the John who authored the canonical book of Revelation, recounting a vision of Jesus and the coming judgment from the island of Patmos (Revelation1:9). While biblical scholars see the disciple John, the author of the Gospel of John (and the letters of 1–3 John), and the author of Revelation as different people, Christian tradition has often elided these Johns together. See Cavan Concannon, "In the Great City of the Ephesians: Contestations over Apostolic Memory and Ecclesial Power in the *Acts of Timothy*," *Journal of Early Christian Studies* 24, no. 3 (2016), 419–46.

42. Paul's narration also invokes the power of writing in the spread of the good news: "and when I could not travel, I wrote."

43. This is further reinforced by choosing John as the narrator. John identifies himself as an eyewitness to Jesus's life, which renders him a credible narrator of the events of the early church. Further, John is shown writing, which reinforces the connection between the story that is being narrated and the text of the Bible. John saw Jesus directly and then later wrote it down. John's character thus embodies evangelical beliefs about the Bible: it was written by trustworthy eyewitnesses, passed on faithfully as it moved around the ancient world, and properly shows that Jesus was divine.

44. See Steve Green's own articulation of this narrative in *This Beautiful Book: An Exploration of the Bible's Incredible Story Line and Why It Matters Today* (with Bill High; Grand Rapids: Zondervan, 2019). We address the Green family's publications further in Chapter 5.

45. Shelly Matthews has helpfully quipped that the MOTB's brand of supersessionism is "not your grandmother's supersessionism," inasmuch as it is deeply entwined with (evangelical) Zionism. We explore this connection in what follows.

46. Morag Kersel has pointed out that museums, including MOTB, rarely use modern state names. We follow her example of reflecting the MOTB's own language, while recognizing that such language occludes issues of ownership and contemporary politics. Kersel reasons: "My use of the term Holy Land was and continues to be a deliberate reflection of the geopolitical eliding of regional states, which results in an annexing of artifacts and an avoidance of

issues related to territorial ownership. The terms Israel, Jordan, Palestine are rarely if ever, used in museum exhibits. Instead, sanitized euphemisms like the Land of Israel, the Land of the Bible, the West Bank, the Levant, and the Holy Land are preferred labels with museums presenting an apolitical stance and reinforcing the universal museum concept of 'all for antiquities and antiquities for all', the material manifestations of the region speak to and belong to everyone". Morag M. Kersel, "Redemption for the Museum of the Bible? Artifacts, Provenance, the Display of Dead Sea Scrolls, and Bias in the Contact Zone," *Museum Management and Curatorship* 36, no. 3 (2021), 223 n. 1.

47. Thomas Tweed, *Crossing and Dwelling: A Theory of Religion* (Cambridge, MA: Harvard University Press, 2008).

48. On the institutional connections between MOTB and Christian Zionist advocacy, see Mark A. Chancey, "When Hobby Lobby Tours the Holy Land: The Back Story of Passages, Museum of the Bible's Christian Zionist Pilgrimage," The Bible and Interpretation website, September 2017, http://www.bibleinterp.arizone.edu/articles/2017/09/cha418027 (a revised and expanded version of this article was published as "Museum of the Bible's Politicized Holy Land Trip for Students," in Hicks-Keeton and Concannon [eds.], *Museum of the Bible: A Critical Introduction*, 275–94). On Christian Zionists more generally, see Sean Durbin, *Righteous Gentiles: Religion, Identity, and Myth in John Hagee's Christians United for Israel* (Leiden: Brill, 2019); Yaakov Ariel, *An Unusual Relationship: Evangelical Christians and Jews* (New York: New York University Press, 2013); Stephen Spector, *Evangelicals and Israel: The Story of American Christian Zionism* (Oxford: Oxford University Press, 2008); and Victoria Clark, *Allies for Armageddon: The Rise of Christian Zionism* (New Haven: Yale University Press, 2007).

49. On Christian Nationalism, see Michelle Goldberg, *Kingdom Coming: The Rise of Christian Nationalism* (New York: W. W. Norton, 2006); Kathleen Belew, *Bring the War Home: The White Power Movement and Paramilitary America* (Cambridge, MA: Harvard University Press, 2019); Andrew Whitehead and Samuel Perry, *Taking America Back for God: Christian Nationalism in the United States* (Oxford: Oxford University Press, 2020); and C. Van Engen, *City on a Hill: A History of American Exceptionalism* (New Haven: Yale University Press, 2020).

50. Museum of the Bible website, www.museumofthebible.org/museum/explo re/floor-5.

51. Julie Stahl and Chris Mitchell, "How the Museum of the Bible Lets Visitors Literally Touch the Jewish Temple," *CBN* (November 14, 2017), www1 .cbn.com/cbnnews/israel/2017/november/how-the-museum-of-the-bible-lets-visitors-literally-touch-the-jewish-temple

52. Museum of the Bible, Virtual Reality Explore Promo, YouTube (August 28, 2020), www.youtube.com/watch?v=efbaFtPyJCc

53. Museum of the Bible website, www.museumofthebible.org/visit/current-attractions/vr-tour

54. Porter, "Land of Israel," 125–27.

55. Bielo, *Ark Encounter*, 35.
56. Cary Summers, *Lifting Up the Bible: The Story Behind Museum of the Bible* (Franklin: Worthy Books/Museum of the Bible, 2017), 158.
57. Porter, "Land of Israel," 130–35.
58. Bielo, *Ark Encounter*, 24–25.
59. As anthropologist Tanya Luhrmann has shown, imagination is a crucial component in evangelical perception of the divine. In one of her experiments, she found that the regular practice of imaginatively immersing oneself in the Bible produced an increase in new sensory experiences (T. M. Luhrmann, *When God Talks Back: Understanding the American Evangelical Relationship with God* [New York: Vintage, 2012], 189–226).
60. Porter, "Land of Israel," 131.
61. This is similar to what Kaell has observed about the kinds of curated interactions preferred by American Christian pilgrims in the Holy Land: "Though pilgrims avoid conversations that they deem too political, they often nurture a spiritual relatedness with Holy Land people: Israeli Jews, Messianic Jews, and Christian Palestinians. They see each of these groups as intrinsic to the land and thus a potential conduit through which Americans can cement their own ties to the place and even to a genealogical lineage that they believe extends to Jesus himself" (Hillary Kaell, *Walking Where Jesus Walked: American Christians and Holy Land Pilgrimage* [New York: New York University Press, 2014], 202–03). These pilgrims want a sanitized experience of life in Israel and don't want to be confronted by complications that might upset the process of identifying with the place.
62. Kaell, *Walking Where Jesus Walked*, 88.
63. Kaell, *Walking Where Jesus Walked*, 84.
64. Kaell, *Walking Where Jesus Walked*, 85.
65. Kaell, *Walking Where Jesus Walked*, 86.
66. A similar management of the panoramic gaze can be found in the "Bible Now" exhibit on the Impact floor. Here visitors enter into a circular space with walls that intermittently display a panoramic view of Jerusalem, with geotagged typing that points out where sacred sites are located within the contemporary landscape. The stability of the camera, mounted high above the western side of the Old City, and the lack of sound allow the viewer to experience the present as static while also seeing how the present landscape connects with sacred sites from the past.
67. Porter, "Land of Israel," 135.
68. This concern with fostering intimacy with the Holy Land is reflected in the MOTB's past support for Christian Zionist pilgrimage trips to Israel, as described by Mark Chancey, "Museum of the Bible's Politicized Holy Land Trip for Students," in Hicks-Keeton and Concannon (eds.), *Museum of the Bible: A Critical Introduction*, 275–94.
69. See Museum of the Bible website, www.museumofthebible.org/visit/current-attractions/washington-revelations
70. Lauren R. Kerby, *Saving History: How White Evangelicals Tour the Nation's Capital and Redeem a Christian America* (Chapel Hill: University of North Carolina Press, 2020).

71. Kerby, *Saving History*, 23.
72. Kerby, *Saving History*, 22.
73. See for example the MOTB's relationship with ethically and legally problematic excavations in the West Bank: Michael D. Press, "An Illegal Archeological Dig in the West Bank Raises Questions about the Museum of the Bible," *Hyperallergic* (June 22, 2018), https://hyperallergic.com/447909/an-illegal-archeological-dig-in-the-west-bank-raises-questions-about-the-museum-of-the-bible/. See also the earlier work by Dylan Bergeson, "The Biblical Pseudo-Archeologists Pillaging the West Bank," *The Atlantic* (February 28, 2013), www.theatlantic.com/international/archive/2013/02/the-biblical-pseudo-archeologists-pillaging-the-west-bank/273488/.
74. In a MOTB-produced video published on the museum's Facebook page in April 2020, lead curator of Art and Exhibitions Amy Van Dyke discussed the history and artistic techniques of Tiffany while also awkwardly addressing Jesus's light skin tone: "It depicts Jesus resurrected on Easter morning, dressed in brilliant white, his face radiant. This was done in the traditional European nineteenth-century style with long wavy hair and light skin, and this was normal for the artist to have depicted him this way. This was part of Tiffany's cultural traditions and normal views of the world. In other cultures it might be different. Jesus may have darker skin, different colored eyes, different clothing, different hair. So for this time and place, for Tiffany, this was an appropriate way to show Jesus" (www.facebook.com/watch/?v=222367185517582).

CHAPTER 5 BIBLICAL CAPITAL

1. Inspire Experiences website, https://inspireexperiences.org/
2. The identifier "Founding Family, Museum of the Bible" appears just below Steve's and Jackie's names on the front cover of their book released in tandem with the MOTB's 2017 opening (*This Dangerous Book: How the Bible Has Shaped Our World and Why It Still Matters Today* [with Bill High; Grand Rapids: Zondervan, 2017]).
3. See, for example, Pierre Bourdieu, "The Forms of Capital," in *Handbook of Theory and Research for the Sociology of Education*, edited by J. Richardson (New York: Greenwood, 1986), 241–58.
4. For Bourdieu's comprehensive analysis of how distinction, as a form of symbolic capital, is constructed in a broad array of contexts, see his *Distinction: A Social Critique of the Judgment of Taste* (Cambridge, MA: Harvard University Press, 1984).
5. For a helpful discussion of this, see Rob Moore, "Capital," in *Pierre Bourdieu: Key Concepts*, edited by Michael Grenfell (New York: Routledge, 2014), 100–3. It is this feature of capital that prompted Marx to describe it as "the visible divinity, the transformation of all human and natural qualities into their opposites, the universal confusion and inversion of things; it brings together impossibilities" ("Money," in *Marx on Religion*, edited by John Raines [Philadelphia: Temple University Press, 2002], 141).

6. Pierre Bourdieu, *The Field of Cultural Production: Essays on Art and Literature* (New York: Columbia University Press, 1993), 81.

7. Candida Moss and Joel Baden, *Bible Nation: The United States of Hobby Lobby* (Princeton: Princeton University Press, 2017), 6–7.

8. For the 2010 tax filing, see https://projects.propublica.org/nonprofits/dis play_990/273444987/2011_12_EO%2F27-3444987_990EZ_201106. See Moss and Baden, *Bible Nation.*

9. On the tax implications of the museum donations, see the evidence documented by Candida Moss and Joel Baden, "The Museum of the Bible is Exploiting Jewish Tradition – and Saving Its Evangelical Christian Donors Millions," *The Daily Beast* (September 1, 2018).

10. Jackie Green and Lauren Green McAfee, *Only One Life: How a Woman's Every Day Shapes an Eternal Legacy* (Grand Rapids: Zondervan, 2018), 192–93.

11. Daniel Vaca, *Evangelicals Incorporated: Books and the Business of Religion in America* (Cambridge, MA: Harvard University Press, 2019), 4.

12. Vaca, *Evangelicals Incorporated,* 5–6.

13. Vaca, *Evangelicals Incorporated,* 14.

14. Vaca, *Evangelicals Incorporated,* 14.

15. *This Dangerous Book,* 16. In the foreword, megachurch pastor Rick Warren writes of the Greens: "This book is the captivating story of a normal family who decided, as much as possible, to build their lives, their family, and their family business on the Bible, God's Word" (9).

16. *This Dangerous Book,* 18. Even in an attempt to appreciate difference when they later describe partnering with both Protestants and Catholics, the Greens focus on what they perceive as characteristic of all people: "Over the years, we've learned – and continue to learn – that people of various denominations and faith traditions have more things in common than we might think. They love their families and want the best for their kids" (103).

17. Michael McAfee and Lauren Green McAfee, *Not What You Think: Why the Bible Might Be Nothing We Expected Yet Everything We Need* (Grand Rapids: Zondervan, 2019), 92.

18. McAfee and Green McAfee, *Not What You Think,* 35.

19. McAfee and Green McAfee, *Not What You Think,* 40.

20. McAfee and Green McAfee, *Not What You Think,* 27.

21. Green and Green, *This Dangerous Book,* 172.

22. The press release, entitled "Statement on Past Acquisitions" and dated March 26, 2020, can be found on the Museum of the Bible website as of the time of writing; see www.museumofthebible.org/press/press-releases/st atement-on-past-acquisitions. The *New York Times,* for example, ran a sympathetic story reproducing the narrative in the museum's press release (Tom Mashberg, "Bible Museum, Admitting Mistakes, Tries to Convert Its Critics," *New York Times* [April 5, 2020]). For a critique of the redemption arc in such stories, see Candida Moss, "Hobby Lobby Sues Christie's, Wants Us to Feel Sorry for Them," *The Daily Beast* (May 19, 2020), www.thedailybeast.com /hobby-lobby-sues-christies-wants-us-to-feel-sorry-for-them.

23. Green and Green, *This Dangerous Book,* 26.

24. See especially Malka Z. Simkovich, *Discovering Second Temple Literature: The Scriptures and Stories That Shaped Early Judaism* (Philadelphia: Jewish Publication Society, 2018), 3–40.

25. Eva Mroczek, "Batshit Stories: New Tales of Discovering Ancient Texts," *Marginalia* (June 22, 2018), https://marginalia.lareviewofbooks.org/batshit-stories-new-tales-of-discovering-ancient-texts/.; Eva Mroczek, *Out of the Cave: The Possibility of a New Biblical Past* (Yale University Press, forthcoming).

26. Given that the Greens celebrate European colonialism here, one might guess that the "we" is not expansive to include those who have not benefited from European colonialism.

27. Green and Green, *This Dangerous Book*, 44–45.

28. On the deep entanglement of white American Christianity and white supremacy with particular attention to the valorization of Columbus, see Eric A. Weed, *The Religion of White Supremacy in the United States* (Lanham: Lexington Books, 2017), especially 3–14.

29. Green and Green, *This Dangerous Book*, 59.

30. Green and Green, *This Dangerous Book*, 78.

31. McAfee and Green McAfee also make use of "discovery" language in *Not What You Think*: "Let's get something straight from the start: this book is more about our questions than our answers. We are there with you, exploring and wrestling and discovering together the value of the Bible and what it might mean for your life and our lives. We share some as well, and throughout the book we will tell you how we've wrestled with them. But in the midst of legitimate uncertainty about the Bible, we have discovered it to be a dazzling oasis of beauty and wisdom" (31–32).

32. Green and Green, *This Dangerous Book*, 113.

33. Green and Green, *This Dangerous Book*, 180.

34. Jill Hicks-Keeton, "The Museum of Whose Bible? On the Dangers of Turning Theology into History," *Ancient Jew Review* (January 24, 2018).

35. Green and Green, *This Dangerous Book*, 113.

36. The full sentence reads: "According to the most widely accepted theory, a select group of Essenes lived at the Qumran site from about 100–50 BCE until 68 CE (according to the revised chronology of Magness, p. 65) and when moving to the desert, they took with them scrolls deriving from various places in Israel. At the same time, they also composed compositions and copied scrolls at Qumran itself" (Emanuel Tov, "The Dead Sea Scrolls," in *The Book of Books: Biblical Canon, Dissemination and Its People*, edited by Jerry Pattengale, Lawrence H. Schiffman, and Filip Vukosavovic [Israel: Bible Lands Museum, 2013], 28).

37. Pattengale, Schiffman, and Vukosavovic (eds.), *Book of Books*, 26–30. Many of the authors have at one time been formally connected to the MOTB or the Green Scholars Initiative. Steve Green authored the preface.

38. Tov, "Dead Sea Scrolls," 30.

39. Green and Green, *This Dangerous Book*, 114.

40. Green and Green, *This Dangerous Book*, 171.

41. Vaca, *Evangelicals Incorporated*, 2.

42. Vaca, *Evangelicals Incorporated*, 3.

43. Kristin Kobes Du Mez, *Jesus and John Wayne: How White Evangelicals Corrupted a Faith and Fractured a Nation* (New York: Liveright Publishing, 2020), 301.

44. Kobes Du Mez, *Jesus and John Wayne*, 300.

45. The concept of the evangelical industrial complex was introduced by Skye Jethani, "The Evangelical Industrial Complex & Rise of Celebrity Pastors, Parts 1 and 2," *Christianity Today* (February 2012). See also the expansion of Jethani's argument by Jessica Johnson, "Megachurches, Celebrity Pastors, and the Evangelical Industrial Complex," in *Religion and Popular Culture in America*, edited by Bruce D. Forbes and Jeffrey Mahan (Berkeley: University of California Press, 2017), 159–76.

46. The Greens are no strangers to book publishing. David Green, the family's patriarch and original founder of Hobby Lobby, has published two books on his history with Hobby Lobby and his Christian capitalist philosophy (David Green, with Dean Merrill, *More Than a Hobby: How a $600 Startup Became America's Home and Craft Superstore* [Nashville: Thomas Nelson, 2005], and David Green, with Bill High, *Giving It All Away . . . and Getting It All Back Again: The Way of Living Generously* [Grand Rapids: Zondervan, 2017]). Steve Green also authored two books prior to the opening of the MOTB, one focused on lauding the family's Christian nationalist newspaper advertisements and the other a Christian nationalist rereading of American history (*Faith in America: The Powerful Impact of One Company Speaking Out Boldly* [Decatur: Looking Glass Books, 2011] and *The Bible in America: What We Believe about the Most Important Book in Our History* [with Todd Hillard; DustJacket Press, 2013]). While David's books were published by the biggest names in evangelical publishing, Zondervan and Thomas Nelson, Steve's pre-MOTB books had less impressive pedigrees. *Faith in America*'s publisher's address is a residential home in Decatur, Georgia, and the publisher of *The Bible in America* lacks a functioning website. The books published by Steve and his immediate family in the MOTB era have all been published by Zondervan. As with other segments of the evangelical industrial complex, these decisions reflected less the quality of the writing or the novelty of each book's ideas than the guaranteed market offered by the Greens' stores, which now include the MOTB's bookstore.

47. Green and Green, *This Dangerous Book*, 97.

48. Green and Green, *This Dangerous Book*, 171. In the Greens' logic, this must be true because if there is more than one truth or more than one legitimate understanding of the Bible, "that would render the Bible's contents meaningless" (171). To render the Bible meaningless does not appear as a live option.

49. Green and Green, *This Dangerous Book*, 72. The appended footnote cites a compendium of presidential quotations, coauthored by Rand Paul, whose purpose is to demonstrate faith on the part of America's presidents and commend it as indispensable to the success of the nation (Rand Paul and James Randall Robison, *Our Presidents and Their Prayers: Proclamations of Faith by America's Leaders* [New York: Center Street, 2015]). The description reads, in part: "In OUR PRESIDENTS & THEIR PRAYERS, Senator Paul stands up to the doubters in this most timely and important affirmation of how faith and prayer have always guided us, and why they must

continue to do so as we face major decisions for the future of our country."

50. Green does not explain how an event that happened in 1972 caused the changes he reports perceiving in the twenty years following 1988.

51. Green and Green, *This Dangerous Book*, 73–74 (quotation on 74).

52. Green and Green, *This Dangerous Book*, 74.

53. Green and Green, *This Dangerous Book*, 75–76.

54. Meredith Warren, "Why 'Judeo-Christian Values' Are a Dog-Whistle Myth Peddled by the Far Right," *The Conversation* (November 17, 2017), https://theconversation.com/why-judeo-christian-values-are-a-dog-whistle-myth-peddled-by-the-far-right-85922.

55. K. Healen Gaston, *Imagining Judeo-Christian America: Religion, Secularism, and the Redefinition of Democracy* (Chicago: University of Chicago Press, 2019).

56. Green and Green, *This Dangerous Book*, 75–76.

57. These case studies have been adapted and expanded from Jill Hicks-Keeton and Cavan Concannon, "On Good Government and Good Girls: How the Museum of the Bible's Founding Family Turned Themselves into Bible Experts," *The Revealer* (March 20, 2019), https://therevealer.org/on-good-government-good-girls-how-the-museum-of-the-bibles-founding-family-turned-themselves-into-bible-experts/

58. Quoted on Bible: For All Things Bible Online, https://get.bible/register. On the potential problems of ABS's ownership of the domain, see Marc Zvi Brettler, "Who Owns the .bible?" *Religion News Service* (March 8, 2018), https://religionnews.com/2018/03/08/who-owns-the-bible/. Despite the reservations of professional biblical scholars, there remains a Code of Conduct for any use of the domain .bible (see https://get.bible/policy). The policy is extremely constricting. One is prohibited from publishing any of the following: "(A) Any content that communicates disrespect for God as He is revealed in the Bible; (B) Any content that communicates disrespect for the Bible, or for any doctrine, symbol or principles of faith derived from the Bible; (C) Any content that communicates disrespect for the Jewish faith or the orthodox Christian faith in any of their historic expressions, or that advocates belief in any religious or faith tradition other than orthodox Christianity or Judaism." As of the time of writing, www.lauren.bible redirects to www.laurenmcafee.com and museum.bible redirects to the MOTB homepage. Any name of a biblical book attached to .bible (e.g., romans.bible or ruth.bible) goes to the YouVersion site for that book.

59. Michael McAfee, Western Conservative Summit 2018, YouTube (July 10, 2018), www.youtube.com/watch?v=YFYDkp6lyt0. Just one week earlier, to the outrage of many, then attorney general Jeff Sessions invoked Romans 13 to justify the Trump administration's child separation policy at the United States' southern border. See Julie Zauzmer and Keith McMillan, "Sessions Cites Bible passage used to defend slavery in defense of separating immigrant families," *Washington Post* (June 15, 2018). For a critique of Sessions's use of Romans 13 by two biblical scholars who are also Christians, see Margaret Aymer and Laura Nasrallah, "What Jeff Sessions Got Wrong when Quoting the Bible," *Washington Post* (June 15, 2018).

60. This description for the Western Conservative Summit 2018 appeared on the events page of the Centennial Institute's website. As of the time of writing, it can be viewed at www.ccu.edu/centennial/event/western-conservative-summit-2018/

61. This description is under Our Vision on the Centennial Institute's about us page, on its website. As of the time of writing, it can be viewed at www.ccu.edu/centennial/about-us/. On the historical connections between evangelical Christianity and corporate capitalists, see particularly Kevin M. Kruse, *One Nation Under God: How Corporate America Invented Christian America* (New York: Basic Books, 2015).

62. There are, in fact, several other ways by which McAfee's participation at the summit could have been explained. He serves, for example, as a teaching pastor at Council Road Baptist Church in Oklahoma City. He is a PhD student in ethics and public policy at the fundamentalist Southern Baptist Theological Seminary. It was the connection to the MOTB that was leveraged as authorizing him to speak.

63. On the Christian right's frequent (yet unpersuasive) characterization of their own voices as outside of politics, see Chrissy Stroop, "Christian Right Claims to Be 'Above' Politics Are Unbelievable," *Religion Dispatches* (September 16, 2020), https://religiondispatches.org/christian-right-claims-to-be-above-politics-are-bogus/

64. Eli Clifton, "Hobby Lobby's Secret Agenda: How it's Quietly Funding a Vast Right-Wing Movement," *Salon* (March 27, 2014), www.salon.com/2014/03/27/hobby_lobbys_secret_agenda_how_its_secretly_funding_a_vast_right_wing_movement/

65. McAfee offers only one other example: that of Masterpiece Cakeshop owner Jack Phillips, who won from the Supreme Court the right to refuse service to a gay couple because of his own religious objections to marriage equality.

66. See similar arguments from the Revolutionary War era in James P. Byrd, *Sacred Scripture: Sacred War: The Bible and the American Revolution* (New York: Oxford University Press, 2012).

67. To our knowledge, "author" here refers to her authorship of *Only One Life* and to her coauthorship, with Steve Green, of *This Dangerous Book.*

68. Kate Bowler, *The Preacher's Wife: The Precarious Power of Evangelical Women Celebrities* (Princeton: Princeton University Press, 2019), 96–97. Jackie Green has also been introduced as the cofounder of MOTB over and over again in promotional media interviews, including for The 700 Club, Huckabee, Pure Talk by Pure Flix, and a podcast called "Jesus Calling." She appeared on Huckabee on June 9, 2018 (www.youtube.com/watch?v=CmJfcB3-EVQ). She was a guest on Pure Talk by Pure Flix, broadcast live from the museum on July 1, 2018 (www.facebook.com/PureFlix/videos/2216147238401875/), and was featured on the podcast "Jesus Calling" on July 7, 2018 (www.facebook.com/JesusCalling/videos/270509153805180/?v=27050915 3805180) and on social media of The 700 Club on August 31, 2018 (www.youtube.com/watch?v=joyXDeupcgs). Her guest post (coauthored with Lauren) for the biblegateway.com blog appeared on May 29, 2018.

69. As Bowler has written: "The woman who professionalized her role as wife or family member could build a career of her own. It was a convenient arrangement for both churches that affirmed women in ministry and those that did not, because audiences presumed that a wife's actions were subject to her husband's approval and therefore sanctioned" (*Preacher's Wife*, 14).

70. Green and McAfee, *Only One Life*, 241.

71. On the discourse of aliens and exiles, see Benjamin Dunning, *Aliens and Sojourners: Self as Other in Early Christianity* (Philadelphia: University of Pennsylvania Press, 2009).

72. See, for example, Ericka S. Dunbar, "For Such a Time as This? #UsToo: Representations of Sexual Trafficking, Collective Trauma, and Horror in the Book of Esther," *The Bible and Critical Theory* 15, no. 2 (2019), 29–48.

73. As an example, see Russell Moore's appearance in the YouTube video Gender Roles (July 2, 2019), www.youtube.com/watch?v=cmeTPNLHw18

74. Elizabeth H. Flowers, *Into the Pulpit: Southern Baptist Women and Power since World War II* (Chapel Hill: University of North Carolina Press, 2012).

75. Green and McAfee, *Only One Life*, 59.

76. Green and McAfee, *Only One Life*, 70–71.

77. Green and McAfee, *Only One Life*, 74.

78. Green and McAfee, *Only One Life*, 150.

79. Green and McAfee, *Only One Life*, 73.

80. Green and McAfee, *Only One Life*, 139. For a critique of how Florence Nightingale is portrayed in MOTB exhibits, see Jessica Baron, "Feminist Icon Florence Nightingale Would Be Horrified at the Bible Museum's Depiction of Her," *The Daily Beast* (September 15, 2018), www .thedailybeast.com/feminist-icon-florence-nightingale-would-be-horrified-at -the-bible-museums-depiction-of-her

81. Green and McAfee, *Only One Life*, 145.

82. Green and McAfee, *Only One Life*, 195–96.

83. Green and McAfee, *Only One Life*, 233–34.

84. Green and McAfee, *Only One Life*, 116.

85. Green and McAfee, *Only One Life*, 116.

86. Green and McAfee, *Only One Life*, 186.

87. Joy A. Schroeder, *Deborah's Daughters: Gender Politics and Biblical Interpretation* (Oxford: Oxford University Press: 2014), especially 236–38.

88. For a cultural history of Jael with particular attention to gender, see Colleen M. Conway, *Sex and Slaughter in the Tent of Jael: A Cultural History of a Biblical Story* (Oxford: Oxford University Press), 2017.

89. See Schroeder, *Deborah's Daughters*, for a comprehensive critical examination of how Deborah has been used through the centuries in political and religious debates related to gender and authority.

90. Green and McAfee, *Only One Life*, 97, 119.

91. Green and McAfee, *Only One Life*, 178.

92. Green and McAfee, *Only One Life*, 186.

93. Green and McAfee, *Only One Life*, 39. At first blush, Moon is an exceedingly odd choice for Green and McAfee to use, as she was in reality an enterprising spitfire who, as historian Regina D. Sullivan has demonstrated in her myth-

busting book on the missionary, "relied on a religious ideology and woman's rights language to argue for an expansion of women's sphere, for female equality in mission work, and for female organization" (*Lottie Moon: A Southern Baptist Missionary to China in History and Legend* [Baton Rouge: Louisiana State University Press, 2011], 1). In a seemingly bizarre research choice, the only secondary source Green and McAfee cite on Moon is an online review of Sullivan's book, but *Only One Life* does not accurately represent either what is in Sullivan's book or in the review of her book, choosing instead to repeat the inaccurate material that the book demonstrates is myth and the review points out as such. We observe, then, that the myth of Lottie Moon among white Southern Baptists is so entrenched that Green and McAfee can perpetuate it while simultaneously citing evidence to the contrary as if it supports their understanding.

94. Green and McAfee, *Only One Life*, 96.
95. Amy DeRogatis, *Saving Sex: Sexuality and Salvation in American Evangelicalism* (Oxford: Oxford University Press, 2014), 10–41.
96. Green and McAfee, *Only One Life*, 27.
97. Green and McAfee, *Only One Life*, 27.
98. Green and McAfee, *Only One Life*, 162.
99. Green and McAfee, *Only One Life*, 67–68.

CONCLUSION

1. This is central to the history of evangelicalism offered in Andrew Sutton's *American Apocalypse: A History of Modern Evangelicalism* (Cambridge, MA: Harvard University Press, 2014).
2. Timothy Gloege, *Guaranteed Pure: The Moody Bible Institute, Business, and the Making of Modern Evangelicalism* (Chapel Hill: University of North Carolina Press, 2015).
3. Gloege, *Guaranteed Pure*, 162–92.
4. This is a central observation of James Bielo, who notes: "Reading across 60 different articles from diverse venues, the language used to discuss the design of exhibits, renovated space, and architecture is thoroughly superlative ... Whatever critics or advocates claim the MOTB to (not) be or to (not) be guilty of, they never claim it to be boring or shabby" ("Quality: D.C.'s Museum of the Bible and Aesthetic Evaluation," *Material Religion* 15, no. 1 [2019], 131).
5. Kathryn Lofton, *Consuming Religion* (Chicago: University of Chicago Press, 2017), 6.
6. Kristin Kobes Du Mez, *Jesus and John Wayne: How White Evangelicals Corrupted a Faith and Fractured a Nation* (New York: Liveright, 2020); Daniel Vaca, *Evangelicals Incorporated: Books and the Business of Religion in America* (Cambridge, MA: Harvard University Press, 2019).
7. Lofton, *Consuming Religion*, 214–16.
8. Lofton, *Consuming Religion*, 7.
9. As an important complement to Lofton's work, Bethany Moreton has shown how Wal-Mart took cues from the tradition of Christian service to brand its products as safe for Christian consumers, thus baptizing consumer capitalism

(*To Serve God and Wal-Mart: The Making of Christian Free Enterprise* [Cambridge, MA: Harvard University Press, 2009], 89).

10. Steven J. Friesen has helpfully suggested that the MOTB is functionally a parachurch organization ("Museum of the Bible"? Response to Panel," Southwest Commission on Religious Studies, annual meeting, March 9, 2019), www.academia.edu/38522896/_Museum_of_the_Bible_Response_t o_Panel_Southwest_Commission_on_Religious_Studies.

11. Christopher P. Scheitle, *Beyond the Congregation: The World of Christian Nonprofits* (Oxford: Oxford University Press, 2010).

12. Lauren R. Kerby, *Saving History: How White Evangelicals Tour the Nation's Capital and Redeem a Christian America* (Chapel Hill: University of North Carolina Press, 2020).

13. This event took place on June 1, 2019. MOTB press release, May 8, 2019, www .museumofthebible.org/newsroom/museum-of-the-bible-to-unfold-mile-long -wiedmann-bible-on-the-national-mall

14. The effects of amplification, echo chambers, and interconnected assemblages is helpfully explored in William E. Connolly's *Capitalism and Christianity, American Style* (Durham: Duke University Press, 2008).

15. Hershel Hepler, a curator at MOTB, once suggested this idea to us in private conversation.

16. See the now classic formulation of this problem in Russell McCutcheon, *Critics Not Caretakers: Redescribing the Public Study of Religion* (Albany: State University of New York Press, 2001).

17. Lofton, *Consuming Religion*, 25.

18. Knust, "Editing without Interpreting," 145–70.

19. On this see also Gregory L. Cuéllar, *Empire, the British Museum, and the Making of the Biblical Scholar in the Nineteenth Century: Archival Criticism* (London: Palgrave Macmillan, 2019).

20. Jennifer Wright Knust, "Editing without Interpreting: The Museum of the Bible and New Testament Textual Criticism," in *The Museum of the Bible: A Critical Introduction*, edited by Jill Hicks-Keeton and Cavan Concannon (Lanham: Lexington Books/Fortress Academic, 2019)145–70.

21. In this we are following Vincent Wimbush, *White Men's Magic: Scripturalization as Slavery* (Oxford: Oxford University Press, 2012); and Cavan Concannon, *Profaning Paul* (Chicago: University of Chicago Press, 2021).

Acknowledgments

We are immensely grateful to our friends and colleagues who thought with us about the Museum of the Bible as we completed this project, whether by reading drafts of material, participating in roundtables on the topic, hosting public talks, or talking with us in a variety of settings. We have benefited greatly from conversations with Sam Adams, Joey Albin, Joel Baden, Carol Bakhos, Bryan Bibb, James Bielo, Marc Brettler, Bob Cargill, Mark Chancey, Lynda Coon, Carly Crouch, Reyhan Durmaz, Robert Eisen, Neil Elliott, John Fea, Taylor Foss, Steve Friesen, Greg Given, Jennifer Graber, Esther Hamori, Chris Hays, Sonia Hazard, Lynn Huber, Jeremy Hutton, Terrence Johnson, Årstein Justnes, Robert Kashow, Morag Kersel, Jenny Knust, Brett Krutzsch, Brent Landau, Mark Letteney, Mark Leuchter, Alan Levenson, Liv Ingeborg Lied, Jim Linville, Jessica Marglin, Shelly Matthews, Roberta Mazza, Margaret Mitchell, Candida Moss, Richard Newton, Brent Nongbri, Bradley Onishi, Rodger Payne, Sarah Porter, Andrew Porwancher, Rebecca Raphael, Christopher Rollston, Rob Seesengood, Donovan Schaefer, Katherine Shaner, Phillip Michael Sherman, Noam Sienna, Ed Silver, Geoff Smith, Tiffany Stanley, Jolyon Thomas, Kimberly Wagner, Julie Ward, Tim Wardle, Steven Weitzman, Ben Wright, Stephen Young, and the sommelier at Bad Saint. We would also like to thank our editor, Beatrice Rehl, for her enthusiasm about this project. Thanks are due to Hilary Hammond for her excellent editorial work and Travis Ables for his work on the index. Financial support for this project was provided at various stages from the School of Religion at the University of Southern California; the Office of the Vice

President for Research and the Office of the Provost, University of Oklahoma; the Department of Religious Studies, University of Oklahoma; the Humanities Forum, University of Oklahoma; the College of Arts & Sciences, University of Oklahoma.

Index